Teach Yourself VISUALLY™

Macs

3rd Edition

Visual™

Paul McFedries

WILEY

John Wiley & Sons, Inc.

Teach Yourself VISUALLY™ Macs, 3rd Edition

Published by
John Wiley & Sons, Inc.
10475 Crosspoint Boulevard
Indianapolis, IN 46256

www.wiley.com

Published simultaneously in Canada

Copyright © 2013 by John Wiley & Sons, Inc., Indianapolis, Indiana

Wiley publishes in a variety of print and electronic formats and by print-on-demand. Some material included with standard print versions of this book may not be included in e-books or in print-on-demand. If this book refers to media such as a CD or DVD that is not included in the version you purchased, you may download this material at http://booksupport.wiley.com. For more information about Wiley products, visit www.wiley.com.

Library of Congress Control Number: 2012948912

ISBN: 978-1-118-35465-0

Manufactured in the United States of America

10 9 8 7 6 5 4 3 2 1

Trademark Acknowledgments

Contact Us

For general information on our other products and services please contact our Customer Care Department within the U.S. at 877-762-2974, outside the U.S. at 317-572-3993 or fax 317-572-4002.

For technical support please visit www.wiley.com/techsupport.

Credits

Acquisitions Editor
Aaron Black

Project Editor
Lynn Northrup

Technical Editor
Dennis R. Cohen

Copy Editor
Scott Tullis

Editorial Director
Robyn Siesky

Business Manager
Amy Knies

Senior Marketing Manager
Sandy Smith

**Vice President and Executive
Group Publisher**
Richard Swadley

**Vice President and Executive
Publisher**
Barry Pruett

Senior Project Coordinator
Kristie Rees

Graphics and Production Specialist
Carrie A. Cesavice

Quality Control Technicians
Melissa Cossell
John Greenough
Lauren Mandelbaum

Proofreading
Melissa D. Buddendeck

Indexing
BIM Indexing & Proofreading Services

About the Author

Paul McFedries is a technical writer who has been authoring computer books since 1991. He has more than 75 books to his credit, which together have sold more than four million copies worldwide. These books include the Wiley titles *MacBook Air Portable Genius, 4th Edition; iPhone 4S Portable Genius; Macs Portable Genius, 2nd Edition*; and *The Facebook Guide for People Over 50*. Paul also runs Word Spy, a website dedicated to tracking new words and phrases (see www.wordspy.com). Please visit Paul's personal website at www.mcfedries.com, or follow him on twitter at www.twitter.com/paulmcf and www.twitter.com/wordspy.

Author's Acknowledgments

The book you hold in your hands is not only an excellent learning tool, but it is truly beautiful, as well. I am happy to have supplied the text that you will read, but the beautiful layout and colors come from Wiley's crack team of graphics specialists and illustrators. The scope of the tasks, the accuracy of the spelling and grammar, and the veracity of the information are all the result of hard work performed by project editor Lynn Northrup, copy editor Scott Tullis, and technical editor Dennis Cohen. Thanks to all of you for your excellent work. My thanks, as well, to acquisitions editor Aaron Black for asking me to write this book.

How to Use This Book

Who This Book Is For

This book is for the reader who has never used this particular technology or software application. It is also for readers who want to expand their knowledge.

The Conventions in This Book

① Steps

This book uses a step-by-step format to guide you easily through each task. **Numbered steps** are actions you must do; **bulleted steps** clarify a point, step, or optional feature; and **indented steps** give you the result.

② Notes

Notes give additional information — special conditions that may occur during an operation, a situation that you want to avoid, or a cross-reference to a related area of the book.

③ Icons and Buttons

Icons and buttons show you exactly what you need to click to perform a step.

④ Tips

Tips offer additional information, including warnings and shortcuts.

⑤ Bold

Bold type shows command names or options that you must click or text or numbers you must type.

⑥ Italics

Italic type introduces and defines a new term.

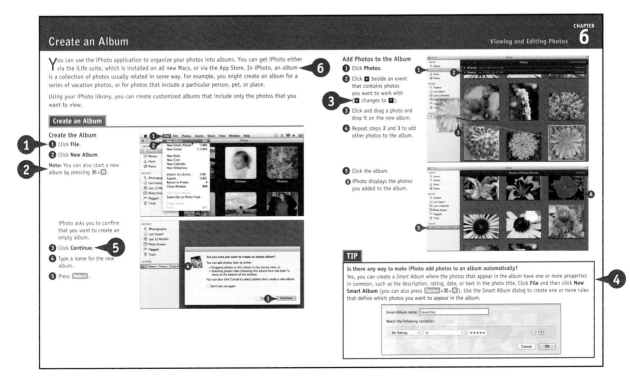

Table of Contents

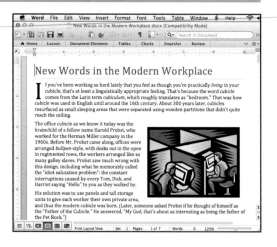

Chapter 3   Connecting Devices

Chapter 4   Learning Mac Basics

Agenda for 2013 Conference

Day 1

MORNING SESSION
9:00 - 9:15	Welcome
9:15 - 10:00	Keynote Speech
10:00 - 10:30	Q & A Session
10:30 - 10:50	Coffee Break
10:50 - 12:00	Panel Session
12:00 - 1:30	Lunch

AFTERNOON SESSION
1:30 - 2:30	Guest Speaker
2:30 - 3:00	Q & A Session
3:00 - 3:20	Coffeee Break
3:20 - 4:00	A Look at the Future
4:00 - 5:00	Breakout Sessions

Table of Contents

Table of Contents

Chapter 12　Working with Your iCloud Account

Table of Contents

Chapter 15   Maintaining Your Mac

CHAPTER 1

Reviewing Mac Types

Are you ready to learn about the Mac? This chapter gets you off to a great start by showing you the different types of Macs available. You learn about the general Mac types and find out about the specific Mac models and what features they offer.

Understanding Mac Types

Before you learn about the specific Mac models Apple offers, you should take a step back and look at the general types of Macs available. For example, you need to understand the difference between a desktop Mac and a notebook Mac. You should also understand the difference between older Macs that use the PowerPC processor, and newer Macs that use processors made by Intel.

Desktop Macs

A desktop Mac is a Macintosh computer designed to sit on your desk. In most cases, you connect the desktop Mac to a separate keyboard, mouse, and monitor. The exception here is the iMac model, which comes with a built-in monitor. Also, the Mac Pro model is quite large, so many people place the system unit on the floor.

Notebook Macs

A portable Mac is a Macintosh computer that you can take with you when you leave your home or office. A portable Mac — also called a laptop or notebook Mac — comes with a keyboard, mouse, and monitor built in, making it easy to use in almost any location. A portable Mac also comes with a battery, so you can use it even in places without an available power outlet.

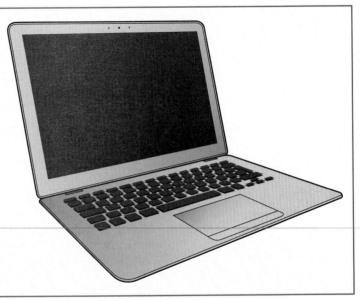

PowerPC Macs

From about 1994 to early 2006, all Mac models used a central processing unit (CPU, the "brain" of the computer) called the PowerPC, which was made jointly by IBM and Motorola. Apple no longer uses PowerPC CPUs, but if you are in the market for a used Mac, note that it may come with the PowerPC chip.

Intel Macs

All of the current Mac models use a CPU made by Intel. Apple began the transition from PowerPC to Intel in 2006, and every Mac made since about August 2006 comes with an Intel CPU. The Intel processors are faster than the PowerPC chips, and they use less power, which improves battery life in portable Macs.

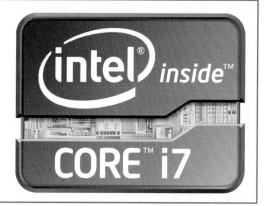

Determine the Mac CPU

If you have a Mac and you do not know whether it has an Intel or PowerPC CPU, you can find out. Start your Mac, click the **Apple** icon (![apple]) in the top left corner, and then click **About This Mac**. In the About This Mac window that appears, examine the Processor value.

Learn About the iMac

If you are thinking of purchasing an iMac, or just want to know more about this Mac model, this section explains the iMac's features and concepts. You get an overview of the iMac, and then you learn some iMac specifics, such as the types of processors the iMac models use, the iMac's main internal features, and the other equipment that comes standard with an iMac. You also identify the iMac ports and learn what each of them is used for.

iMac Overview

The iMac is an "all-in-one" computer that combines the system components (the CPU, memory, hard drive, and other internal components) and the screen in a single unit. The resulting console is amazingly thin, so the iMac does not take up very much room on your desk.

iMac Features

The current version of the iMac uses an Intel Core i5 or Intel Core i7 processor; a high-resolution, widescreen display (21.5 or 27 inches wide); a powerful graphics card; a built-in FaceTime HD camera and microphone; built-in stereo speakers; wired and wireless networking support; and an optical disc drive and burner.

21.5-inch iMac
Starting at $1199

- 21.5-inch (viewable) LED–backlit glossy widescreen TFT display with support for millions of colors
- Resolution: 1920 by 1080 pixels

27-inch iMac
Starting at $1699

- 27–inch (viewable) LED–backlit glossy widescreen TFT display with support for millions of colors
- Resolution: 2560 by 1440 pixels

iMac Ports

The back of the iMac has a generous supply of ports that enable you to connect a wide variety of devices.

A Audio Out

You use the audio out port to play music or other audio through speakers or headphones.

B Audio In

You use the audio in port to bring speech or other audio into the iMac using a microphone, musical instrument, or audio player.

C USB

You use the iMac's four USB ports to connect devices that support USB, including keyboards, mice, printers, cameras, external drives, iPods, iPads, and iPhones.

D FireWire 800

You use the FireWire 800 port to connect devices that support FireWire 800 or FireWire 400 (with an adapter), including external hard drives, external DVD drives, and video cameras.

E Thunderbolt

You use the two Thunderbolt ports to connect the iMac to Thunderbolt-compatible devices, such as an additional display or an external hard drive.

F Network

You use the network port to connect the iMac to a wired network.

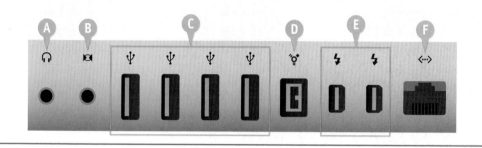

Delve into the Mac mini

If you are thinking of purchasing a Mac mini, or just want to know more about this Mac model, this section explains the Mac mini's features and concepts. You get an overview of the Mac mini, and then you learn some Mac mini specifics, such as the types of processors the Mac mini models use, the Mac mini's main internal features, and the other equipment that comes standard with a Mac mini. You also identify the Mac mini ports and learn what each of them is used for.

Mac mini Overview

The Mac mini is a scaled-down version of a Mac that includes all the standard components — CPU, memory, one or two hard drives, and a video card — in a unit that measures only about 7.7 inches square (and about 1.4 inches tall). This makes the Mac mini perfect for a small work area.

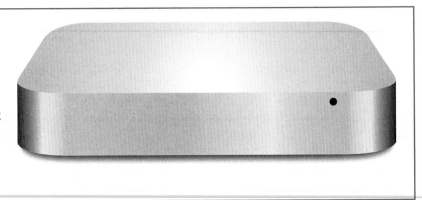

Mac mini Features

The current version of the Mac mini uses an Intel Core i5 processor; a 500GB hard drive; wired and wireless networking support; and numerous ports (see the following section, "Mac mini Ports"). You need to supply your own keyboard, mouse, and monitor.

2.3GHz Mac mini

Height: 1.4 inches (3.6 cm)
Width: 7.7 inches (19.7 cm)
Depth: 7.7 inches (19.7 cm)
Weight: 2.7 pounds (1.22kg)[1]

2.5GHz Mac mini

Height: 1.4 inches (3.6 cm)
Width: 7.7 inches (19.7 cm)
Depth: 7.7 inches (19.7 cm)
Weight: 2.7 pounds (1.22kg)[1]

Mac mini Ports

The back of the Mac mini has a number of ports that enable you to connect a wide variety of devices.

A Network

You use the network port to connect the Mac mini to a wired network.

B FireWire 800

You use the FireWire 800 port to connect devices that support FireWire 800 or FireWire 400 (with an adapter), including external hard drives, external DVD drives, and video cameras.

C HDMI Video Out

You use the HDMI video out port to connect the Mac mini to an HD TV or other display that uses an HDMI connector.

D Thunderbolt

You use the Thunderbolt port to connect the Mac mini to Thunderbolt-compatible devices, such as an additional display or an external hard drive.

E USB

You use the Mac mini's four USB ports to connect devices that support USB, including keyboards, mice, printers, cameras, external drives, iPods, iPads, and iPhones.

F SDXC Card Slot

You use the SDXC card slot to insert a Secure Digital Extended Capacity memory card.

G Audio In

You use the audio in port to bring speech or other audio into the Mac mini using a microphone, musical instrument, or audio player.

H Audio Out

You use the audio out port to play music or other audio through speakers or headphones.

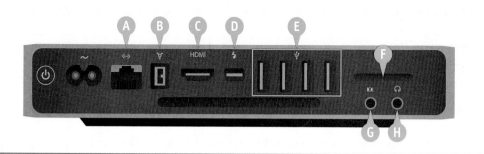

Get to Know the Mac Pro

If you are thinking of purchasing a Mac Pro, or just want to know more about this Mac model, this section explains the Mac Pro's features and concepts. You get an overview of the Mac Pro, and then you learn some Mac Pro specifics, such as the types of processors the Mac Pro models use, the Mac Pro's main internal features, and the other equipment that comes standard with a Mac Pro. You also identify the Mac Pro ports and learn what each of them is used for.

Mac Pro Overview

The Mac Pro is the fastest and most powerful of all the Mac models. With a fast CPU, lots of memory, a large hard drive, powerful graphics, and a wide variety of expansion options, the Mac Pro is designed for power users who need maximum performance and expandability.

Mac Pro Features

The Mac Pro uses either one Intel Xeon Quad-Core processor, which gives the Mac Pro the power of four individual CPUs, or two Intel Xeon 6-Core processors, which is the equivalent of 12 individual CPUs. It also comes with 6GB or 12GB of memory, a 1TB hard drive, wired and optional wireless networking support, a CD and DVD burner, and numerous ports. You can upgrade the Mac Pro with a faster CPU, more memory (up to 64GB), and multiple hard drives.

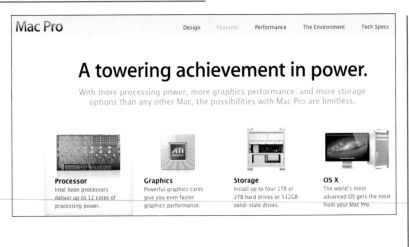

Mac Pro

Design   Features   Performance   The Environment   Tech Specs

A towering achievement in power.

With more processing power, more graphics performance, and more storage options than any other Mac, the possibilities with Mac Pro are limitless.

Processor
Intel Xeon processors deliver up to 12 cores of processing power.

Graphics
Powerful graphics cards give you even faster graphics performance.

Storage
Install up to four 1TB or 2TB hard drives or 512GB solid-state drives.

OS X
The world's most advanced OS gets the most from your Mac Pro.

Mac Pro Ports

The back of the Mac Pro has a number of ports that enable you to connect a wide variety of devices. Note that the Mac Pro also has several ports on the front.

Ⓐ DVI Video Out

You use the DVI video out port to connect the Mac Pro to a computer monitor, TV, or other display.

Ⓑ Mini DisplayPort Video Out

You use the two Mini DisplayPort video out ports to connect the Mac Pro to one or two high resolution displays.

Ⓒ USB

You use the Mac Pro's five USB ports (three on the back, two on the front) to connect devices that support USB, including keyboards, mice, printers, cameras, external drives, and iPods.

Ⓓ FireWire 800

You use the four FireWire 800 ports (two on the back, two on the front) to connect devices that support FireWire 800 or FireWire 400 (with an adapter), including external hard drives, external DVD drives, and video cameras.

Ⓔ Optical Audio In

You use the optical audio in port to bring digital audio into the Mac Pro using digital audio devices that support optical connections.

Ⓕ Optical Audio Out

You use the optical audio out port to send digital audio from the Mac Pro to digital audio devices that support optical connections.

Ⓖ Audio In

You use the audio in port to bring speech or other audio into the Mac Pro using a microphone, musical instrument, or audio player.

Ⓗ Audio Out

You use the two audio out ports (one on the back, one on the front) to play music or other audio through speakers or headphones.

Ⓘ Network

You can use the two network ports to connect the Mac Pro to two different wired networks.

Check Out the MacBook Pro

I f you are thinking of purchasing a MacBook Pro, or just want to know more about this Mac model, this section explains the MacBook Pro's features and concepts. You get an overview of the MacBook Pro, and then you learn some MacBook Pro specifics, such as the types of processors the MacBook Pro models use, the MacBook Pro's main internal features, and the other equipment that comes standard with a MacBook Pro. You also identify the MacBook Pro ports and learn what each of them is used for.

MacBook Pro Overview

The MacBook Pro is a portable computer that combines the monitor and keyboard into a single unit. Instead of a mouse, the MacBook Pro uses a trackpad where you move the pointer by sliding your finger along the pad. The latest MacBook Pro models use Multi-Touch trackpads, where you use gestures to scroll, rotate, and zoom screen objects.

MacBook Pro Features

The MacBook Pro with Retina display uses an Intel Core i7 processor; a 15-inch ultra-high resolution widescreen display measured diagonally; 8GB of memory; and a 256GB or 512GB solid-state hard drive. The regular MacBook Pro models use an Intel Core i7 processor; a widescreen display (13 or 15 inches measured diagonally); 8GB of memory; and a 256GB or 512GB solid-state hard drive. All MacBook Pro models also come with a built-in FaceTime HD camera and microphone, stereo speakers, and wireless networking support. Note that the latest MacBook Pro models do *not* come with wired networking support or an optical drive.

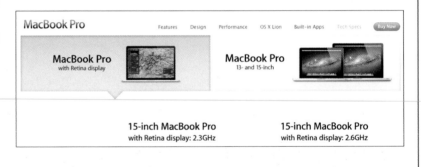

12

MacBook Pro Ports

The sides of the MacBook Pro have a number of ports that enable you to connect a wide variety of devices. Note that the different versions of the MacBook Pro (15-inch with Retina display, and 13- and 15-inch with regular display) have slightly different port configurations. A 15-inch MacBook Pro with Retina display is shown here.

Ⓐ SDXC Card Slot

You use the SDXC card slot to insert a Secure Digital Extended Capacity memory card.

Ⓑ HDMI Video Out

You use the HDMI video out port to connect the MacBook Pro to an HD TV or other display that uses an HDMI connector.

Ⓒ USB

You use the MacBook Pro's two USB ports to connect devices that support USB, including keyboards, mice, printers, cameras, external drives, and iPods. The latest version of the MacBook Pro supports USB 3.0.

Ⓓ Thunderbolt

You use the two Thunderbolt ports to connect the MacBook Pro to Thunderbolt-compatible devices, such as an additional display or an external hard drive.

Ⓔ Audio Out

You use the audio out port to play music or other audio through speakers or headphones.

Tour the MacBook Air

If you are thinking of purchasing a MacBook Air, or just want to know more about this Mac model, this section explains the MacBook Air's features and concepts. You get an overview of the MacBook Air, and then you learn some MacBook Air specifics, such as the types of processors the MacBook Air models use, the MacBook Air's main internal features, and the other equipment that comes standard with a MacBook Air. You also identify the MacBook Air ports and learn what each of them is used for.

MacBook Air Overview

The MacBook Air is a notebook computer that combines the monitor and keyboard into a single unit. Instead of a mouse, the MacBook Air uses a Multi-Touch trackpad where you move the pointer by sliding your finger along the pad, and where you use gestures to scroll, rotate, and zoom screen objects. With a height of just 0.68 inches, the MacBook Air is the world's thinnest notebook computer.

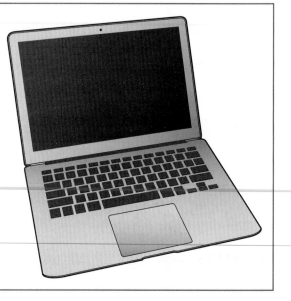

MacBook Air Features

The MacBook Air uses an Intel Core i5 processor (an upgrade to an Intel Core i7 processor is available); an 11.6- or 13.3-inch widescreen display (measured diagonally); 4GB of memory; a 64GB, 128GB, or 256GB solid-state hard drive; a built-in FaceTime HD camera and microphone; and wireless networking support. Note that the MacBook Air does *not* come with wired networking support or an optical drive.

11-inch MacBook Air		13-inch MacBook Air	
$999	$1099	$1199	$1499

11.6-inch (diagonal) high-resolution LED-backlit glossy widescreen display with support for millions of colors	13.3-inch (diagonal) high-resolution LED-backlit glossy widescreen display with support for millions of colors

MacBook Air Ports

The sides of the MacBook Air have a number of ports that enable you to connect a wide variety of devices. Note that the different versions of the MacBook Air (11- and 13-inch display) have slightly different port configurations. A 13-inch MacBook Air is shown here.

Ⓐ SD Card Slot

You use the SD card slot (available only on the 13-inch model) to insert a Secure Digital memory card.

Ⓑ USB

You use the MacBook Air's USB ports to connect devices that support USB, including DVD drives, keyboards, mice, printers, cameras, external drives, and iPods. The latest version of the MacBook Air supports USB 3.0.

Ⓒ Thunderbolt

You use the Thunderbolt port to connect the MacBook Air to Thunderbolt-compatible devices, such as an additional display or an external hard drive.

Ⓓ Audio Out

You use the audio out port to play music or other audio through speakers or headphones.

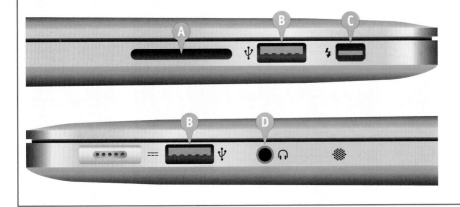

CHAPTER 2

Learning What You Can Do with a Mac

Are you ready to learn about what you can do with your Mac? In this chapter you find out about the wide variety of tasks you can perform with your Mac.

Create Documents

Whether you use your Mac at home, at the office, or on the road, you can use your Mac to create a wide variety of documents. In general terms, a *document* is a file that contains information, which is usually text, but it may also consist of pictures, charts, lines, and other nontext items. With your Mac, you can create documents such as lists, letters, memos, budgets, forecasts, presentations, and web pages.

Text Documents

You can use text editing software on your Mac to create simple documents such as lists, notes, instructions, and other items that do not require fonts, colors, or other types of formatting. With your Mac, you can use the TextEdit application to create plain text documents, and the Stickies application to create electronic sticky notes.

Word Processing Documents

You can use word processing software on your Mac to create letters, resumes, memos, reports, newsletters, brochures, business cards, menus, flyers, invitations, and certificates. Anything that you use to communicate on paper, you can create using your Mac. You can also use TextEdit to create formatted documents. Other examples include Microsoft Word for the Mac and Apple iWork Pages.

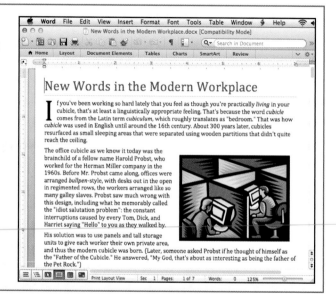

Spreadsheets

A spreadsheet application is a software program that enables you to manipulate numbers and formulas to quickly create powerful mathematical, financial, and statistical models. Your Mac comes with a test drive version of the Apple iWork Numbers application. Another example is Microsoft Excel for the Mac.

Presentations

A presentation program enables you to build professional-looking slides that you can use to convey your ideas to other people. Your Mac comes with a test drive version of the Apple iWork Keynote application. Another example is Microsoft PowerPoint for the Mac.

Web Pages

You can use web page editing software on your Mac to create your own pages to publish to the web. You can create a personal home page, a blog, or pages to support your business. Your Mac does not come with a program for creating web pages, but the App Store contains several excellent apps, including TextWrangler, BBEdit, and Web Form Builder Lite.

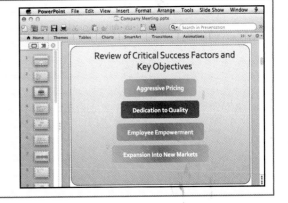

Play and Record Music

Your Mac is a veritable music machine that you can use to build, organize, play, and share your digital music collection. You can get music onto your Mac by copying it from audio CDs, or by purchasing music online. If you are musically inclined, you can even record or compose new tunes using an application called GarageBand (part of the Apple iLife suite). Once you have a collection of music on your Mac, you can use your Mac to create custom music CDs, or copy some or all of the music to a device such as an iPod or iPad.

iTunes

Your Mac comes with the iTunes application, which stores your library of digital music files. With iTunes you can play albums and songs, organize tunes into related playlists, copy music to a CD, download and edit track information, and organize your music to suit your style. You can also use iTunes to listen to Internet-based radio stations.

iTunes Store

You can use the iTunes application to connect directly to the online iTunes Store, where you can purchase individual songs, usually for 99 cents per song, or entire albums, usually for $9.99 per album. Your Mac downloads the purchased music to your iTunes library, and you can listen to the music on your Mac or add the music to your iPod, iPhone, or iPad.

Import Music from a CD

You can add tracks from a music CD to the iTunes library. This enables you to listen to an album without having to put the CD into your CD or DVD drive each time. In iTunes, the process of copying tracks from a CD to your Mac is called *importing* or *ripping*.

Record Music

If your Mac came with the iLife suite, you can use the GarageBand program to record or compose your own tunes. You can attach an instrument such as a guitar or keyboard to your Mac and record your playing. You can also use GarageBand to add accompanying instruments such as drums, bass, piano, or another guitar.

Burn Music to a CD

You can copy, or *burn*, music files from your Mac onto a CD. Burning CDs is a great way to create customized CDs that you can listen to on the computer or in a portable device. You can burn music files using the iTunes application.

Synchronize with an iPod, iPhone, or iPad

You can use the iTunes application to copy some or all of your music library to an iPod, iPhone, or iPad; this enables you to play your music wherever you are or on another audio device that connects to the device. When you attach the iPod, iPhone, or iPad to your Mac, iTunes automatically synchronizes the device according to the settings you specify.

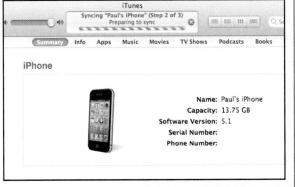

View and Organize Your Photos

Your Mac is perfect for showing your digital photos in their best light. Your Mac comes with tools that enable you to view individual photos and to run slide shows of multiple photos. Your Mac also enables you to organize your digital photos, import images from a digital camera or similar device (such as an iPhone or iPad), and edit your photos. Many Macs also come with a built-in camera that you can use to take simple snapshots.

View Photos

Your Mac gives you many ways to view your digital photos. You can view photos within Finder using the Cover Flow view, or by selecting the photos and pressing Spacebar. You can also double-click a photo file to open it using the Preview application, or you can open a file using the iPhoto application, if it is installed on your Mac. Also, both Preview and iPhoto enable you to run photo slide shows.

Organize Photos

If your Mac comes with iPhoto, part of the Apple iLife suite, you can use it to organize your collection of digital photos. For example, you can create albums of related photos, and you can create folders in which to store photos. You can also rename and rate photos, apply keywords to photos, flag important photos, and sort photos in various ways.

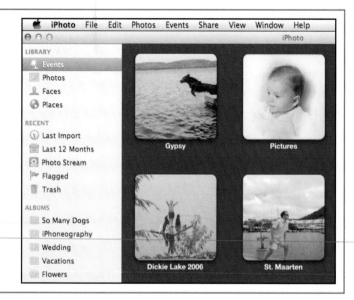

Import Photos to Your Mac

If you have a digital camera attached to your Mac, you can use either the Image Capture application or the iPhoto application, part of the Apple iLife suite, to import some or all of the camera's images to your Mac.

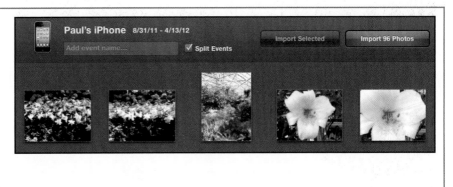

Take Snapshots

If your Mac includes an iSight camera or has a digital video camera connected, you can use the Photo Booth application to take snapshots of whatever subject is currently displayed in the camera. You can also apply various effects to the photos.

Edit Photos

If your Mac comes with the iPhoto application, you can use it to edit your digital photos. You can rotate, crop, or straighten a photo; you can modify a photo's exposure, contrast, and sharpness; you can fix problems such as red eye and blemishes; and you can apply special effects to a photo.

Play and Make a Movie or Slide Show

Your Mac's solid graphical underpinnings mean that it is a great tool for video playback. For example, your Mac comes with tools that enable you to watch movies on DVD. You can play digital video such as movies, TV shows, and podcast files that you download from the Internet, or digital video that you import from a camera. You can also use your Mac to create your own digital movies and your own photo slide shows.

Play a DVD

If your Mac has a DVD drive, you can use the DVD Player application to play a DVD movie. You can either use full-screen mode to watch the movie using the entire screen, or watch the movie in a window while you work on other things. DVD Player has features that enable you to control the movie playback and volume.

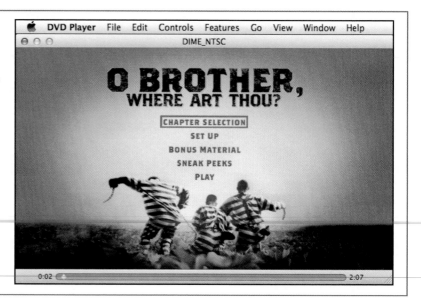

Play a Video File

Your Mac comes with an application called QuickTime Player that enables you to open video files and control the playback and volume. QuickTime Player also includes many extra features, including the ability to record movies and audio, cut and paste scenes, and publish your videos on services such as YouTube and Facebook.

24

Play a Movie, TV Show, or Podcast

You most often use iTunes to play music, but you can also use it to play movies, video files stored on your Mac, and TV shows that you purchase from the iTunes Store, as well as podcasts that you download from the iTunes Store or subscribe to online.

Make a Movie

Most Macs come with an application called iMovie, part of the Apple iLife suite, which enables you to make your own digital movies. You can import clips from a video camera or video file, add clips to the movie, and rearrange and trim those clips as needed. You can also add transitions between scenes, music and sound effects, titles, and more.

Make a Slide Show

You can use your Mac to create your own photo slide shows. Using the iPhoto application, part of the Apple iLife suite, you can create a slide show of your photos that includes animation effects, transition effects, and music. You can enhance the slide show with photo titles and sophisticated background and text themes.

Take Advantage of the Web

You can use your Mac to connect to your Internet account. Once the connection has been established, you can use the built-in web browser to access almost any site available on the web. This means you can use your Mac to search for information, read the latest news, research and purchase goods and services, sell your own items, socialize with others, and more.

Surf the Web

Your Mac comes with a browser application called Safari that you use to surf the web. Safari offers several ways to load and navigate web pages. You can also use Safari to save your favorite web pages as bookmarks, view multiple pages in a single window using tabs, download files to your Mac, and much more.

Search for Information

If you need information on a specific topic, free websites called *search engines* enable you to quickly search the web for pages that have the information you require. You can search the web either by going directly to a search engine site or by using the search feature built into Safari.

Read News

The web is home to many sites that enable you to read the latest news. For example, many print sources have websites, some magazines exist only online, and there are more recent innovations such as blogs and RSS feeds. Some media sites require that you register to access the articles, but on most sites the registration is free.

Buy and Sell

e-Commerce — the online buying and selling of goods and services — is a big part of the web. You can use web-based stores to purchase books, theater tickets, and even cars, which gives you the convenience of shopping at home, easily comparing prices and features, and having goods delivered to your door. Many sites also enable you to sell or auction your products or household items.

Socialize

The web offers many opportunities to socialize, whether you are looking for a friend or a date, or you just want some good conversation. However, you should observe some common-sense precautions. For example, arrange to meet new friends in public places, supervise all online socializing done by children, and do not give out personal information to strangers.

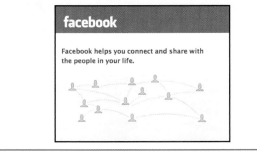

Take Advantage of iCloud

You can use your Mac to set up a free web-based iCloud account that enables you to perform many activities online, including exchanging email, maintaining contacts, and tracking appointments. You can also use your iCloud account to synchronize data between your Mac and other Macs, Windows PCs, as well as devices such as iPods, iPhones, and iPads.

Communicate with Others

You can use your Mac to communicate with other people using online and wireless technologies. For example, once you have connected your Mac to the Internet, you can start sending and receiving email, using either your Internet service provider (ISP) account or a web-based account. You can also use your Internet connection to exchange instant messages and perform audio and video chats. If you have a camera attached to your Mac, you can also place video calls to other people through your wired or wireless network.

Exchange Email

Email is the Internet system that enables you to electronically exchange messages with other Internet users anywhere in the world. To use email, you must have an email account, which is usually supplied by your ISP or email service. The account gives you an email address to which others can send messages. You then set up that account in the OS X Mail application.

Exchange Email over the Web

You can also set up a web-based email account. Although you can do this using services such as Hotmail.com and Yahoo.com, many Mac users create iCloud accounts, which include web-based email. A web-based account is convenient because it enables you to send and receive messages from any computer that has access to the Internet.

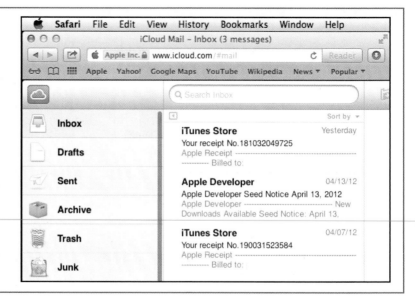

Exchange Instant Messages

Instant messaging allows you to contact other people who are online, thus enabling you to have a real-time exchange of messages. Communicating in real time means that if you send a message to another person who is online, that message appears on the person's computer right away. If that person sends you a response, it appears on your computer right away. In OS X Mountain Lion, you use the Messages application to exchange instant messages.

Share via Twitter

If you have an account on Twitter, you can configure your Mac with your Twitter credentials. You can then share information with your Twitter followers by sending tweets from a number of Mac applications, including Safari and iPhoto. You can also use the Photo Booth application to take your picture, and then use that photo as your Twitter profile picture.

Place Video Calls

OS X Mountain Lion comes with a program called FaceTime that enables you to make video calls to other people. With a video call, your image is captured by a video camera — such as the iSight or FaceTime HD camera built into many Macs — and a microphone captures your voice. Both the video and audio streams are sent to the other person, who could be using FaceTime on a Mac, an iPhone 4 or later, a fourth-generation iPod touch or later, or an iPad 2 or later. The other person can also see and hear you.

Organize Your Contacts and Appointments

You can use your Mac to help you organize various aspects of your life. For example, your Mac comes with tools that enable you to enter, edit, organize, and work with your contacts, which means you can maintain a convenient digital version of your address book. Other Mac tools enable you to schedule events such as appointments, meetings, and trips. You can even configure your Mac to synchronize your contacts and schedule among multiple devices.

Maintain Your Contact List

Your Mac comes with an application called Contacts that enables you to store information about your contacts. For each contact, you can store data such as the person's name, address, telephone number, email address, and birthday.

Work with Contacts

You can use your Contacts list to perform many different contact-related tasks. For example, you can use Mail to send a message either to individual contacts or to a contact group, which is a Contacts item that contains multiple contacts. Also, you can use Calendar to set up a meeting with one or more contacts.

Schedule an Appointment

You can help organize your life by using your
Mac to record your
appointments on the date
and time they occur. You
do this using the Calendar
application, which uses
an electronic calendar to
store your appointments.
You can even configure
Calendar to display a
reminder before an
appointment occurs.

Schedule an All-Day Event

If an appointment has no set time — for example,
a birthday, anniversary, or multiple-day event such
as a sales
meeting or
vacation — you
can use Calendar
to set up the
appointment as
an all-day event.

Schedule a Repeating Appointment

If an appointment occurs
regularly — for example, once a
week or once every three
months — you do not need to
schedule every appointment
manually. Instead, you can use
Calendar to configure the
activity as a repeating
appointment, where you specify
the repeat interval. Calendar
then creates all the future
appointments automatically.

Synchronize with iCloud

If you have an iCloud account, you can synchronize
your Mac contacts and appointments so that they also
appear in the iCloud Contacts and Calendar. If you
have an iPod touch, iPhone, or iPad, you can use
iCloud to sync those same contacts and appointments
to your device. If you have a second Mac or a
Windows PC, you can use iCloud to keep your contacts
and appointments in sync on both computers.

CHAPTER 3

Connecting Devices

When you plug a device into your Mac, most of the time the device works right away. However, some devices require a bit of extra effort on your part to get them connected and configured. This chapter takes you through a few such devices, including an external display, printer, fax, iPod, iPhone, iPad, Bluetooth device, and even another Mac.

Connect Your Mac to an External Display

You can connect your Mac to an external display such as a monitor or a TV. This is essential for machines such as the Mac mini and Mac Pro that do not come with a screen. However, you can also connect an iMac or portable Mac to a larger screen for more viewing area.

The Mac Connection

Thunderbolt Port

All current Mac models, with the exception of the Mac Pro, come with at least one Thunderbolt port for connection to Thunderbolt-compatible monitors.

HDMI Port

The latest models of the MacBook Pro and the Mac mini come with an HDMI port for connection to a monitor, TV, or projector that has an HDMI port.

DVI Port

The Mac Pro, and older models of the Mac mini and MacBook Pro, use a regular DVI port to output video.

Mini DisplayPort

The Mac Pro and older models of all the other Mac types come with a Mini DisplayPort. Apple offers separate adapters for connecting these ports to regular DVI displays.

The Display Connection

DVI Port

Most computer monitors come with at least one DVI port, although the configuration (the number of holes) may not match what you have on your Mac. Therefore, the cable you use must have connectors that match the ports on both the Mac and the monitor.

VGA Port

Most computer monitors come with at least one VGA port. To use such a port with your Mac, you need a cable adapter that converts DVI or Mini DisplayPort to VGA. Note that Mini DisplayPort cables also work with Thunderbird ports.

Composite or S-Video Port

Most televisions come with either or both an S-Video port or a composite video port. To use such a port with your Mac, you need a cable adapter that converts DVI or Mini DisplayPort to either S-Video or composite video.

Cable Adapters

If you have a Mac that uses an HDMI port, you may need to purchase an adapter that enables you to connect your Mac to VGA or regular DVI display. You can also purchase from Apple an adapter that enables you to connect your Mac to a composite or S-Video display.

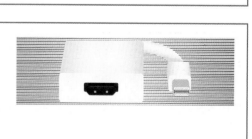

Connect a Printer

If you have a printer that you want to use to make hard copies of your documents, you must first connect the printer to your Mac. In most cases, a few moments after you connect the printer, your Mac will recognize the printer and install it right away. However, you should check that your printer installed correctly. If it did not, then you must add your printer to OS X by hand. In rare cases, you may need to insert the installation disc that came with your printer.

Connect a Printer

1 Connect the printer's USB cable to a free USB port on your Mac, and then turn on the printer.

2 Click the Apple icon ().

3 Click **System Preferences**.

Note: You can also click the System Preferences icon (■) in the Dock.

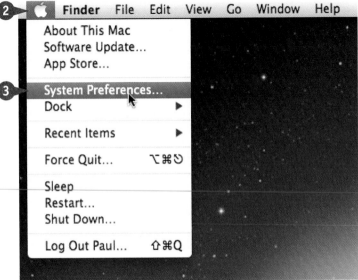

The System Preferences appear.

④ Click **Print & Scan**.

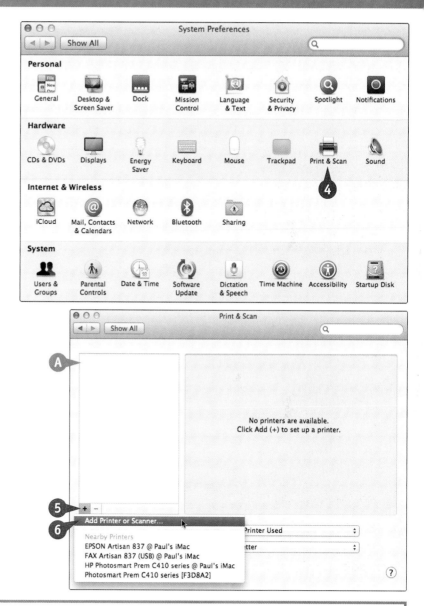

The Print & Scan preferences appear.

Ⓐ If you see your printer in the Printers list, skip the rest of the steps in this section.

⑤ Click **Add** (⊞).

⑥ Click **Add Printer or Scanner**.

The Add Printer dialog appears.

continued ▶

TIP

What do I do if my printer has a parallel port instead of a USB port?

Although all new printers come with USB ports, many older printers use a parallel (also called LPT) port instead. No Mac has a corresponding printer port, so you need to purchase a parallel-to-USB adapter cable, which has a parallel connector on one end and a USB connector on the other.

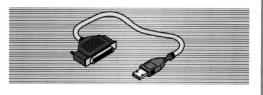

Connect a Printer (continued)

Fortunately, the vast majority of the time your Mac recognizes your printer immediately after you attach it to the USB port, so in most cases you will not need to use the extra steps in this section. You can also connect to a printer that has been shared on your local network. To learn how to make the connection to a network printer, see Chapter 14, "Networking with Your Mac."

Connect a Printer (continued)

⑦ Click **Default**.

⑧ In the Printer Name list, click your printer.

⑨ Use the Name text box to edit the printer name.

⑩ If the Use list shows the wrong printer, click 🔽 and then click the correct printer.

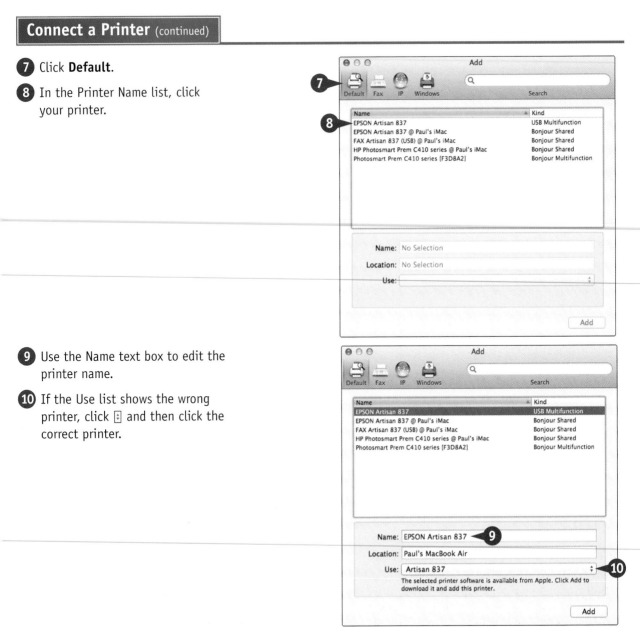

11 Click **Add**.

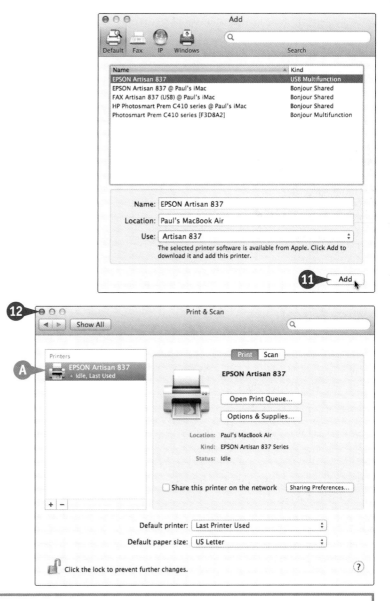

A OS X installs the printer and then adds the printer to the Printers list.

12 Click **Close** (⊜).

TIPS

What should I do if I do not see my printer in the Print Using list?

First, insert the disc that came with your printer and then run the installation program. If that does not work, follow steps **1** to **8** and then, in the Use list, click ⊡ and then click **Other**. Click the printer disc, locate and choose the printer driver, and then click **Open**.

What if I do not have a printer disc?

If you do not have a printer disc, or if the disc does not contain Mac drivers, visit the printer manufacturer's website and download the drivers you need. If you cannot get drivers for the printer (many printer manufacturers do not bother writing Mac drivers), you may still be able to use the printer by following steps **1** to **8** and then choosing **Generic PostScript Printer** in the Use list.

Connect a Fax Modem

If you want to send or receive faxes using your Mac, you must connect an external fax modem. Faxing has long been superseded by email as the preferred way of sending documents and images. However, faxing still has a place for those times when you need to send a document that shows your signature or contains handwritten annotations.

Some older Macs came with an internal fax modem already installed, so you may not need to connect an external modem. Also note that Apple's USB Modem is not compatible with OS X Lion or Mountain Lion.

Connect a Fax Modem

① Connect the fax modem to a free USB port on your Mac.

② Follow steps **2** to **5** in the previous section to display the Add Printer dialog.

③ Click **Fax**.

Note: If you are using a version of OS X earlier than Leopard (10.5), click **Default Browser** instead.

④ In the Printer Name list, click your modem.

5 Use the Name text box to edit the modem name.

6 Click **Add**.

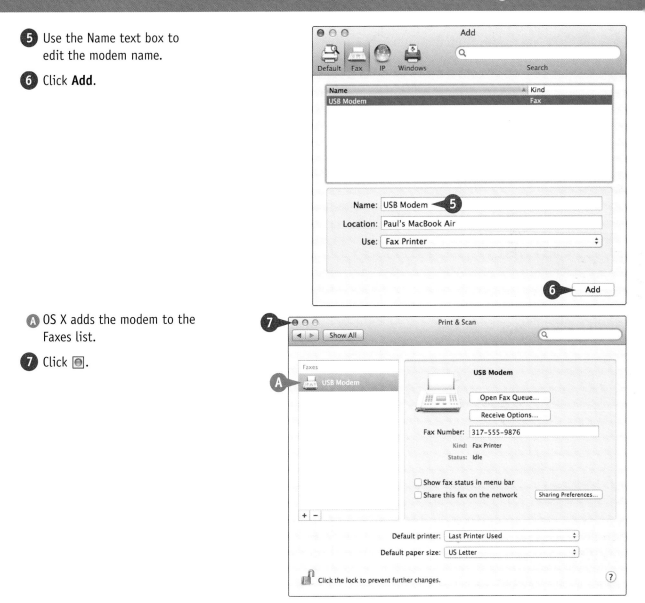

A OS X adds the modem to the Faxes list.

7 Click ⊙.

What do I do if my modem has a serial port instead of a USB port?

Although almost all new modems come with USB ports, many older modems use a serial port instead. No Mac has a corresponding serial port, so you need to purchase a serial-to-USB adapter or cable, which has a serial connector on one end and a USB connector on the other.

Connect an iPod

To synchronize some or all of your iTunes library with your iPod or iPod touch, you can connect the device to your Mac. With the latest versions of iOS, the iPod touch can synchronize with your Mac over Wi-Fi. However, if your iPod touch and your Mac are not on the same network, or you want to synchronize an older iPod, you need to make a physical connection between the device and your Mac.

To connect an iPod or iPod touch, you need the USB cable that came with the device's package. You also need a free USB port on your Mac.

Connect an iPod

Connect the iPod

1 Attach the USB cable's 30-pin connector to the iPod's port.

Note: If your iPod is flat on the desk, make sure you insert the 30-pin connector with the icon pointing up.

Note: If you have an iPod touch or iPod nano that was released in 2012, you use the 8-pin Lightning connector instead.

2 Attach the cable's USB connector to a free USB port on your Mac.

Your Mac launches iTunes and automatically begins synchronizing the iPod.

Disconnect the iPod

1 In iTunes, click the **Eject** button (⏏) beside your iPod's name.

iTunes begins releasing the iPod.

Note: See the following tip to learn when it is safe to disconnect the cable from the iPod.

2 Pinch the sides of the 30-pin connector and then pull the connector away from the iPod.

3 Disconnect the USB connector from the Mac's USB port.

Note: If your Mac has two or more free USB ports and you synchronize your iPod frequently, consider leaving the cable plugged in to a USB port for easier iPod connections in the future.

TIP

Do I always have to eject my iPod before disconnecting it?
For an iPod touch, you can disconnect the device at any time as long as there is no sync in progress. For an older iPod, you must first eject the iPod if the iPod screen says "Do not disconnect," "Eject Before Disconnecting," or "Sync in Progress." You can safely disconnect the cable from your iPod if the iPod screen says "OK to disconnect," "Charging," "Charged," or you see the iPod main menu screen.

Connect an iPhone

To synchronize your iTunes library, Contacts, Calendar appointments, Safari bookmarks, and email account settings with your iPhone, you can connect the iPhone to your Mac. Recent versions of iOS have enabled the iPhone to use Wi-Fi to synchronize with your Mac. However, if your iPhone is not running a recent version of iOS, or if your Mac and your iPhone are not on the same network, you must physically connect your iPhone to your Mac using the USB cable that came with the iPhone package. You can also connect an iPhone using an optional dock.

Connect an iPhone

Connect the iPhone Directly

1 Attach the USB cable's 30-pin connector to the iPhone's port.

Note: If your iPhone is flat on the desk, make sure you insert the 30-pin connector with the icon pointing up.

Note: If you have an iPhone 5, you use the 8-pin Lightning connector instead.

2 Attach the cable's USB connector to a free USB port on your Mac.

Your Mac launches iTunes and automatically begins synchronizing the iPhone.

Connect the iPhone Using the Dock

 Attach the USB cable's 30-pin connector to the iPhone dock's port.

Note: Make sure you insert the 30-pin connector with the icon pointing up.

Note: If you have an iPhone 5–compatible dock, you use the 8-pin Lightning connector instead.

2 Insert the iPhone into the dock.

3 Attach the cable's USB connector to a free USB port on your Mac.

Your Mac launches iTunes and automatically begins synchronizing the iPhone.

TIP

How do I disconnect the iPhone?

In iTunes, click the **Eject** button (⏏) beside your iPhone's name. If you are using the USB cable, pinch the sides of the cable's 30-pin connector and then pull the connector away from the iPhone. If you are using the dock, lift the iPhone out of the dock.

Connect an iPad

To synchronize some or all of your iTunes library, Calendar events, Contacts, Safari bookmarks, and more with your iPad, you can connect the iPad to your Mac. The most recent iOS versions have included a feature that enables you to synchronize an iPad over a Wi-Fi connection. However, if your iPad is running an older version of iOS, or if your iPad and your Mac are not on the same network, you must physically connect your iPad to your Mac.

To connect an iPad, you need the USB cable that came with the iPad package. You can also connect an iPad using an optional dock.

Connect an iPad

Connect the iPad Directly

1 Attach the USB cable's 30-pin connector to the iPad's port.

Note: If your iPad is flat on the desk, make sure you insert the 30-pin connector with the icon pointing up.

2 Attach the cable's USB connector to a free USB port on your Mac.

Your Mac launches iTunes and automatically begins synchronizing the iPad.

Connect the iPad Using the Dock

1 Attach the USB cable's 30-pin connector to the iPad dock's port.

Note: Make sure you insert the 30-pin connector with the icon pointing up.

2 Insert the iPad into the dock.

3 Attach the cable's USB connector to a free USB port on your Mac.

Your Mac launches iTunes and automatically begins synchronizing the iPad.

TIP

How do I disconnect the iPad?
In iTunes, click the **Eject** button (⏏) beside your iPad's name. If you are using the USB cable, pinch the sides of the iPad connector and then pull the connector away from the iPad. If you are using the dock, lift the iPad out of the dock.

Connect a Bluetooth Device

You can make wireless connections to devices such as mice, keyboards, headsets, and cell phones by using the Bluetooth networking technology. Bluetooth works by creating a temporary wireless network between your Mac and the device. Networking requires special equipment, but with Bluetooth devices, the networking is built in, so no extra equipment is needed.

For Bluetooth connections to work, your Mac must support Bluetooth (all newer Macs do) and your device must be Bluetooth enabled. Also, your Mac and the Bluetooth device must remain within about 30 feet of each other.

Connect a Bluetooth Device

Connect a Bluetooth Device without a Passkey

1 Click **System Preferences** (◙) in the Dock.

2 Click **Bluetooth**.

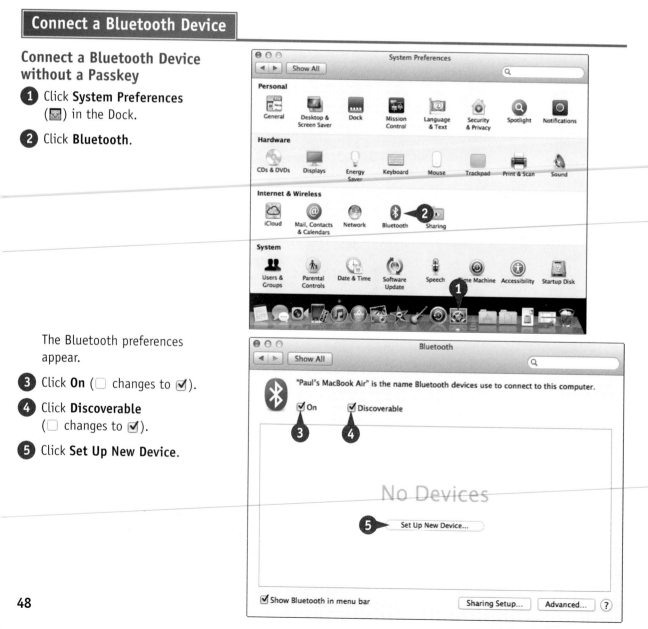

The Bluetooth preferences appear.

3 Click **On** (☐ changes to ☑).

4 Click **Discoverable** (☐ changes to ☑).

5 Click **Set Up New Device**.

The Bluetooth Setup Assistant appears.

⑥ Perform whatever steps are necessary to make your Bluetooth device discoverable.

Note: For example, if you are connecting a Bluetooth mouse, the device often has a separate switch or button that makes the mouse discoverable, so you need to turn on that switch or press that button.

Ⓐ A list of the available Bluetooth devices appears here.

⑦ Click the Bluetooth device you want to connect.

⑧ Click **Continue**.

⑨ Perform the steps required to pair your Mac and your device.

Your Mac connects with the device.

⑩ Click **Quit**.

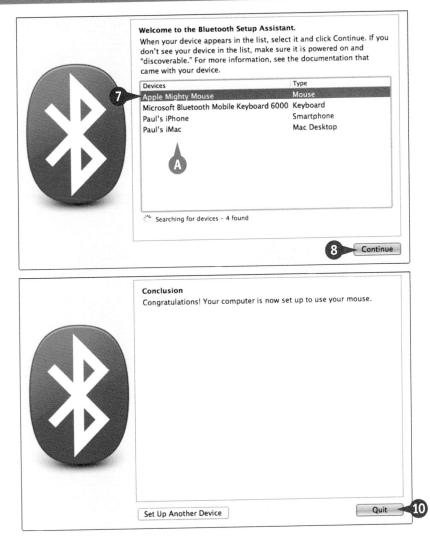

Welcome to the Bluetooth Setup Assistant.
When your device appears in the list, select it and click Continue. If you don't see your device in the list, make sure it is powered on and "discoverable." For more information, see the documentation that came with your device.

Devices	Type
Apple Mighty Mouse	Mouse
Microsoft Bluetooth Mobile Keyboard 6000	Keyboard
Paul's iPhone	Smartphone
Paul's iMac	Mac Desktop

Searching for devices – 4 found

Continue

Conclusion
Congratulations! Your computer is now set up to use your mouse.

Set Up Another Device   Quit

TIPS

What does it mean to make a device "discoverable"?
This means that you configure the device to broadcast its availability for a Bluetooth connection. This is important because you usually want to use a Bluetooth device such as a mouse or keyboard with a single computer. By controlling when the device is discoverable, you ensure that it works only with the computer you want it to.

What does "pairing" mean?
As a security precaution, many Bluetooth devices do not connect automatically to other devices. This makes sense because otherwise it means a stranger with a Bluetooth device could connect to your cell phone or even your Mac. To prevent this, most Bluetooth devices require you to enter a passcode before the connection is made. This is known as *pairing* the two devices.

continued ▶

A Bluetooth mouse and a Bluetooth headset do not require any extra pairing steps, although with a headset you must configure your Mac to use it for sound output. However, pairing devices such as a Bluetooth keyboard and a Bluetooth cell phone does require an extra step.

In most cases, pairing is accomplished by your Mac generating a 6- or 8-digit *passkey* that you must then type into the Bluetooth device (assuming that it has some kind of keypad). In other cases, the device comes with a default passkey that you must enter into your Mac to set up the pairing.

Connect a Bluetooth Device (continued)

Connect a Bluetooth Device with a Passkey

1 Turn the device on, if required.

2 Turn on the switch or press the button that makes the device discoverable, if required.

3 Follow steps **1** and **2** from earlier in this section and click **Add** (⊞).

The Bluetooth Setup Assistant appears.

4 Click your Bluetooth device.

5 Click **Continue**.

The Bluetooth Setup Assistant displays a passkey.

6 Use the Bluetooth device to type the displayed passkey.

7 Press Return.

Bluetooth Setup Assistant

Welcome to the Bluetooth Setup Assistant.
When your device appears in the list, select it and click Continue. If you don't see your device in the list, make sure it is powered on and "discoverable." For more information, see the documentation that came with your device.

Devices	Type
Microsoft Bluetooth Mobile Keyboard 6000	Keyboard
Paul's iPhone	Smartphone
Paul's iMac	Mac Desktop

Searching for devices – 3 found

5 Continue

Bluetooth Setup Assistant

Attempting to pair with "Microsoft Bluetooth Mobile Keyboard 6000."
Your device may ask you to enter a passkey. Check your device to see if it is ready to accept a passkey. When your device is ready, enter in the following passkey followed by the Return key:

6 → 7 2 5 5 6 5 9 8   return

Once you have entered the passkey on your device the pairing process will be completed.

Listen to Audio Through Bluetooth Headphones

1 Click **System Preferences** () in the Dock.

2 Click **Sound**.

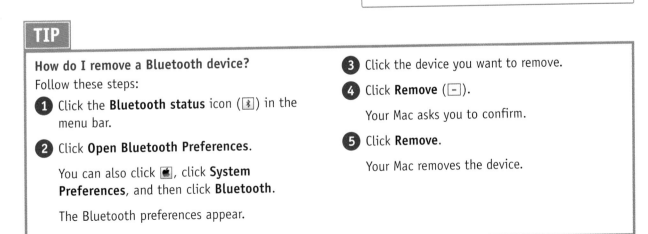

The Sound preferences appear.

3 Click **Output**.

4 Click the Bluetooth headphones.

How do I remove a Bluetooth device?

Follow these steps:

1 Click the **Bluetooth status** icon (🚹) in the menu bar.

2 Click **Open Bluetooth Preferences**.

You can also click 🍎, click **System Preferences**, and then click **Bluetooth**.

The Bluetooth preferences appear.

3 Click the device you want to remove.

4 Click **Remove** (⊟).

Your Mac asks you to confirm.

5 Click **Remove**.

Your Mac removes the device.

Connect Your Mac to Another Mac

You can share data such as documents, bookmarks, and downloads between two Macs by connecting those Macs using a Thunderbolt cable or a network cable. The Thunderbolt connection is the better option because it is about ten times faster than the network connection. With the exception of the Mac Pro, all the latest versions of the Mac come with at least one Thunderbolt port.

This section assumes that you do not have a local area network set up, so you need to connect the two Macs directly. In either case, you must enable file sharing to share data between the Macs.

Connect Your Mac to Another Mac

Connect Using a Thunderbolt Cable

1 Attach one of the Thunderbolt cable's connectors to the Thunderbolt port on one of the Macs.

2 Attach the other Thunderbolt cable connector to the Thunderbolt port on the other Mac.

Connect Using a Network Cable

1 Attach one of the network cable's connectors to the network port on one of the Macs.

2 Attach the other network cable connector to the network port on the other Mac.

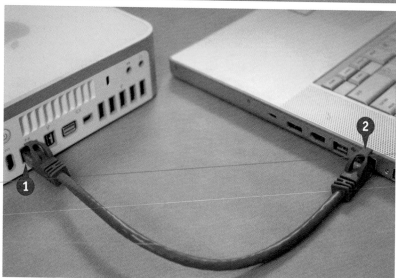

Enable File Sharing

1 Click .

2 Click **System Preferences**.

The System Preferences window appears.

3 Click **Sharing**.

Can I use a regular network cable?

Yes, for many Macs. However, some older Macs require a special crossover cable. You must use such a cable if you want to connect any of the following Macs:

eMac	iMac (Summer 2001)
iBook	Power Mac G4 (AGP Graphics)
iBook (FireWire)	Power Mac G4 (PCI Graphics)
iMac (17-inch Flat Panel)	Power Mac G4 Cube
iMac (Early 2001)	Power Macintosh G3 (Blue and White)
iMac (Flat Panel)	PowerBook (FireWire)
iMac (Slot Loading)	PowerBook G3 Series (Bronze Keyboard)
iMac (Summer 2000)	

continued ▶

The purpose of connecting one Mac to another is to share documents, photos, and other data between the two Macs. By default, a Mac is not configured to share its data with other computers, so you must enable file sharing on both Macs.

Once file sharing is turned on, after you make the Thunderbolt or network cable connection you can see the files shared on the other Mac by accessing Finder's Network folder. You can also control which folders each Mac shares.

Connect Your Mac to Another Mac (continued)

The Sharing preferences appear.

4 Click **File Sharing** (☐ changes to ☑).

Note: See the tip on the following page to learn how to share other folders on your Mac.

5 Click ⊙.

View the Other Mac's Files

1 Click **Finder** (🖥).

2 Click the icon for the other Mac.

Note: If you do not see an icon for the other Mac, click **Go** and then click **Network**, or press Shift+⌘+K.

A Your Mac connects to the other Mac using the Guest account.

3 Click **Connect As**.

Your Mac prompts you to log in to the other Mac.

4 Click **Registered User** (○ changes to ◉).

5 Type the user name of an account on the other Mac.

6 Type the account password.

7 Click **Remember this password in my keychain** (☐ changes to ☑).

8 Click **Connect**.

Your Mac logs in to the other Mac.

B You see the folder associated with the user account that you used to log in to the other Mac.

9 Click a folder to see and work with its contents.

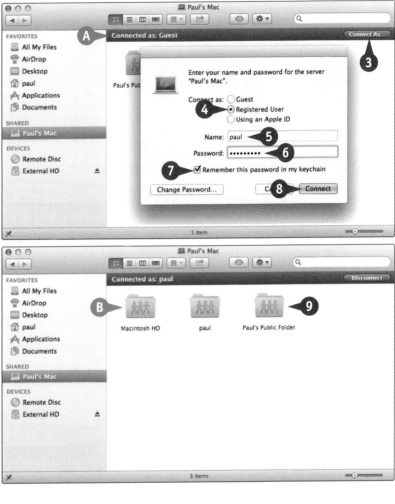

TIP

How do I share other folders?

1 Click 🍎.

2 Click **System Preferences**.

3 Click **Sharing**.

4 Click **File Sharing**. Under the Shared Folders list, click 📷.

5 Click the folder you want to share.

6 Click **Add**.

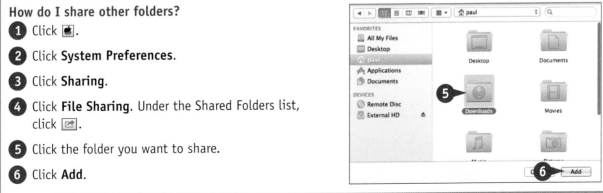

CHAPTER 4

Learning Mac Basics

Much of the work you do on your Mac will involve applications and documents, which are files that contain text, images, and other data. These tasks include saving, opening, and editing documents, as well as copying and renaming files. To perform these and other tasks, you should have a basic understanding of how to work with and manage applications and documents on your Mac.

Explore the OS X Screen

Before you can begin to understand how the OS X operating system works, you should become familiar with the basic screen elements. These elements include the menu bar, the desktop, desktop icons, and the Dock. Understanding where these elements appear on the screen and what they are used for will help you work through the rest of the sections in this book and help you navigate your Mac and its applications on your own.

Ⓐ Menu Bar

The menu bar contains the pull-down menus for OS X and most Mac software.

Ⓑ Desktop

This is the OS X work area, where you work with your applications and documents.

Ⓒ Mouse Pointer

When you move your mouse or move your finger on a trackpad, the pointer moves along with it.

Ⓓ Desktop Icon

An icon on the desktop represents an application, a folder, a document, or a device attached to your Mac, such as a disk drive, a CD or DVD, or an iPod.

Ⓔ Dock

The Dock contains several icons, each of which gives you quick access to some commonly used applications.

Tour the Dock

The Dock is the strip that runs along the bottom of the Mac screen. The Dock is populated with several small images, called *icons*. Each icon represents a particular component of your Mac, and clicking the icon opens the component. This makes the Dock one of the most important and useful Mac features because it gives you one-click access to applications, folders, and documents. The icons shown here are typical, but your Mac may display a different arrangement.

A Finder

Work with the files on your computer.

B Launchpad

View, organize, and start your applications.

C Mission Control

Locate and navigate running applications.

D Safari

Browse the World Wide Web on the Internet.

E Mail

Send and receive email messages.

F Contacts

Store and access people's contact information.

G Calendar

Record upcoming meetings and other events.

H Reminders

Set reminders for upcoming tasks.

I Notes

Record to-do lists and other short notes.

J Messages

Send instant messages to other people.

K FaceTime

Place video calls to other FaceTime users.

L Photo Booth

Take a picture using the camera on your Mac.

M iTunes

Play music and other media and add media to your iPod, iPhone, or iPad.

N App Store

Install new applications and upgrade existing ones.

O iPhoto

Import and edit digital photos and other images.

P iMovie

Import video footage and edit digital movies.

Q GarageBand

Create songs, podcasts, and other audio files.

R Time Machine

Create and access backups of your files.

S System Preferences

Customize and configure your Mac.

T Applications

Display the contents of your Applications folder.

U Documents

Display the contents of your Documents folder.

V Downloads

Display the contents of your Downloads folder.

W Trash

Delete files, folders, and applications.

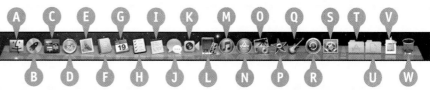

Start an Application

To perform tasks of any kind on your Mac, you use one of the applications installed on your Mac. The application you use depends on the task you want to perform. For example, if you want to surf the World Wide Web, you use a web browser application, such as the Safari program that comes with your Mac. Before you can use an application, however, you must first tell your Mac which application you want to run. Your Mac launches the application and displays it on the desktop. You can then use the application's tools to perform your tasks.

Start an Application

1 Click the Launchpad icon ().

The Launchpad screen appears.

2 If the application you want to start resides in a different Launchpad screen, click the dot that corresponds to the screen.

Launchpad switches to the screen and displays the applications.

③ If the application you want to start resides within a folder, click the folder.

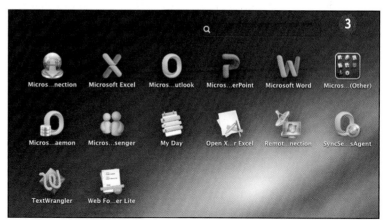

Launchpad opens the folder.

④ Click the icon of the application you want to start.

Your Mac starts the application.

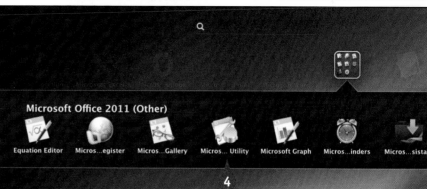

The dots that represent each Launchpad screen are quite small, making them hard to click with the mouse. Is there an easier way to navigate the Launchpad screens?
You can press ⌘+▶ and cmd+◀ to navigate the screens. You can also place two fingers on either the trackpad or the surface of a Magic Mouse and then swipe right or left. Note, too, that you can also use a trackpad gesture to open Launchpad: Place four fingers lightly on the trackpad and pinch them together.

How do I shut down a running application?
The easiest way is to right-click the application's Dock icon and then click **Quit**. Alternatively, you can switch to the application and press ⌘+Q.

Switch Between Applications

If you plan on running multiple applications at the same time, you need to know how to easily switch from one application to another. On your Mac, after you start one application, you do not need to close that application before you open another one. Your Mac supports a feature called *multitasking*, which means running two or more applications at once. This is handy if you need to use several applications throughout the day. For example, you might keep your word processing application, your web browser, and your email application open all day.

Switch Between Applications

1 Click the Dock icon of the application that you want to switch to.

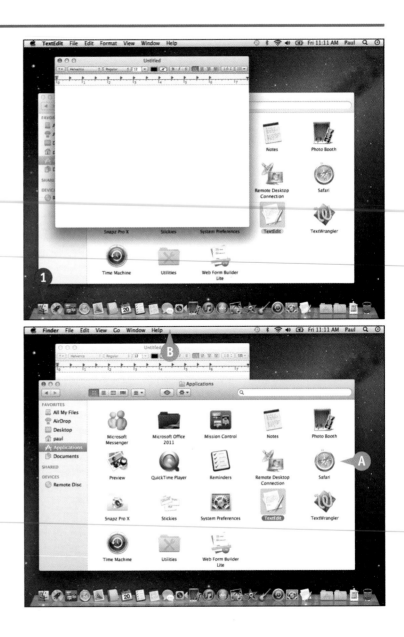

A Your Mac brings the application window(s) to the foreground.

B The menu bar displays the menus associated with the application.

Note: To switch between applications from the keyboard, press and hold ⌘ and repeatedly press Tab until the application that you want is highlighted in the list of running applications. Release ⌘ to switch to the application.

Tour an Application Window

When you start an application, it appears on the Mac desktop in its own window. Each application has a unique window layout, but almost all application windows have a few features in common. To get the most out of your applications and to start working quickly and efficiently in an application, you need to know what these common features are and where to find them within the application window.

Ⓐ Close Button

Click the **Close** button (Ⓐ) to remove the application window from the desktop, usually without exiting the application.

Ⓑ Minimize Button

Click the **Minimize** button (Ⓐ) to remove the window from the desktop and display an icon for the currently open document in the right side of the Dock. The window is still open, but not active.

Ⓒ Zoom Button

Click the **Zoom** button (Ⓐ) to enlarge the window so that it can display all of its content, or as much of its content as can fit the screen.

Ⓓ Toolbar

The toolbar contains buttons that offer easy access to common application commands and features, although not all applications have toolbars.

Ⓔ Status Bar

The status bar displays information about the current state of the application or document.

Ⓕ Vertical Scroll Bar

Click and drag the vertical scroll bar to navigate up and down in a document.

Ⓖ Horizontal Scroll Bar

Click and drag the horizontal scroll bar to navigate left and right in a document.

Ⓗ Resize Control

Click and drag any edge or corner of the window to make the window larger or smaller.

Select a Command from a Pull-Down Menu

When you are working in an application, you can use the menu bar to access the application's commands and features. Each item in the menu bar represents a *pull-down menu*, a collection of commands usually related to each other in some way. For example, the File menu commands usually deal with file-related tasks such as opening and closing documents. The items in a menu are either commands that execute an action in the application, or features that you can turn on and off.

Select a Command from a Pull-Down Menu

Execute Commands

1 Click the name of the menu that you want to display.

Ⓐ The application displays the menu.

2 Click the command that you want to execute.

The application executes the command.

Ⓑ A command followed by an ellipsis (...) means the command displays a dialog.

Ⓒ A command followed by an arrow (▶) means the command displays a submenu. Click the command to open the submenu and then click the command that you want to run.

Turn Features On and Off

1 Click the name of the menu that you want to display.

Ⓓ The application displays the menu.

2 Click the menu item.

You may have to click for a submenu if your command is not on the main menu.

The application turns the feature either on (a check mark, ☑, appears the next time you open the menu) or off (no check mark appears the next time you open the menu).

Select a Command Using a Toolbar

You can access many application commands faster by using the toolbar. Many applications come with a toolbar, which is a collection of buttons, lists, and other controls displayed in a strip, usually across the top of the application window. Because the toolbar is always visible, you can always use it to select commands, which means that the toolbar often gives you one-click access to the application's most common features. This is faster than using the menu bar method, which often takes several clicks, depending on the command.

Select a Command Using a Toolbar

Turn Features On and Off

1 Click the toolbar button that represents the feature you want to turn on.

A The application turns the feature on and indicates this state by highlighting the toolbar button.

B When a feature is turned off, the application does not highlight the button.

Execute Commands

1 Click the toolbar button that represents the command that you want.

2 If the button displays a menu, click the command on the menu.

C The application executes the command.

Select Options with Dialog Controls

You often interact with an application by selecting options or typing text using a *dialog* — a window that appears when an application has information for you, or needs you to provide information. For example, when you select the File menu's Print command to print a document, you use the Print dialog to specify the number of copies that you want to print. You provide that and other information by accessing various types of dialog controls.

To provide information to an application quickly and accurately, you need to know what these dialog controls look like and how they work.

Ⓐ Command Button

Clicking a command button executes the command printed on the button face. For example, you can click **OK** to apply settings that you have chosen in a dialog, or you can click **Cancel** to close the dialog without changing the settings.

Ⓑ Text Box

A text box enables you to enter typed text. Use **Del** to delete any existing characters, and then type your text.

Ⓒ List Box

A list box displays a list of choices from which you select the item you want. Use the vertical scroll bar to bring the item you want into view, and then click the item to select it.

Enter the URL of the calendar you want to subscribe to.

Calendar URL: http://cal.server.com/mycalendar.ics Ⓑ

Cancel   Subscribe Ⓐ

Spelling and Grammar

fleet   Change

Find Next

glee
glees Ⓒ
Glenn
glen
fleet
gleed

Ignore
Learn
Define
Guess

Automatic by Language   ☐ Check grammar

Ⓓ Tabs

Many dialogs offer a large number of controls, so related controls appear on different tabs, and the tab names and icons appear across the top of the dialog. Click a tab to see its controls.

Ⓔ Pop-Up Menu

A pop-up menu displays a list of choices from which you select the item you want. Click ⊡ to pop up the menu, and then click the item that you want to select.

Ⓕ Check Box

Clicking a check box toggles an application feature on and off. If you are turning on a feature, the check box changes from ☐ to ☑; if you are turning off the feature, the check box changes from ☑ to ☐.

Ⓖ Radio Button

Clicking a radio button turns on an application feature. Only one radio button in a group can be turned on at a time. When you click a radio button that is currently off, it changes from ◯ to ◉; the radio button that was on changes from ◉ to ◯.

Save a Document

After you create a document and make changes to it, you can save the document to preserve your work. When you work on a document, your Mac stores the changes in your computer's memory. However, your Mac erases the contents of the Mac's memory each time you shut down or restart the computer. This means that the changes you have made to your document are lost when you turn off or restart your Mac. However, saving the document preserves your changes on your Mac's hard drive.

Save a Document

1 Click **File**.

2 Click **Save**.

In most applications, you can also press ⌘+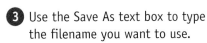.

If you have saved the document previously, your changes are now preserved, and you do not need to follow the rest of the steps in this section.

If this is a new document that you have never saved before, the Save dialog appears.

3 Use the Save As text box to type the filename you want to use.

Ⓐ To store the file in a different folder, you can click ⬦ in the Where list and then click the location that you prefer.

4 Click **Save**.

The application saves the file.

Open a Document

To work with a document that you have saved in the past, you can open it in the application that you used to create it. When you save a document, you save its contents to your Mac's hard drive, and those contents are stored in a separate file. When you open the document using the same application that you used to save it, your Mac loads the file's contents into memory and displays the document in the application. You can then view or edit the document as needed.

Open a Document

1 Start the application that you want to work with.

2 Click **File**.

3 Click **Open**.

In most applications, you can also press ⌘+O.

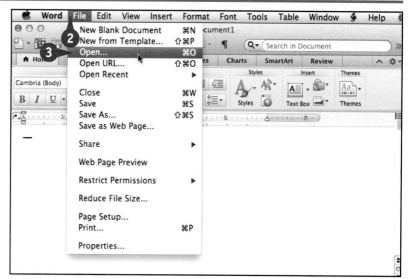

The Open dialog appears.

A To select a different folder from which to open the file, you can click ⬆ and then click the location that you prefer.

4 Click the document.

5 Click **Open**.

The document appears in a window on the desktop.

Print a Document

When you need a hard copy of your document, either for your files or to distribute to someone else, you can send the document to your printer. Most applications that deal with documents also come with a Print command. When you run this command, the Print dialog appears. You use the Print dialog to choose the printer you want to use, as well as to specify how many copies you want to print. Many Print dialogs also enable you to see a preview of your document before printing it.

Print a Document

1 Turn on your printer.

2 Open the document that you want to print.

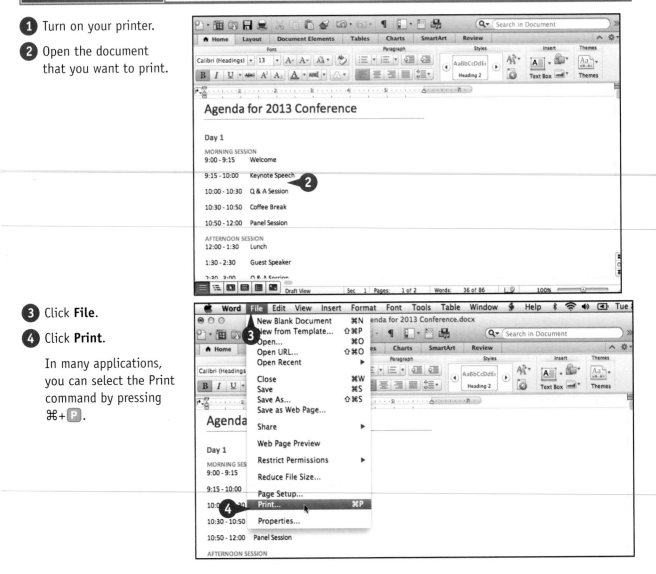

3 Click **File**.

4 Click **Print**.

In many applications, you can select the Print command by pressing ⌘+P.

The Print dialog appears.

The layout of the Print dialog varies from application to application. The version shown here is a typical example.

5 If you have more than one printer, click ⬦ in the Printer list to select the printer that you want to use.

6 To print more than one copy, use the Copies text box to type the number of copies to print.

7 Click **Print**.

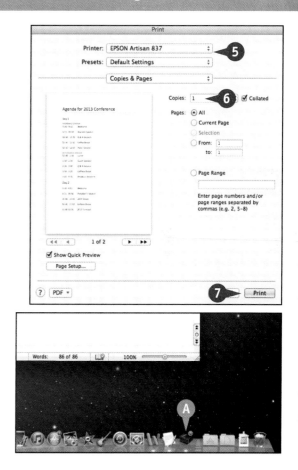

A Your Mac prints the document. The printer's icon appears in the Dock while the document prints.

TIP

Can I print only part of my document?

Yes, although the options for printing only part of a document vary from application to application. In most applications, you can print a range of pages by selecting the **From** option (◯ changes to ◉) and then using the two text boxes to type the numbers of the first and last pages you want to print.

If you just want to print one page, click anywhere within the page before running the Print command; then either select the **Current Page** option (◯ changes to ◉) or click **From** (◯ changes to ◉) and type the page number in both text boxes.

If you just want to print a section of the document, select the text before running the Print command, and then click the **Selection** option (◯ changes to ◉).

Edit Document Text

When you work with a character-based file, such as a text or word processing document or an email message, you need to know the basic techniques for editing, selecting, copying, and moving text. The text that you enter into a document is rarely perfect the first time through. It is likely to contain errors that require correcting, or words, sentences, or paragraphs that appear in the wrong place.

To get your document text the way you want it, you need to know how to edit text, including deleting characters, selecting the text you want to work with, and copying and moving text.

Edit Document Text

Delete Characters

1 In a text document, click immediately to the right of the last character that you want to delete.

A The cursor appears after the character.

Agenda for 2013 Conference

Day 1

MORNING SESSION
9:00 - 9:15	Welcome
9:15 - 10:00	Keynote Speech
10:00 - 10:30	Q & A Session
10:30 - 10:50	Coffee Break
10:50 - 12:00	Panel Session
12:00 - 1:30	Lunch

AFTERNOON SESSION
1:30 - 2:30	Guest Speaker
2:30 - 3:00	Q & A Session
3:00 - 3:20	Coffeee Break
3:20 - 4:00	A Look at the Future of the Industry
4:00 - 5:00	Breakout Sessions

---

2 Press **Del** until you have deleted all the characters you want.

If you make a mistake, immediately click **Edit**, and then click **Undo**. You can also press ⌘+**Z**.

Agenda for 2013 Conference

Day 1

MORNING SESSION
9:00 - 9:15	Welcome
9:15 - 10:00	Keynote Speech
10:00 - 10:30	Q & A Session
10:30 - 10:50	Coffee Break
10:50 - 12:00	Panel Session
12:00 - 1:30	Lunch

AFTERNOON SESSION
1:30 - 2:30	Guest Speaker
2:30 - 3:00	Q & A Session
3:00 - 3:20	Coffeee Break
3:20 - 4:00	A Look at the Future
4:00 - 5:00	Breakout Sessions

Select Text for Editing

1 Click and drag across the text that you want to select.

Agenda for 2013 Conference

Day 1

MORNING SESSION ◄ **1**

9:00 - 9:15	Welcome
9:15 - 10:00	Keynote Speech
10:00 - 10:30	Q & A Session
10:30 - 10:50	Coffee Break
10:50 - 12:00	Panel Session
12:00 - 1:30	Lunch

AFTERNOON SESSION

---

2 Release the mouse button.

B The application highlights the selected text.

Agenda for 2013 Conference

2 ay 1

MORNING SESSION ◄ **B**

9:00 - 9:15	Welcome
9:15 - 10:00	Keynote Speech
10:00 - 10:30	Q & A Session
10:30 - 10:50	Coffee Break
10:50 - 12:00	Panel Session
12:00 - 1:30	Lunch

AFTERNOON SESSION

TIP

Are there any shortcut methods for selecting text?

Yes, most Mac applications have shortcuts you can use. Here are the most useful ones:

- Double-click a word to select it.
- Press and hold **Shift** and press ➡ or ⬅ to select entire words.
- Press and hold **Shift** and ⌘ and press ➡ to select to the end of the line, or ⬅ to select to the beginning of the line.
- Triple-click inside a paragraph to select it.
- Click **Edit** and then click **Select All**, or press ⌘+**A** to select the entire document.

Edit	View	Insert	Format	Font	To
Undo Typing					⌘Z
Repeat Typing					⌘Y
Cut					⌘X
Copy					⌘C
Copy to Scrapbook					^⌥C
Paste					⌘V
Paste Special...					^⌘V
Paste and Match Formatting					⌥⇧⌘V
Clear					▶
Select All					⌘A
Find					▶
Links...					
Object					

continued ▶

Edit Document Text (continued)

Once you select text, you can then copy or move the text to another location in your document. Copying text is often a useful way to save work. For example, if you want to use the same passage of text elsewhere in the document, you can copy it rather than typing it from scratch. If you need a similar passage in another part of the document, copy the original and then edit the copy as needed. If you entered a passage of text in the wrong position within the document, you can fix that by moving the text to the correct location.

Edit Document Text (continued)

Copy Text

1. Select the text that you want to copy.

2. Click **Edit**.

3. Click **Copy**.

In most applications, you can also press ⌘+C.

4. Click inside the document where you want the copied text to appear.

The cursor appears in the position where you clicked.

5. Click **Edit**.

6. Click **Paste**.

In most applications, you can also press ⌘+V.

Ⓐ The application inserts a copy of the selected text at the cursor position.

Move Text

1 Select the text that you want to move.

2 Click **Edit**.

3 Click **Cut**.

In most applications, you can also press ⌘+X.

The application removes the text from the document.

4 Click inside the document where you want to move the text.

The cursor appears at the position where you clicked.

5 Click **Edit**.

6 Click **Paste**.

In most applications, you can also press ⌘+V.

B The application inserts the text at the cursor position.

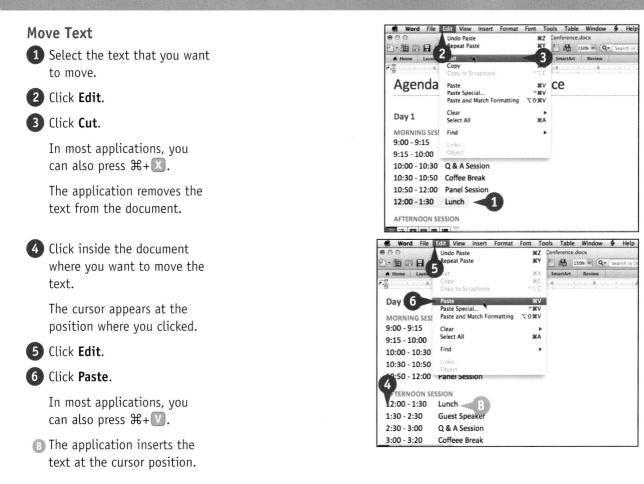

| TIP |

How do I move and copy text with my mouse?

First, select the text that you want to move or copy. To move the selected text, position the mouse pointer over the selection and then click and drag the text to the new position within the document.

To copy the selected text, position the mouse pointer over the selection, press and hold Option, and then click and drag the text (the mouse ▶ changes to ▸) to the new position within the document.

Copy a File

You can use your Mac to make an exact copy of a file. This is useful when you want to make an extra copy of an important file to use as a backup. Similarly, you might require a copy of a file if you want to send the copy on a disk to another person. Finally, copying a file is also a real timesaver if you need a new file very similar to an existing file: You copy the original file and then make the required changes to the copy.

You can copy either a single file or multiple files. You can also use this technique to copy a folder.

Copy a File

1 Locate the file that you want to copy.

2 Open the folder to which you want to copy the file.

To open a second folder window, click **File** and then click **New Finder Window**, or press ⌘+N.

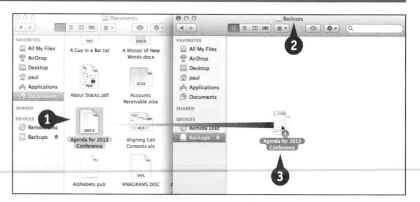

3 Press and hold Option, and then click and drag the file and drop it inside the destination folder.

A The original file remains in its folder.

B A copy of the original file appears in the destination folder.

You can also make a copy of a file in the same folder, which is useful if you want to make major changes to the file and you would like to preserve a copy of the original. Click the file, click **File**, and then click **Duplicate**, or press ⌘+D. Your Mac creates a copy with the word "copy" added to the filename.

Move a File

When you need to store a file in a new location, the easiest way is to move the file from its current folder to another folder on your Mac. When you save a file for the first time, you specify a folder on your Mac's hard drive. This original location is not permanent, however. Using the technique in this section, you can move the file to another location on your Mac's hard drive. You can use this technique to move a single file, multiple files, and even a folder.

Move a File

1 Locate the file that you want to move.

2 Open the folder to which you want to move the file.

To create a new destination folder in the current folder, click **File** and then click **New Folder**, or press `Shift`+⌘+`N`.

3 Click and drag the file and drop it inside the destination folder.

Note: If you are moving the file to another disk drive, you must press and hold ⌘ while you click and drag the file.

Ⓐ The file disappears from its original folder.

Ⓑ The file moves to the destination folder.

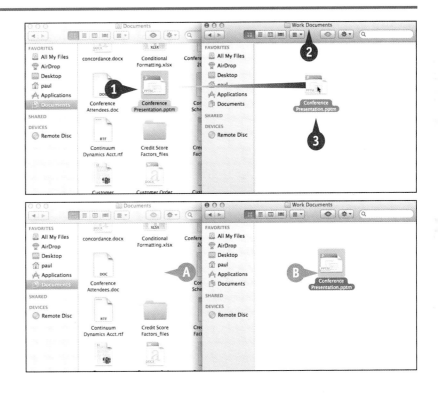

Rename a File

You can change the name of a file, which is useful if the current filename does not accurately describe the contents of the file. By giving your document a descriptive name, you make it easier to find the file later.

You should rename only those documents that you have created or that have been given to you by someone else. Do not try to rename any of the OS X system files or any files associated with your applications, or your computer may behave erratically, or even crash.

Rename a File

1 Open the folder containing the file that you want to rename.

2 Click the file.

3 Press **Return**.

A A text box appears around the filename.

You can also rename any folders that you have created.

4 Edit the existing name or type a new name that you want to use for the file.

If you decide that you do not want to rename the file after all, you can press **Esc** to cancel the operation.

5 Press **Return** or click an empty section of the folder.

B The new name appears under the file icon.

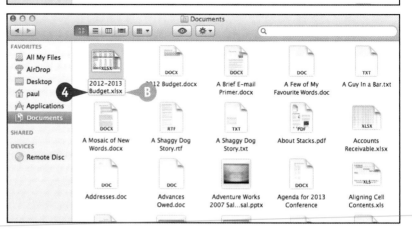

Delete a File

When you no longer need a file, you can delete it. This helps to prevent your hard drive from becoming cluttered with unnecessary files. You should ensure that you delete only those documents that you have created or that have been given to you by someone else. Do not delete any of the OS X system files or any files associated with your applications, or your computer may behave erratically, or even crash.

Delete a File

1 Locate the file that you want to delete.

2 Click and drag the file and drop it on the Trash icon in the Dock.

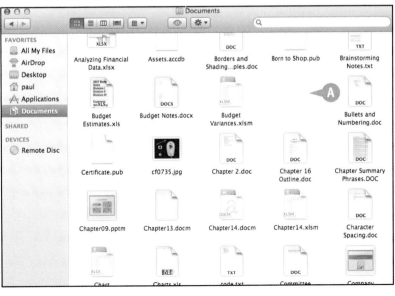

A The file disappears from the folder.

You can also delete a file by clicking it and then pressing ⌘+**Del**.

If you delete a file accidentally, you can restore it. Simply click the Dock's Trash icon to open the Trash window. Click and drag the file from the Trash window and drop it back in its original folder.

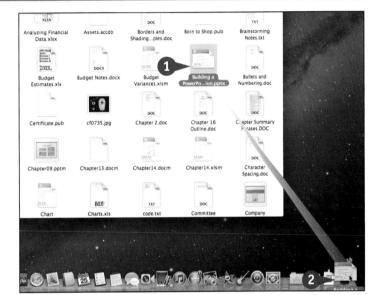

CHAPTER 5

Listening to Music

Using iTunes, you can create a library of music and use that library to play songs, albums, and collections of songs called playlists. You can also use iTunes to listen to music CDs, import tracks from music CDs, create your own CDs, and more.

Open and Close iTunes

Your Mac includes iTunes to enable you to play back and manage various types of audio files. iTunes also includes features for organizing and playing videos, watching movies and TV shows, and organizing e-books, but this chapter focuses on the audio features in iTunes.

To begin using the program, you must first learn how to find and open the iTunes window. When you finish using the program, you can close the iTunes window to free up computer processing power.

Open and Close iTunes

Open iTunes

1 In the Dock, click **iTunes** (icon).

The iTunes window appears.

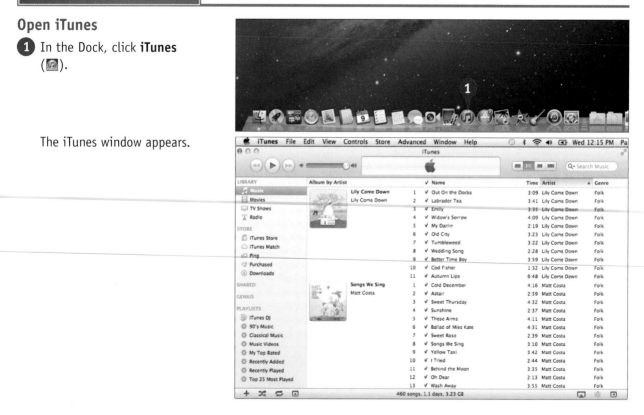

Close iTunes

1 Click **iTunes**.

2 Click **Quit iTunes**.

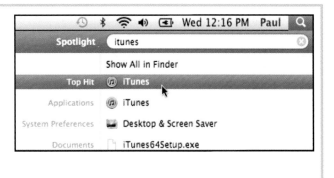

TIP

Are there other methods I can use to open iTunes?

Yes. If you have removed the 🎵 icon from the Dock, there are a couple of other quick methods you can use to start iTunes. If you have used iTunes recently, a reasonably fast method is to click the **Apple** icon (), click **Recent Items**, and then click **iTunes**. You can also click **Spotlight** (), type **itunes**, and then click **iTunes** in the search results.

Understanding the iTunes Library

Most of your iTunes time will be spent in the library, so you need to understand what the library is and how you work with it. In particular, you need to understand the various categories — such as music and audiobooks — that iTunes uses to organize the library's audio content. Also, to make it easier to navigate the library, you need to know how to configure the library to show only the categories that you will be working with.

The iTunes Library

The iTunes library is where your Mac stores the files that you can play and work with in the iTunes application. Although iTunes has some video components, its focus is on audio features, so most of the library sections are audio related. These sections enable you to work with music, podcasts, audiobooks, ringtones, and Internet radio.

Understanding Library Categories

The left side of the iTunes window is called the Source list and it displays the various categories available in the iTunes library. In the Library list, the audio-related categories include Music, Podcasts, Books (for audiobooks), Ringtones, and Radio. The Store list includes items you have purchased from the iTunes Store.

Each category shows you the contents of that category and the details for each item. For example, in the Music category, you can see details such as the name of each album and the artist who recorded it.

Configuring the Library

You can configure which categories of the iTunes library appear in the Library list on the left side of the iTunes window. Click **iTunes** and then click **Preferences** to open the iTunes preferences; then click the **General** tab. In the Show section, click the check box for each type of content you want to work with (☐ changes to ☑), and then click **OK**.

Navigate the iTunes Window

Familiarizing yourself with the various elements of the iTunes window is a good idea so that you can easily navigate and activate elements when you are ready to play audio files, music CDs, or podcasts; import and burn audio CDs; create your own playlists; or listen to Internet radio.

In particular, you need to learn the iTunes playback controls because you will use them to control the playback of almost all music you work with in iTunes. It is also worthwhile to learn the different View options because these often come in handy when navigating the iTunes library.

A Playback Controls

These buttons control media playback and enable you to adjust the volume.

B Sort Buttons

These buttons sort the contents of the current iTunes category.

C Status Area

This area displays information about the item currently playing or the action that iTunes is currently performing.

D View Options

These buttons control how the contents of the current category appear. Click **List** (▤) to view the contents as a list by song; click **Album List** (▤) to view the contents as a list by album; click **Grid** (▦) to view the contents as thumbnails; or click **Cover Flow** (▤) to view the contents as scrolling thumbnails.

E Genius Sidebar

This area displays a list of songs, albums, or other iTunes Store content similar to the current item in the library. Click **Store** and then click **Turn On Genius** to use this feature.

F Contents

The contents of the current iTunes library source appear here.

G Categories

This area displays the iTunes library categories that you can view.

Play a Song

You use the Music category of the iTunes library to play a song stored on your computer. Although iTunes offers several methods to locate the song you want to play, the easiest method is to display the albums you have in your iTunes library, and then open the album that contains the song you want to play.

While the song is playing, you can control the volume to suit the music or your current location. If you need to leave the room or take a call, you can also pause the currently playing song.

Play a Song

1 Click **Music**.

2 Click **Albums**.

3 Double-click the album that contains the song you want to play.

A If you want to play the entire album, click **Play Album**.

4 Click the song you want to play.

5 Click the **Play** button (▶).

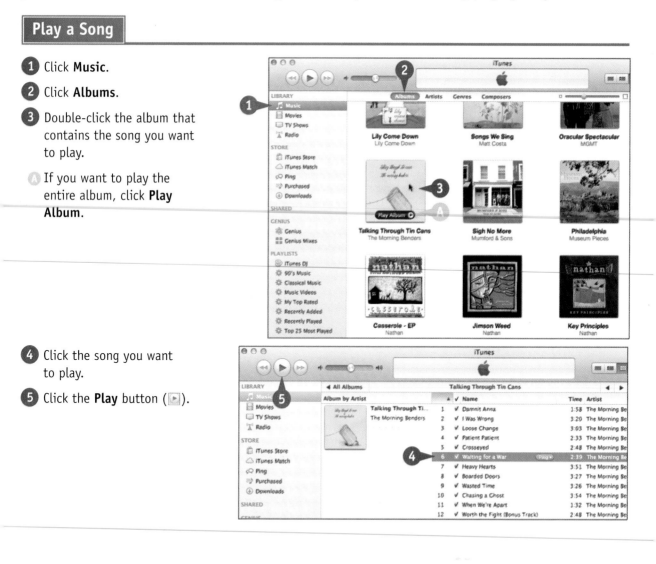

iTunes begins playing the song.

B Information about the song playback appears here.

C iTunes displays a speaker icon (🔊) beside the currently playing song.

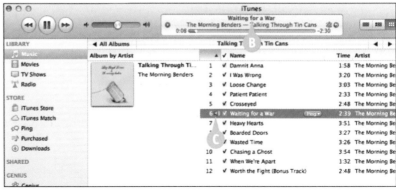

D If you need to stop the song temporarily, click the **Pause** button (⏸).

Note: You can also pause and restart a song by pressing the `Spacebar`.

E You can use the Volume slider to adjust the volume (see the tip).

Note: See the section "Play a Music CD" to learn more about the playback buttons.

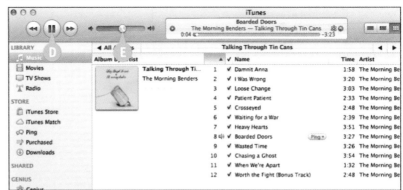

TIP

How do I adjust the volume?
To turn the volume up or down, click and drag the **Volume** slider to the left (to reduce the volume) or to the right (to increase the volume). You can also press ⌘+⬇ to reduce the volume, or ⌘+⬆ to increase the volume.

To mute the volume, either drag the **Volume** slider all the way to the left, or press `Option`+⌘+⬇. To restore the volume, adjust the **Volume** slider or press `Option`+⌘+⬆.

Play a Music CD

Y ou can play your favorite music CDs in iTunes. If your Mac has an optical drive (that is, a drive capable of reading CDs and DVDs), you can insert an audio disc in the drive and the CD appears in the Devices section of the iTunes library. When you click the CD, the iTunes contents area displays the individual tracks on the CD, and if you have an Internet connection you usually see the name of each track as well as other track data.

Play a Music CD

Play a CD

1 Insert a music CD into your Mac's optical drive.

A The music CD appears in the iTunes Devices category.

iTunes asks if you want to import the CD.

2 Click **No**.

Note: To learn how to import a CD, see the section "Import Tracks from a Music CD."

B If you have an Internet connection, iTunes shows the contents of the CD.

Note: iTunes shows the contents for most CDs, but it may not show the correct information for some discs, particularly noncommercial mixed CDs.

3 Click ▶.

iTunes begins playing the CD from the first track.

Skip a Track

1 Click the **Next** button (⏭) to skip to the next track.

Note: You can also skip to the next track by pressing ⌘+➡.

2 Click the **Previous** button (⏮) to skip to the beginning of the current track; click ⏮ again to skip to the previous track.

Note: You can also skip to the previous track by pressing ⌘+⬅.

Pause and Resume Play

1 Click ⏸ (⏸ changes to ▶).

iTunes pauses playback.

2 Click ▶.

iTunes resumes playback where you left off.

continued ▶

TIPS

Can I change the CD's audio levels?

Yes, iTunes has a graphic equalizer component that you can use to adjust the levels. To display the equalizer, click **Window** and then click **Equalizer** (or press `Option`+⌘+`2`). In the Equalizer window, use the sliders to set the audio levels, or click the pop-up menu (⏷) to choose an audio preset.

Can I display visualizations during playback?

Yes. You can click **View** and then click **Show Visualizer** (you can also press ⌘+`T`). To change the currently displayed visualizer, click **View**, click **Visualizer**, and then click the visualization you want to view.

iTunes gives you more options for controlling the CD playback. For example, you can easily switch from one song to another on the CD. You can also use the Repeat feature to tell iTunes to start the CD over from the beginning after it has finished playing the CD. iTunes also offers the Shuffle feature, which plays the CD's tracks in random order.

When the CD is done, you can use iTunes to eject it from your Mac. If you want to learn how to import music from the CD to iTunes, see the section "Import Tracks from a Music CD."

Play a Music CD (continued)

Play Another Song

1 In the list of songs, double-click the song you want to play.

iTunes begins playing the song.

Repeat the CD

1 Click the **Repeat** button (🔁 changes to 🔁).

iTunes restarts the CD after the last track finishes playing.

To repeat just the current song, click 🔁 again (🔁 changes to 🔁).

Play Songs Randomly

 Click the **Shuffle** button
(⤭ changes to ⤭).

iTunes shuffles the order
of play.

Eject the CD

1 Click the **Eject** button (⏏)
beside the CD.

Note: You can also eject the CD
by pressing and holding ⏏ on
the keyboard.

iTunes ejects the CD from
your Mac's optical drive.

TIP

Why do I not see the song titles after I insert my music CD?
When you play a music CD, iTunes tries to gather information about the album from the Internet. If you still
see only track numbers, it may be that you do not have an Internet connection established, that you
inserted a noncommercial mixed CD, or that the online music database does not include the CD. Connect to
the Internet, click **Advanced**, and then click **Get CD Track Names**.

Import Tracks from a Music CD

You can add tracks from a music CD to the iTunes library. This enables you to listen to an album without having to put the CD into your Mac's optical drive each time. The process of adding tracks from a CD is called *importing*, or *ripping*, in OS X.

After you import the tracks from a music CD, you can play those tracks from the Music category of the iTunes library. You can also use the tracks to create your own playlists and to create your own custom CDs.

Import Tracks from a Music CD

1 Insert a CD into your Mac's CD or DVD drive.

A The music CD appears in the iTunes Devices category.

iTunes asks if you want to import the CD.

2 Click **No**.

B If you want to import the entire CD, click **Yes** and skip the rest of the steps in this section.

C iTunes shows the contents of the CD.

3 Uncheck the box next to each CD track that you do not want to copy (☑ changes to ☐).

4 Click **Import CD**.

92

iTunes begins importing the check-marked track or tracks.

D This area displays the copy progress for each track.

E When iTunes is importing a track, it displays ⊡ beside the track number.

F When iTunes is finished importing a track, it displays ⊡ beside the track number.

G When iTunes has completed the import, you see ⊡ beside the track numbers of all the tracks you selected.

5 Click the **Eject** button (⊡) beside the CD, or press ⊡.

I ripped a track by accident. How do I remove it from the library?
Click the **Music** category, open the album you imported, right-click the track that you want to remove, and then click **Delete** from the shortcut menu. When iTunes asks you to confirm the deletion, click **Remove**. When iTunes asks if you want to keep the file, click **Move to Trash**.

Can I specify a different quality when importing?
Yes. You do that by changing the *bit rate*, which is a measure of how much of the CD's original data is copied to your computer. This is measured in kilobits per second (Kbps): The higher the value, the higher the quality, but the more disk space each track takes up. Click **Import Settings** to open the Import Settings dialog. In the **Settings** pop-up menu, click ⊡, click **Custom**, and then use the Stereo Bit Rate pop-up to click the value you want.

Create a Playlist

A *playlist* is a collection of songs that are related in some way. Using your iTunes library, you can create customized playlists that include only the songs that you want to hear. For example, you might want to create a playlist of upbeat or festive songs to play during a party or celebration. Similarly, you might want to create a playlist of your current favorite songs to burn to a CD. Whatever the reason, once you create the playlist you can populate it with songs using a simple drag-and-drop technique.

Create a Playlist

Create the Playlist

1 Click **File**.

2 Click **New Playlist**.

Note: You can also choose the New Playlist command by pressing ⌘+N.

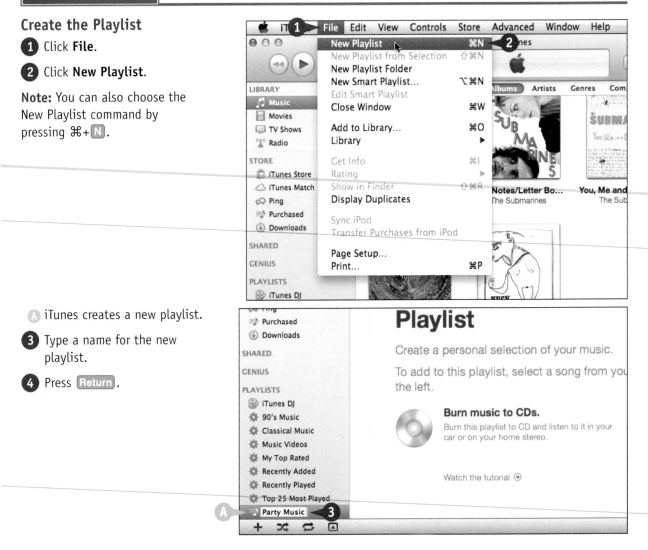

A iTunes creates a new playlist.

3 Type a name for the new playlist.

4 Press Return.

Add Songs to the Playlist

1 Click **Music**.

2 Open an album that has one or more songs you want to add to the playlist.

3 Click a song that you want to add to the playlist.

Note: If you want more than one song from the album's playlist, press and hold ⌘ and click each of the songs you want to add.

4 Drag the selected track (or tracks) and drop them on your playlist.

5 Repeat steps **2** to **4** to add more songs to the playlist.

6 Click the playlist.

Ⓑ iTunes displays the songs you added to the playlist.

Ⓒ If you want to listen to the playlist, click ▶.

Is there a faster way to create and populate a playlist?

Yes. First, click **Music** to open the Music category of the iTunes library. Press and hold ⌘ and then click each song that you want to include in your playlist. When you are done, click **File** and then click **New Playlist from Selection**. (You can also press Shift +⌘+N.) Type the new playlist name and then press Return.

Is there any way to make iTunes add songs to a playlist automatically?

Yes, you can create a *Smart Playlist* where the songs that appear in the list have one or more properties in common, such as the genre, rating, artist, or text in the song title. Click **File** and then click **New Smart Playlist** (you can also press Option+⌘+N). Use the Smart Playlist dialog to create one or more rules that define which songs you want to appear in the playlist.

Burn Music Files to a CD

You can copy, or *burn*, music files from your Mac onto a CD. Burning CDs is a great way to create customized CDs that you can listen to on the computer or on any device that plays CDs.

You can burn music files from within the iTunes window. The easiest way to do this is to create a playlist of the songs you want to burn to the CD. You then organize the playlist by sorting the tracks in the order you want to hear them. To burn music files to a CD, your Mac must have a recordable optical drive.

Burn Music Files to a CD

1 Insert a blank CD into your Mac's recordable disc drive.

2 If you already have iTunes running and your Mac asks you to choose an action, click **Ignore**.

A If you do not yet have iTunes running, use the Action menu to click ⊡, click **Open iTunes**, and then click **OK**.

3 Create a playlist for the songs you want to burn to the disc.

Note: See the section "Create a Playlist" to learn how to build an iTunes playlist.

4 Click the playlist that you want to burn.

You inserted a blank CD. Choose an action from the pop-up menu or click Ignore. **A**

Action: 🎵 Open iTunes ⬍

☐ Make this action the default

(?) [Eject]   **2** ➤ [Ignore] [OK]

PLAYLISTS				
🔵 iTunes DJ	15	✔ Cold December		4:16
⚙ 90's Music	16	✔ Songs We Sing		3:10
⚙ Classical Music	17	✔ The Youth	EXPLICIT	3:49
⚙ Music Videos	18	✔ Kids	EXPLICIT	5:03
⚙ My Top Rated	19	✔ Waiting for a War		2:39
⚙ Recently Added	20	✔ Wasted Time		3:26
⚙ Recently Played	21	✔ The Cave		3:38
⚙ Top 25 Most Played	22	✔ We Search for Arrowheads		3:15
4 ➤ 🎵 **Party Music**	23	✔ Scarecrow		4:25
	24	✔ Trans Am		3:04
	25	✔ The Good In Everyone		2:09
	26	✔ Losing California		3:06
+ ✕ ⇄ ▣			88 songs, 5.5 hours, 681	

5 To modify the play order, click and drag a song and drop it on a new position in the playlist.

6 Repeat step **5** to get the songs in the order in which you want them to appear on the CD.

3	✓	B-B-Bicycles		2:07	The Bicycles	The Good, the Bad,...	Pop
4	✓	Lonely Boy		3:13	The Black Keys	El Camino	Alternative
5	✓	Gold On the Ceiling	Ping▾	3:44	The Black Keys	El Camino	Alternative
6	✓	Furr		4:08	Blitzen Trapper	Furr (Bonus Track V...	Alternative
7	✓	In One Ear		4:02	Cage the Elephant	Cage the Elephant	Rock
8	✓	Ain't No Rest for the Wicked		2:55	Cage the Elephant	Cage the Elephant	Rock
9	✓	Sister Kate		2:25	The Ditty Bops	The Ditty Bops	Folk
10	✓	The Valley Town		3:41	Elliott Brood	Mountain Meadows	Alternative
11	✓	Open Arms		4:59	Hey Rosetta!	Into Your Lungs	Rock
12	✓	The Sound		2:45	Human Highway	Moody Motorcycle	Alternative
13	✓	Moody Motorcycle		3:11	Human Highway	Moody Motorcycle	Alternative
14	✓	Out On the Docks		3:09	Lily Come Down	Lily Come Down	Folk
15	✓	Cold December		4:16	Matt Costa	Songs We Sing	Folk
16	✓	Songs We Sing		3:10	Matt Costa	Songs We Sing	Folk
17	✓	The Youth	EXPLICIT	3:49	MGMT	Oracular Spectacular	Alternative
18	✓	Kids	EXPLICIT	5:03	MGMT	Oracular Spectacular	Alternative
19	✓	Waiting for a War		2:39	The Morning Benders	Talking Through Ti...	Alternative

7 Click **File**.

8 Click **Burn Playlist to Disc**.

The Burn Settings dialog appears.

9 Click **Burn**.

iTunes burns the songs to the CD.

Burn Settings

Disc Burner: OPTIARC DVD RW AD-5630A

Preferred Speed: Maximum Possible

Disc Format: ● Audio CD
    Gap Between Songs: 2 seconds
    ☐ Use Sound Check
    ☐ Include CD Text
  ○ MP3 CD
  ○ Data CD or DVD
    Data discs include all files in the playlist. These discs may not play in some players.

Cancel   Burn

TIPS

Can I control the interval between songs on the CD?
Yes. By default, iTunes adds 2 seconds between each track on the CD. You can change that in the Burn Settings dialog. In the Gap Between Songs pop-up menu, click ▣, and then click the interval you want to use: None, or any time between 1 second and 5 seconds.

What happens if I have more music than can fit on a single disc?
You can still add all the music you want to burn to the playlist. iTunes fills the first disc and then adds the remaining songs to a second disc. After iTunes finishes burning the first disc, it prompts you to insert the next one.

Edit Song Information

For each song in your library or on a music CD, iTunes maintains a collection of information that includes the song title, artist, album title, genre, and more. If a song's information contains errors or omissions, you can edit the data. For example, an album can commonly be categorized under the wrong music genre, so you can edit the album info to give it the correct genre. You can edit one song at a time, or you can edit multiple songs, such as an entire album or music CD.

Edit Song Information

Edit a Single Song

1 Click the song you want to edit.

2 Click **File**.

3 Click **Get Info**.

Note: You can also press ⌘+I. Alternatively, right-click the song and then click **Get Info**.

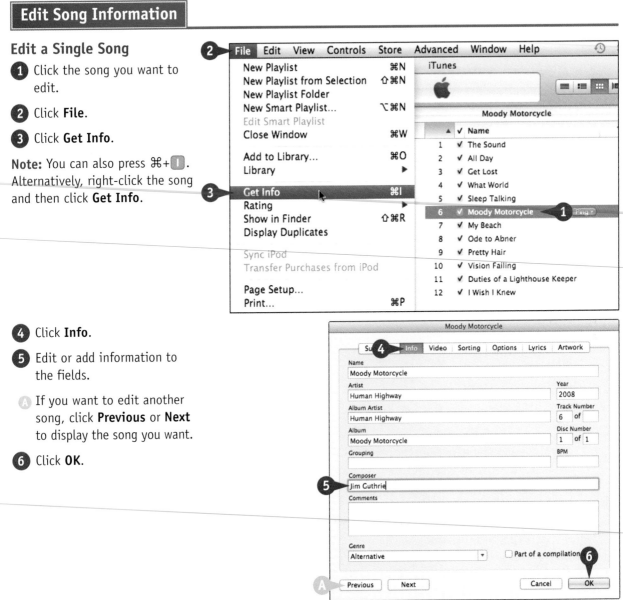

4 Click **Info**.

5 Edit or add information to the fields.

Ⓐ If you want to edit another song, click **Previous** or **Next** to display the song you want.

6 Click **OK**.

Edit Multiple Songs

1 Select all the songs that you want to edit.

Note: To select individual songs, press and hold ⌘ and click each song; to select all songs (on a music CD, for example), press ⌘+A.

2 Click **File**.

3 Click **Get Info**.

Note: You can also press ⌘+I. Alternatively, right-click any selected song and then click **Get Info**.

iTunes asks you to confirm that you want to edit multiple songs.

4 Click **Yes**.

The Multiple Item Information dialog appears.

5 Edit or add information to the fields.

B iTunes displays ✓ beside each modified field.

6 Click **OK**.

iTunes applies the edits to each selected song.

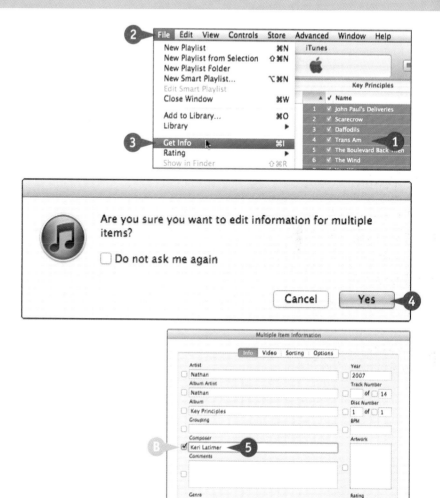

TIP

When I edit multiple songs, why do I not see all the fields in the Multiple Item Information dialog?
When you are editing multiple songs, you can modify only fields that contain data common to all the songs. This makes sense because any changes you make apply to all the selected songs. For example, each song usually has a different title, so you would not want to give every song the same title. This is why you do not see the Name field in the Multiple Item Information dialog. However, you do see fields common to all the selected songs. On a music CD, for example, data such as the artist, album title, and genre are usually the same for all the songs.

Purchase Music from the iTunes Store

You can add music to your iTunes library by purchasing songs or albums from the iTunes Store. iTunes downloads the song or album to your computer and then adds it to both the Music category and the Purchased playlist. You can then play and manage the song or album just like any other content in the iTunes library.

To purchase music from the iTunes Store, you must have an Apple ID, which you can obtain from https://appleid.apple.com. You can also use an AOL account, if you have one.

Purchase Music from the iTunes Store

1 Click **iTunes Store**.

2 Click **Music**.

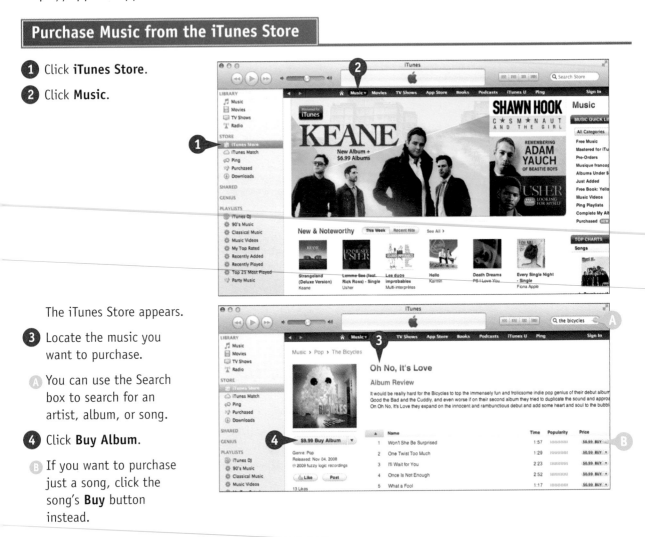

The iTunes Store appears.

3 Locate the music you want to purchase.

A You can use the Search box to search for an artist, album, or song.

4 Click **Buy Album**.

B If you want to purchase just a song, click the song's **Buy** button instead.

iTunes asks you to sign in to your iTunes Store account.

5 If you have not signed in to your account, you must type your Apple ID.

6 Type your password.

7 Click **Buy**.

iTunes charges your credit card and begins downloading the music to your Mac.

C To watch the progress of the download, click **Downloads**.

Sign In to download from the iTunes Store

If you have an Apple ID and password, enter them here. If you've used the iTunes Store or iCloud, for example, you have an Apple ID.

Apple ID
myaccount@me.com **5**

Password Forgot?
•••••••• **6**

☐ Remember password

(?) Create Apple ID Cancel Buy **7**

iTunes
Downloading 15 items
What a Fool / Oh No, It's Love / The Bicycles (processing file)

Q Search

LIBRARY
♫ Music
🎬 Movies
📺 TV Shows
📻 Radio

STORE
🎵 iTunes Store
🔄 iTunes Match
📡 Ping
Purchased
Downloads

SHARED
GENIUS

PLAYLISTS
🎧 iTunes DJ
⚙ 90's Music
Classical Music

Kind Name

Status

♫ One Twist Too Much / Oh No, It's Love / The Bicycles
3.3 MB - Done

♫ I'll Wait for You / Oh No, It's Love / The Bicycles
4.5 MB - Done

♫ Once Is Not Enough / Oh No, It's Love / The Bicycles
3.8 MB - Done

♫ What a Fool / Oh No, It's Love / The Bicycles
2.4 MB of 2.9 MB - processing file

♫ Roland / Oh No, It's Love / The Bicycles
652.0 KB of 3.5 MB

♫ Green Light / Oh No, It's Love / The Bicycles
1.1 MB of 2.6 MB

♫ Walk Away (From a Good Thing) / Oh No, It's Love / The Bicycles
zero KB of 6.7 MB - waiting

♫ Oh No, It's Love / Oh No, It's Love / The Bicycles
zero KB of 3.9 MB - waiting

♫ Stop Calling Me Baby / Oh No, It's Love / The Bicycles
zero KB of 3.9 MB - waiting

♫ Sweet Petite / Oh No, It's Love / The Bicycles
zero KB of 6.0 MB - waiting

TIPS

Can I use my purchased music on other computers and devices?

Yes. Although many iTunes Store media — particularly movies and TV shows — have digital rights management (DRM) restrictions applied to prevent illegal copying, the songs and albums in the iTunes Store are DRM-free, and so do not have these restrictions. This means you can play them on multiple computers and media devices (such as iPods, iPads, and iPhones), and burn them to multiple CDs.

If I want to purchase a number of songs, how do I avoid having many $0.99 charges on my credit card bill?

The easiest way to avoid a lot of small iTunes charges is to purchase an iTunes gift card from an Apple Store or any retailer that sells gift cards. On the back of the card, scratch off the sticker that covers the redeem code. In iTunes, access the iTunes Store and click **Redeem** at the bottom of the store. Type the redeem code, and then click **Redeem**.

Listen to an Internet Radio Station

The Internet offers a number of radio stations that you can listen to. iTunes maintains a list of many of these online radio stations, so it is often easier to use iTunes to listen to Internet radio.

Just like a regular radio station, an Internet radio station broadcasts a constant audio stream, except you access the audio over the Internet instead of over the air. iTunes offers several radio stations in each of its more than two dozen genres, which include Blues, Classic Rock, Classical, Folk, Hip Hop, Jazz, and Pop.

Listen to an Internet Radio Station

1 Click **Radio**.

Note: If you do not see the Radio category, see the first tip on the following page.

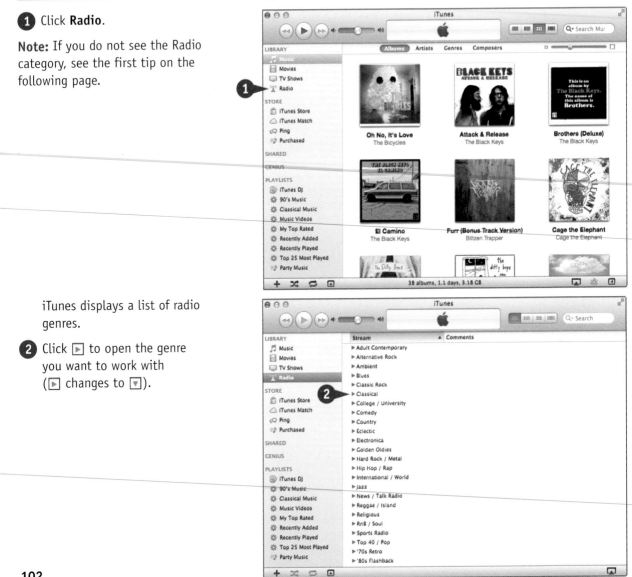

iTunes displays a list of radio genres.

2 Click ▶ to open the genre you want to work with (▶ changes to ▼).

iTunes displays a list of radio station streams in the genre.

③ Click the radio station stream you want to listen to.

④ Click ▶.

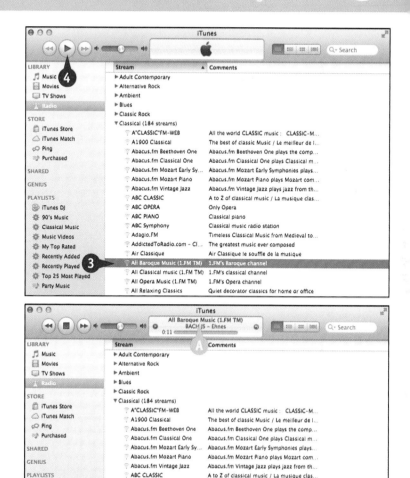

iTunes plays the radio station stream.

Ⓐ The name of the station and the name of the currently playing track usually appear here.

The Radio section of the iTunes library does not appear. Can I still listen to Internet radio?

Yes. By default, iTunes does not show all the available library categories and sources. To display the Radio source, click **iTunes** and then click **Preferences** to open the iTunes preferences. Click the **General** tab, click **Radio** (☐ changes to ☑), and then click **OK**.

Is it possible to use iTunes to save or record a song from a radio station stream?

No, an Internet radio stream is "listen only." iTunes does not give you any way to save the stream to your Mac hard drive or to record the stream as it plays.

CHAPTER 6

Viewing and Editing Photos

Whether you just want to look at your photos, or you want to edit them to crop out unneeded portions or fix problems, your Mac comes with a number of useful tools for this purpose.

View a Preview of a Photo

OS X offers several tools you can use to see a preview of any photo on your Mac. The Finder application has a number of methods you can use to view your photos, but here you learn about the two easiest methods. First, you can preview any saved image file using the OS X Quick Look feature; second, you can see photo previews by switching to the Cover Flow view. You can also preview photos using the Preview application.

View a Preview of a Photo

View a Preview with Quick Look

1 Click **Finder** (📁) in the Dock.

2 Open the folder that contains the photo you want to preview.

3 Click the photo.

4 Click **Quick Look** (👁).

You can also right-click the photo and then click **Quick Look**, or press Spacebar.

Ⓐ Finder displays a preview of the photo.

View a Preview with Cover Flow

1 Click **Finder** (📁) in the Dock.

2 Open the folder that contains the photo you want to preview.

3 Click the photo.

4 Click **Cover Flow** (▦).

Ⓑ Finder displays a preview of the photo.

View a Preview in the Preview Application

1 Click **Finder** (🖼️) in the Dock.

2 Open the folder that contains the photo you want to preview.

3 Click the photo.

4 Click **File**.

5 Click **Open With**.

6 Click **Preview**.

Note: In many cases, you can also simply double-click the photo to open it in the Preview application.

The Preview application opens and displays the photo.

7 Use the toolbar buttons to change how the photo appears in the Preview window. For example, click 🔍 to get a closer look at the photos.

C More commands are available on the **View** menu.

8 When you are finished viewing the photo, click **Close** (◉).

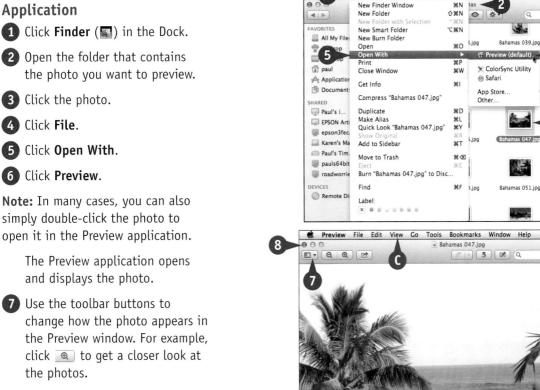

TIPS

Is there an easier way to preview multiple photos using the Preview application?

Yes. Instead of constantly starting and quitting Preview for each photo you want to view, you can load multiple photos into the Preview application. In Finder, navigate to the folder that contains the photos, and then select each file that you want to preview. Either click and drag the mouse (▶) over the photos or press and hold ⌘ and click each one. In Preview, click **Next** and **Previous** to navigate the photos.

Is there a way that I can zoom in on just a portion of a photo?

Yes. In Preview, click **Tools** and then click **Select Tool** (or either press ⌘+ 3 or click **Select** in the toolbar). Click and drag your mouse (▶) to select the portion of the photo that you want to magnify. Click **View** and then click **Zoom to Selection** (or press ⌘+⬚).

View a Slide Show of Your Photos

Instead of viewing your photos one at a time, you can easily view multiple photos by running them in a slide show. You can run the slide show using the Preview application. The slide show displays each photo for a few seconds, and then Preview automatically displays the next photo. Quick Look also offers several on-screen controls that you can use to control the slide show playback. You can also configure Quick Look to display the images full screen.

View a Slide Show of Your Photos

1 Click **Finder** (🔲) in the Dock.

2 Open the folder that contains the photos you want to view in the slide show.

3 Select the photos you want to view.

4 Click **File**.

5 Click **Open With**.

6 Click **Preview**.

The Preview window appears.

7 Click **View**.

8 Click **Slideshow**.

You can also select Slideshow by pressing Shift + ⌘ + F.

108

Preview opens the slide show window.

9 Move the mouse (🖰).

Ⓐ Preview displays the slide show controls.

10 Click **Play** (▶).

Preview begins the slide show.

Ⓑ Click **Next** (⏭) to move to the next photo.

Ⓒ Click **Back** (⏮) to move to the previous photo.

Ⓓ Click **Pause** (⏸) to suspend the slide show.

11 When the slide show is over or when you want to return to Finder, click **Close** (⊗) or press **Esc**.

TIPS

Can I jump to a specific photo during the slide show?
Yes. With the slide show running, press **Return** to stop the show and display thumbnail views of all the slide show images. Use the arrow keys to select the photo that you want to view in the slide show, and then press **Return**. Preview returns you to the slide show and displays the selected photo. Click **Play** to resume the slide show from that photo.

What keyboard shortcuts can I use when viewing a slide show?
Press ➡ or ⬆ to display the next photo, and press ⬅ or ⬇ to display the previous photo. Press **Esc** to end the slide show.

Open and Close iPhoto

Your Mac has iLife installed, and the suite includes the iPhoto application, which offers special tools for viewing, managing, and editing your photos. You can also purchase iPhoto via the App Store. With iPhoto you can import photos from a digital camera, view and organize the photos on your Mac, and edit and repair photos.

To begin using the program, you must first learn how to find and open the iPhoto window. When you finish using the program, you can close the iPhoto window to free up computer processing power.

Open and Close iPhoto

Open iPhoto

1 In the Dock, click
iPhoto (🖼).

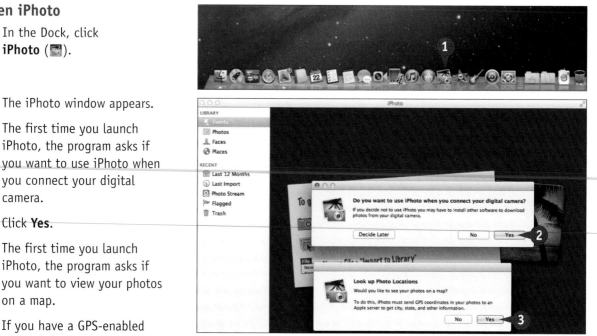

The iPhoto window appears.

The first time you launch iPhoto, the program asks if you want to use iPhoto when you connect your digital camera.

2 Click **Yes**.

The first time you launch iPhoto, the program asks if you want to view your photos on a map.

3 If you have a GPS-enabled camera (such as an iPhone 3G or later, or an iPad 2 or later with 3G or 4G) or if you want to enter location data manually, click **Yes**.

Close iPhoto

1 Click **iPhoto**.

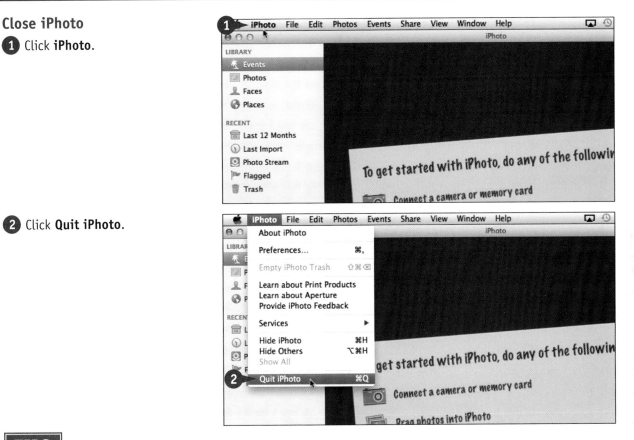

2 Click **Quit iPhoto**.

Are there other methods I can use to open iPhoto?
Yes. If you do not have 🖼 in the Dock, there are a couple of methods you can use to open iPhoto. If you have used iPhoto recently, a reasonably fast method is to click 🍎, click **Recent Items**, and then click **iPhoto**. Alternatively, click **Spotlight** (🔍), type **iphoto**, and then click **iPhoto** in the search results.

Are there faster methods I can use to close iPhoto?
Yes. Probably the fastest method you can use to quit iPhoto is to click 🔘. Alternatively, right-click the **iPhoto** icon (🖼) and then click **Quit**. Finally, if your hands are closer to the keyboard than to the mouse, you can quit iPhoto by switching to the application and pressing ⌘+🇶.

Import Photos from a Digital Camera

You can import photos from a digital camera and save them on your Mac. If you have the iLife suite installed on your Mac, you can use the iPhoto application to handle importing photos. iPhoto is also available via the App Store. iPhoto enables you to add a name and a description to each import, which helps you to find your photos after the import is complete.

To perform the import, you need a cable to connect your digital camera to your Mac. Most digital cameras come with a USB cable.

Import Photos from a Digital Camera

Import Photos from a Digital Camera

① Connect one end of the cable to the digital camera.

② Connect the other end of the cable to a free USB port on your Mac.

③ Turn the camera on and put it in either playback or computer mode.

Your Mac launches the iPhoto application.

Ⓐ Your digital camera appears in the Devices section.

Ⓑ iPhoto displays previews of the camera's photos.

④ Use the Event Name text box to type a name for the group of photos you are going to import.

5 Select the photos that you want to import.

Note: To select photos, either click and drag the mouse (▶) around the photos you want, or press and hold ⌘ and click each photo.

6 Click **Import Selected**.

C If you want to import all the photos from the digital camera, click **Import X Photos**, where X is the number of photos stored in the camera.

iPhoto imports the photos from the digital camera.

iPhoto asks if you want to delete the original photos from the digital camera.

7 If you no longer need the photos on the camera, click **Delete Photos**.

D If you prefer to keep the photos on the camera, click **Keep Photos** instead.

View the Imported Photos

1 Click **Events**.

2 Double-click the event name that you specified in step 4.

TIP

When I connect my digital camera, why do I see Image Capture instead of iPhoto?
You need to configure Image Capture to open iPhoto when you connect your camera. Follow these steps:

1 Connect your digital camera to your Mac.

The Image Capture application opens.

Note: If you do not see the Image Capture application, click **Finder** (▦) in the Dock, click **Applications**, and then double-click **Image Capture**.

2 Click the **Connecting** 🔅 and then click **iPhoto**.

3 Click **Image Capture** in the menu bar.

4 Click **Quit Image Capture**.

View Your Photos

If you want to look at several photos, you can use the iPhoto application, which is available with the Apple iLife suite or via the App Store. iPhoto offers a feature called *full-screen mode*, which hides everything else and displays your photos using the entire screen.

Once you activate full-screen mode, iPhoto offers several on-screen controls that you can use to navigate backward and forward through the photos in a folder. Full-screen mode also shows thumbnail images of each photo, so you can quickly jump to any photo you want to view.

View Your Photos

1 In iPhoto, click **Events**.

2 Double-click the event that contains the photos you want to view.

3 Double-click the first photo you want to view.

iPhoto displays the photo.

④ Click **Next** (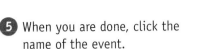) to view the next photo in the event.

Ⓐ You can also click **Previous** (◄) to see the previous photo in the event.

Note: You can also navigate photos by pressing ➡ and ⬅.

⑤ When you are done, click the name of the event.

TIP

Is there a way that I can jump quickly to a particular photo in full-screen mode?

Yes. Follow these steps:

① Move the mouse (▶) to the thumbnails at the bottom of the iPhoto window.

Ⓐ iPhoto displays larger thumbnail images of the event's photos.

② Use the horizontal scroll bar to bring the thumbnail of the photo you want into view.

③ Click the photo's thumbnail.

iPhoto displays the photo in full-screen mode.

Create an Album

You can use the iPhoto application to organize your photos into albums. You can get iPhoto either via the iLife suite, which is installed on all new Macs, or via the App Store. In iPhoto, an *album* is a collection of photos usually related in some way. For example, you might create an album for a series of vacation photos, or for photos that include a particular person, pet, or place.

Using your iPhoto library, you can create customized albums that include only the photos that you want to view.

Create an Album

Create the Album

1 Click **File**.

2 Click **New Album**.

Note: You can also start a new album by pressing ⌘+N.

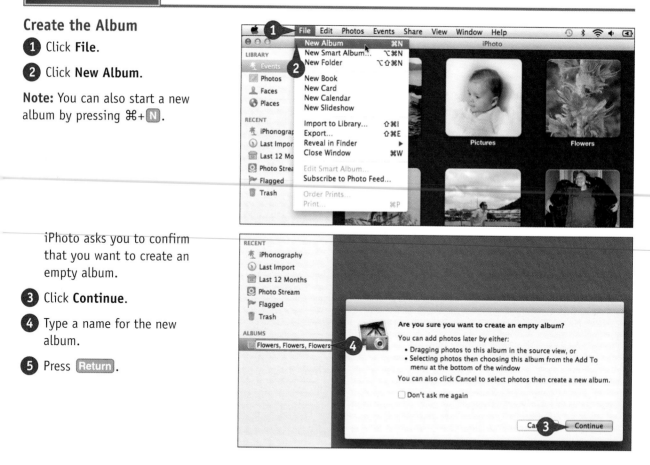

iPhoto asks you to confirm that you want to create an empty album.

3 Click **Continue**.

4 Type a name for the new album.

5 Press Return.

Add Photos to the Album

1. Click **Photos**.

2. Click ▶ beside an event that contains photos you want to work with (▶ changes to ▼).

3. Click and drag a photo and drop it on the new album.

4. Repeat steps **2** and **3** to add other photos to the album.

5. Click the album.

Ⓐ iPhoto displays the photos you added to the album.

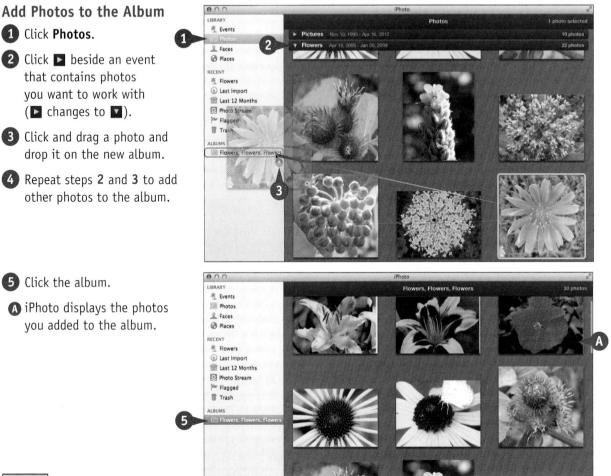

TIP

Is there any way to make iPhoto add photos to an album automatically?

Yes, you can create a *Smart Album* where the photos that appear in the album have one or more properties in common, such as the description, rating, date, or text in the photo title. Click **File** and then click **New Smart Album** (you can also press Option+⌘+N). Use the Smart Album dialog to create one or more rules that define which photos you want to appear in the album.

Smart Album name:	Favorites

Match the following condition:

My Rating	is	★★★★★	⊖ ⊕

Cancel   OK

Crop a Photo

I f you have a photo containing elements that you do not want or need to see, you can often cut out those elements. This is called *cropping*, and you can do this with iPhoto, which comes with the iLife suite, or via the App Store. When you crop a photo, you specify a rectangular area of the photo that you want to keep. iPhoto discards everything outside of the rectangle.

Cropping is a useful technique to know because it can help give focus to the true subject of a photo. Cropping is also useful for removing extraneous elements that appear on or near the edges of a photo.

Crop a Photo

1 Click the photo you want to crop.

2 Click **Edit** (✎).

iPhoto displays its editing tools.

3 Click **Crop** (▣).

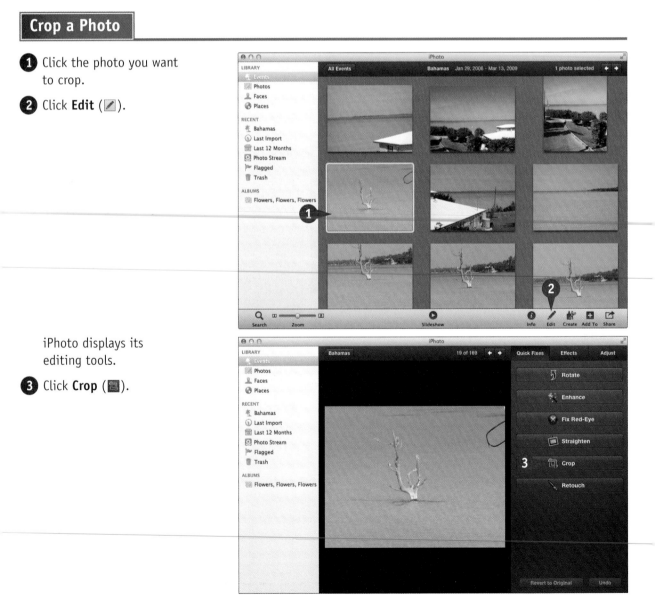

iPhoto displays a cropping rectangle on the photo.

④ Click and drag a corner or side to define the area you want to keep.

Note: Remember that iPhoto keeps the area inside the rectangle.

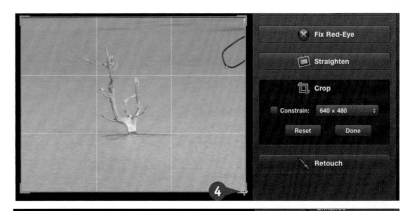

⑤ Click **Done**.

iPhoto saves the cropped photo.

⑥ Click **Edit** ().

iPhoto exits edit mode.

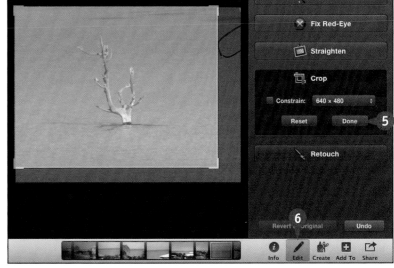

TIP

Is there a quick way to crop a photo to a certain size?

Yes, iPhoto enables you to specify either a specific size, such as 640 × 480, or a specific ratio, such as 4 × 3 or 16 × 9. Follow these steps:

① Follow steps **1** to **3** to display the Crop tool.

② Click the **Constrain** check box (☐ changes to ☑).

③ In the Constrain pop-up menu, click ▣.

④ Click the size or ratio you want to use.

⑤ Click **Done**.

⑥ Click **Edit** ().

iPhoto exits edit mode.

Rotate a Photo

You can rotate a photo using the iPhoto application, which comes with all new Macs as part of iLife, and is also available via the App Store. Depending on how you held your camera when you took a shot, the resulting photo might show the subject sideways or upside down. This may be the effect you want, but more likely this is a problem. To fix the problem, you can use iPhoto to rotate the photo so that the subject appears right-side up. You can rotate a photo either clockwise or counterclockwise.

Rotate a Photo

1 Click the photo you want to rotate.

Note: A quick way to rotate a photo is to right-click the photo and then click **Rotate** ().

2 Click **Edit** (☑).

iPhoto displays its editing tools.

3 Click **Rotate** (🔄).

A iPhoto rotates the photo 90 degrees counterclockwise.

4 Repeat step **3** until the subject of the photo is right-side up.

5 Click **Edit** (✏️).

iPhoto exits edit mode.

TIP

Can I rotate a photo clockwise instead?
Yes, you can. Follow these steps:

1 With the editing tools displayed, press and hold `Option`.

A The Rotate icon changes from 🔄 to 🔃.

2 With `Option` held down, click **Rotate** to rotate the photo clockwise by 90 degrees.

Note: You can also right-click the photo and then click **Rotate Clockwise**.

Straighten a Photo

You can straighten a crooked photo using the iPhoto application, which comes with all new Macs as part of iLife, and is also available via the App Store. If you do not use a tripod when taking pictures, getting your camera perfectly level when you take a shot is very difficult and requires a lot of practice and a steady hand. Despite your best efforts, you might end up with a photo that is not quite level. To fix this problem, you can use iPhoto to nudge the photo clockwise or counterclockwise so that the subject appears straight.

Straighten a Photo

1 Click the photo you want to straighten.

2 Click **Edit** ( ).

iPhoto displays its editing tools.

3 Click **Straighten** ( ).

iPhoto displays a grid over the photo.

4 Click and drag the **Angle** slider.

Drag the slider to the left to angle the photo counterclockwise.

Drag the slider to the right to angle the photo clockwise.

5 Click **Done**.

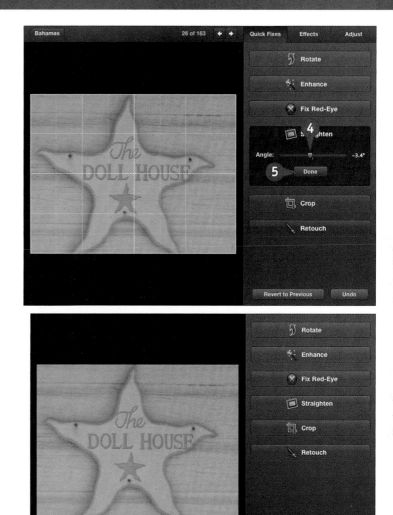

6 Click **Edit** (✏).

iPhoto exits edit mode.

TIP

How do I know when my photo is level?
Use the gridlines that iPhoto places over the photo. Locate a horizontal line in your photo, and then rotate the photo so that this line is parallel to the nearest horizontal line in the grid. You can also match a vertical line in the photo with a vertical line in the grid.

Remove Red Eye from a Photo

You can remove red eye from a photo using the iPhoto application, which comes with all new Macs as part of iLife, and is also available via the App Store. When you use a flash to take a picture of one or more people, in some cases the flash may reflect off the subjects' retinas. The result is *red eye*, where each person's pupils appear red instead of black.

If you have a photo where one or more people have red eyes because of the camera flash, you can use iPhoto to remove the red eye and give your subjects a more natural look.

Remove Red Eye from a Photo

1 Click the photo that contains the red eye.

2 Click **Edit** (✎).

iPhoto displays its editing tools.

A If needed, you can click and drag this slider to the right to zoom in on the picture.

B You can click and drag this rectangle to bring the red eye into view.

3 Click **Fix Red-Eye** (⊗).

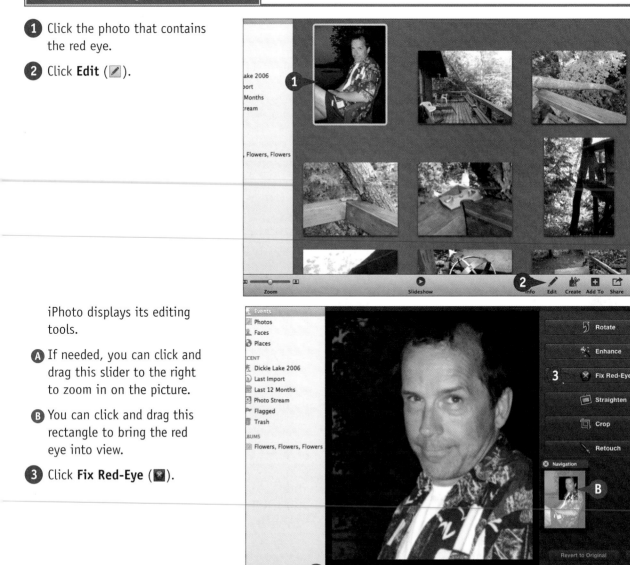

iPhoto displays its Red-Eye controls.

C You may be able to fix the red eye automatically by clicking the **Auto-fix red-eye** check box (☐ changes to ☑). If that does not work, continue with the rest of these steps.

4 Position the red eye pointer over a red eye in the photo.

5 Click the red eye.

D iPhoto removes the red eye.

6 Repeat steps **4** and **5** to fix any other instances of red eye in the photo.

7 Click **Done**.

8 Click **Edit** (✎).

iPhoto exits edit mode.

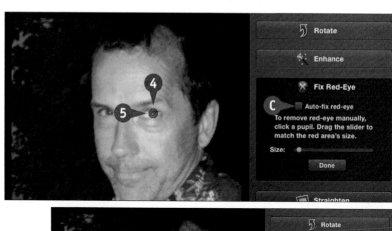

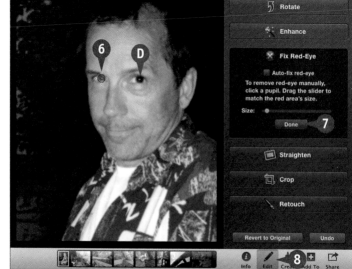

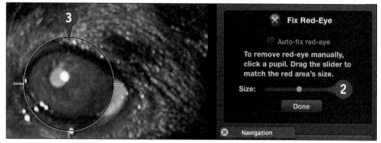

TIP

Why does iPhoto remove only part of the red eye in my photo?
The Red-Eye tool may not be set to a large-enough size. The tool should be approximately the same size as the subject's eye:

1 Follow steps **1** to **3** to display the Red-Eye controls.

2 Click and drag the Size slider until the Red-Eye tool is the size of the red-eye area.

3 Use your mouse to move the circle over the red eye and then click.

iPhoto removes the red eye that occurs within the circle.

Add Names to Faces in Your Photos

You can make your photos easier to manage and navigate by adding names to the faces that appear in each photo. This is sometimes called *tagging*, and it enables you to navigate your photos by name. For example, you can view all your photos in which a certain person appears.

To add names to the faces in your photos, you must be using iPhoto '09 or later. To check this, click **iPhoto** in the menu bar and then click **About iPhoto**.

Add Names to Faces in Your Photos

1 Click the photo that you want to tag.

2 Click **Info** (ⓘ).

3 Click **X unnamed** (where *X* is the number of faces iPhoto identifies in the photo).

iPhoto displays its naming tools.

4 Click **unnamed**.

5 Type the person's name.

6 Press [Return].

7 Repeat steps **3** to **5** to name each person in the photo.

A If iPhoto did not mark a face in the photo, click **Add a face**, size and position the box over the face, and then type the name in the **click to name** box.

8 Click **Info** (■).

iPhoto exits naming mode.

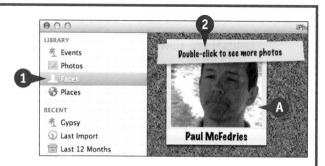

Last Import   2 of 34

Canon PowerShot G6
7.2-28.8 mm
480 x 640   179 KB   JPEG
ISO 50   14.4 mm   0 EV   f/4   1/320

IMG_1075
July 30, 2005 12:11:09 AM
Add a description...

Faces
1 unnamed
Add a face...   A

Paul McFedries

Add a description...

Faces
Paul McFedries
Add a face...

Paul McFedries

Assign a Place...

8

Info   Edit   Create   Add To   Share

TIP

How do I view all the photos that contain a particular person?

One method you can use is to open a photo, click **Info** (■), and then click the **Show All** arrow (■) that appears beside the person's name. You can also follow these steps:

1 Click **Faces** in the iPhoto sidebar.

A iPhoto displays the names and sample photos of each person you have named.

2 Double-click the person you want to view.

iPhoto displays all the photos in which you have tagged that person.

LIBRARY
Events
Photos
Faces
Places

RECENT
Gypsy
Last Import
Last 12 Months

Double-click to see more photos

Paul McFedries

Map Your Photos

You can view your photos by location if you edit each photo to include the location where you took the image. If your camera does not add location data automatically, you can tell iPhoto the locations where your photos were taken, and then display a map that shows those locations. This enables you to view all your photos taken in a particular place.

To map your photos, you must be using iPhoto '09 or later. To check this, click **iPhoto** in the menu bar and then click **About iPhoto**.

Map Your Photos

1 Click the event that you want to map.

If you want to map a single photo, open the event and then open the photo.

2 Click **Info** (🛈).

3 Click **Assign a Place**.

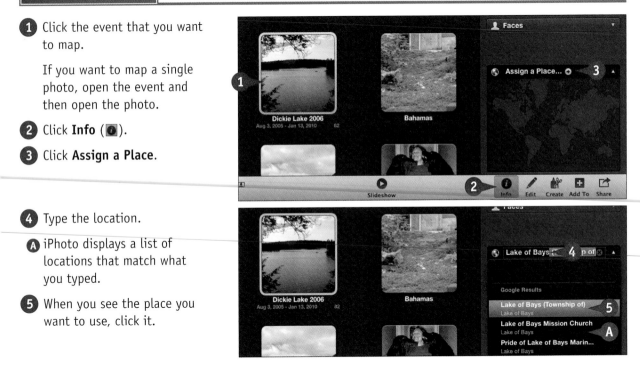

4 Type the location.

Ⓐ iPhoto displays a list of locations that match what you typed.

5 When you see the place you want to use, click it.

iPhoto displays the location on a Google map.

6 Click and drag the pin to the correct location, if necessary.

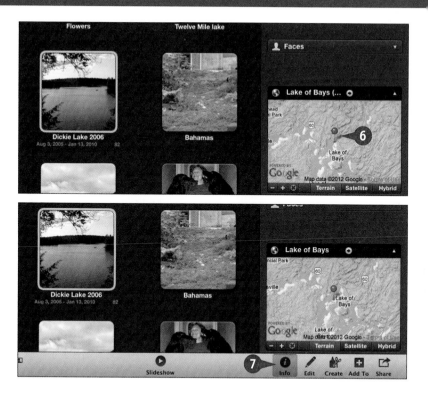

7 Click **Info** (🔵).

iPhoto closes the Info window.

TIPS

Is there a way to have the location data added automatically?
Yes. If you have a GPS-enabled device — such as an iPhone 3G or later, or a 2nd- or 3rd-generation iPad with 3G or 4G — iPhoto automatically picks up location data from the photos. However, for this to work, you must activate this feature. Click **iPhoto** in the menu bar, click **Preferences**, and then click the **Advanced** tab. Click the **Look up Places** and then click **Automatically**. Note that you may still have to add or edit location names for your photos.

How do I view all the photos that were taken in a particular place?
Click **Places** in the iPhoto sidebar to see a map of the world with pins for each of your identified photo locations. Position the mouse (↖) over the location's pin, and then click the **Show All** arrow (🔵). iPhoto displays all the photos that were identified as taken in that location.

Email a Photo

You can use the iPhoto application to create a message to send a photo to another person via email. iPhoto comes with all new Macs as part of iLife, and is also available via the App Store. If you have a photo that you want to share with someone, and you know that person's email address, you can send the photo in an email message. Using iPhoto, you can specify which photo you want to send, and iPhoto creates a new message.

Email a Photo

1 Click the photo you want to send.

2 Click **Share**.

3 Click **Email**.

You can also click **Share** () and then click **Email**.

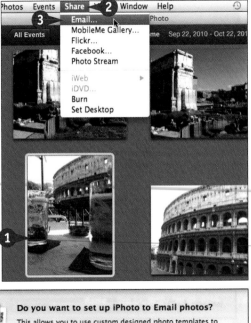

Your Mac asks if you want to set up iPhoto to email photos.

Note: This is a one-time setup task. In the future, you can skip directly to step **7**.

4 Click **Setup**.

Your Mac displays the Add Account dialog.

5 Fill in the email account details, which vary depending on the account type.

6 Click **Save**.

Add iCloud Account

Full Name: Millicent Peeved

Email Address: mpeeved@me.com

Password: •••••••••

Description: iCloud

Cancel **6**   Save

(A) iPhoto creates a new message and adds the photo to the message body.

7 Type the address of the message recipient.

8 Type the message subject.

9 Click here and then type your message text.

(B) You can use these controls to format the text.

(C) You can click these thumbnails to apply a special effect to the message.

10 Click **Send**.

iPhoto sends the message.

TIP

How do I change the size of the photo?

You need to be careful when sending photos because a single image can be several megabytes in size. If your recipient's email system places restrictions on the size of messages it can receive, your message might not go through.

To change the size of the photo, click the **Photo Size** ⬦ and then click the size you want to use for the sent photo, such as Small or Medium. Note that this does not affect the size of the original photo, just the copy sent with the message.

Take Your Picture

If your Mac comes with a built-in iSight or FaceTime HD camera, or if you have an external camera attached to your Mac, you can use the camera to take a picture of yourself using the Photo Booth application. Once you have taken your picture, you can email that picture, add it to iPhoto, or set it as your user account or iChat buddy picture.

Take Your Picture

Take Your Picture with Photo Booth

1 In the Dock, click **Photo Booth** ().

The Photo Booth window appears.

Ⓐ The live feed from the camera appears here.

2 Click **Take a still picture** (🔲).

Ⓑ Click **Take four quick pictures** (▦) if you want Photo Booth to snap four successive photos, each about 1 second apart.

Ⓒ Click **Take a movie clip** (▤) if you want Photo Booth to capture the live camera feed as a movie.

132

Click **Take Photo** (📷).

Note: You can also press ⌘+🅣 or click **File** and then click **Take Photo**.

Photo Booth counts down 3 seconds and then takes the photo.

Note: When the Mac is taking your picture, be sure to look into the camera, not into the screen.

Work with Your Photo Booth Picture

Ⓓ Photo Booth displays the picture.

❶ Click the picture.

❷ Click **Share** (📤).

Ⓔ Click **Add to iPhoto** to add the photo to iPhoto.

Ⓕ Click **Set Account Picture** to set the photo as your user account picture.

Ⓖ Click **Set Buddy Picture** to set the photo as your Messages picture.

Ⓗ Click **Change Twitter Profile Picture** to set the photo as your Twitter avatar.

TIP

Can I make my photos more interesting?
Yes. Photo Booth comes with around two dozen special effects.

❶ Click **View**.

❷ Click **Show Effects**.

❸ Click an icon to select a different page of effects.

Ⓐ You can also use the arrow buttons to change pages.

❹ Click the effect you want to use.

CHAPTER 7

Working with Digital Video

Your Mac comes with the tools you need to play movies and digital video as well as to create your own digital video movies. Using the iMovie application, you can import camcorder video, apply scene transitions, and add titles, credits, and a soundtrack.

Play a DVD Using DVD Player

If your Mac has a DVD drive, you can insert a DVD movie disc into the drive and then use the DVD Player application to play the movie on your Mac. You can either watch the movie in full-screen mode where the movie takes up the entire Mac screen, or play the DVD in a window while you work on other things. DVD Player has features that enable you to control the movie playback and volume.

Play a DVD Using DVD Player

Play a DVD Full-Screen

1 Insert the DVD disc into your Mac's DVD drive.

DVD Player runs automatically and starts playing the DVD full screen.

2 If you get to the DVD menu, click **Play** to start the movie.

3 Move the mouse (🖰) to the bottom of the screen.

The playback controls appear.

Ⓐ Click to pause the movie.

Ⓑ Click to fast-forward the movie.

Ⓒ Click to rewind the movie.

Ⓓ Drag the slider to adjust the volume.

Ⓔ Click to display the DVD menu.

Ⓕ Click to exit full-screen mode.

Play a DVD in a Window

① Insert the DVD disc into your Mac's DVD drive.

DVD Player runs automatically and starts playing the DVD full screen.

② Press ⌘+🇫.

You can also press [Esc] or move the ▸ to the bottom of the screen and then click **Exit full screen**.

DVD Player displays the movie in a window.

🄶 DVD Player displays the Controller.

③ When you get to the DVD menu, click **Play Movie** to start the movie.

🄷 Click to pause the movie.

🄸 Click and hold to fast-forward the movie.

🄹 Click and hold to rewind the movie.

🄺 Drag the slider to adjust the volume.

🄻 Click to display the DVD menu.

🄼 Click to stop the movie.

🄽 Click to eject the DVD.

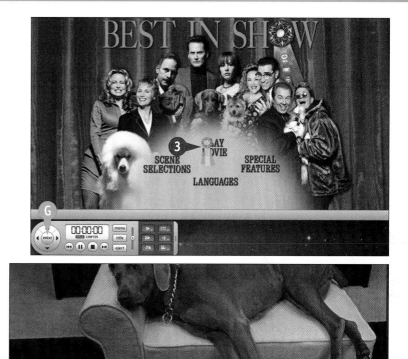

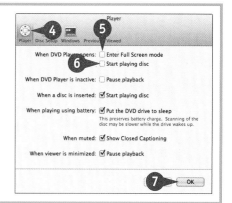

TIP

How can I always start my DVDs in a window?

① Move the (▸) to the top of the screen to display the menu bar.

② Click **DVD Player**.

③ Click **Preferences** to open the DVD Player preferences.

④ Click the **Player** tab.

⑤ Click **Enter Full Screen mode** (☑ changes to ☐).

⑥ If you want to manually control when the playback starts, also click **Start playing disc** (☑ changes to ☐).

⑦ Click **OK** to put the new settings into effect.

Play Digital Video with QuickTime Player

Your Mac comes with an application called *QuickTime Player* that can play digital video files in various formats. You will mostly use QuickTime Player to play digital video files stored on your Mac, but you can also use the application to play digital video from the web. QuickTime Player enables you to open video files, navigate the digital video playback, and control the digital video volume.

Although you learn only how to play digital video files in this section, the version of QuickTime that comes with OS X 10.8 (Mountain Lion) comes with many extra features, including the capability to record movies and audio and to cut and paste scenes.

Play Digital Video with QuickTime Player

1 Click **Finder** (🙂).

2 Click **Applications**.

3 Double-click **QuickTime Player** (◉).

Note: If you see the **QuickTime Player** icon in the Dock, you can also click that icon to launch the program.

The QuickTime Player application appears.

4 Click **File**.

5 Click **Open File**.

You can also press ⌘+O.

The Open dialog appears.

6 Locate and click the video file you want to play.

7 Click **Open**.

QuickTime opens a new player window.

8 Click **Play** (▶).

Ⓐ Click here to fast-forward the video.

Ⓑ Click here to rewind the video.

Ⓒ Click and drag this slider to adjust the volume.

If you want to view the video in full-screen mode, press ⌘+F.

TIP

Can I use QuickTime Player to play a video from the web?
Yes, as long as you know the Internet address of the video, QuickTime Player can play most video formats available on the web. In QuickTime Player, click **File** and then click **Open Location** (or press ⌘+U). In the Open URL dialog, type or paste the video address in the **Movie Location** text box, and then click **Open**.

Create a New Movie Project

The iLife suite installed on your Mac includes iMovie, which is also available via the App Store. iMovie enables you to import video from a digital camcorder or video file and use that footage to create your own movies. You do this by first creating a project that holds your video clips, transitions, titles, and other elements of your movie.

When you first start iMovie, the program creates a new project for you automatically. Follow the steps in this section to create subsequent projects.

Create a New Movie Project

1 Click the **iMovie** icon (⬛) in the Dock.

The iMovie window appears.

2 Click **File**.

3 Click **New Project**.

You can also press ⌘+N.

The New Project dialog appears.

④ Use the Name text box to type a name for your project.

⑤ Click the **Aspect Ratio** ⊡ and then click the ratio you prefer: Widescreen (16:9) or Standard (4:3).

⑥ If you want to apply a theme to your project, click the one you want in the Project Themes list.

Note: See the first tip below to learn more about themes.

⑦ If you want iMovie to automatically insert transitions between all your clips, click **Automatically add** (☐ changes to ☑) and then click ⊡ to choose the type of transition.

⑧ Click **Create**.

iMovie creates your new project.

TIPS

What are the iMovie themes?

One of the goals of iMovie is to make digital video editing as effortless as possible. To that end, iMovie offers several themes that you can apply to a project. Each theme comes with its own set of titles and transitions that are added automatically, saving you a lot of work. There are seven themes in all, including Photo Album, Bulletin Board, Comic Book, and Scrapbook. If one of them is suitable for your project, applying it cuts down on your production time.

How do I switch from one project to another?

You use the Project Library, which is a list of your movie projects. To display it, click **Window** and then click **Show Project Library**. You can also click the **Project Library** button in the top left corner of the iMovie window. In the Project Library, double-click the project you want to work with.

Import a Video File

With the iMovie application, you can import digital video from a camera for use in your movie project. If you have video content on a USB digital camcorder or smartphone (such as an iPhone 3GS or later), you can connect the device to your Mac and then import some or all of the video to your iMovie project.

If your Mac or monitor has a built-in iSight or FaceTime HD camera, you can also use iMovie to import live images from that camera to use as digital video footage in your movie project.

Import a Video File

Import All Clips

1 Connect the video device to your Mac.

iMovie displays its Import From dialog.

2 Click **Import All**.

iMovie prompts you to create a new event.

3 Click **Create new Event** (○ changes to ◉).

4 Use the Create new Event text box to type a name for the import event.

Ⓐ If you want to add the video to an existing event, click **Add to existing Event** (○ changes to ◉) and then choose the event from the pop-up menu.

5 Click **Import**.

Import Selected Clips

1 Connect the video device to your Mac and place it in playback mode, if necessary.

iMovie displays its Import From dialog.

2 Click **Manual**.

3 Deselect the check box under each clip you do not want to import (☑ changes to ☐).

4 Click **Import Checked**.

iMovie prompts you to create a new event.

5 Click **Create new Event** (○ changes to ⊙).

6 Use the Create new Event text box to type a name for the import event.

7 Click **Import**.

iMovie begins importing the clips.

8 Click **OK**.

9 Click **Done**.

How do I import digital video from my iSight or FaceTime HD camera?
Follow these steps:

1 In iMovie, click **File** and then click **Import from Camera**.

2 Click **Capture**.

3 Follow steps **5** and **6** in the "Import Selected Clips" section.

4 Click **Capture**.

5 When you are done, click **Stop**.

6 Click **Done**.

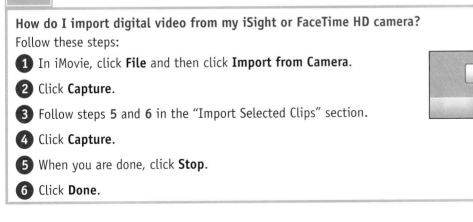

Add Video Clips to Your Project

To create and work with a movie project in iMovie, you must first add some video clips to that project. A *video clip* is a segment of digital video. You begin building your movie by adding one or more video clips to your project.

When you import digital video as described in the previous section, "Import a Video File," iMovie automatically breaks up the video into separate clips, with each clip being the footage shot during a single recording session. You can then decide which of those clips you want to add to your project, or you can add only part of a clip.

Add Video Clips to Your Project

Add an Entire Clip

1 Click the Event Library item that contains the video clip you want to add.

2 Press and hold **Option** and click the clip.

Ⓐ iMovie selects the entire clip.

3 Click and drag the selected clip and drop it in your project at the spot where you want the clip to appear.

Ⓑ iMovie adds the entire video clip to the project.

Ⓒ iMovie adds an orange bar to the bottom of the original clip to indicate that it has been added to the project.

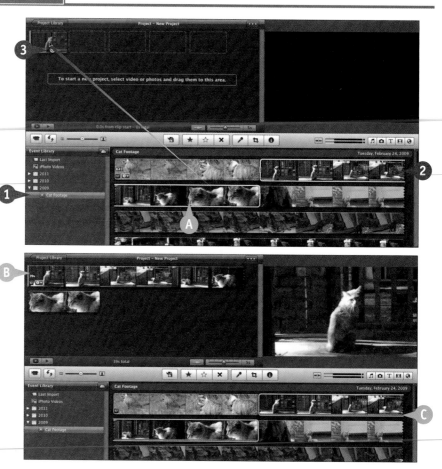

Add a Partial Clip

1 Click the Event Library item that contains the video clip you want to add.

2 Click the clip at the point where you want the selection to begin.

3 Click and drag the right edge of the selection box to the point where you want the selection to end.

4 Click and drag the selected clip and drop it in your project at the spot where you want the clip to appear.

D iMovie adds the selected portion of the video clip to the project.

E iMovie adds an orange bar to the bottom of the original clip to indicate that it has been added to a project.

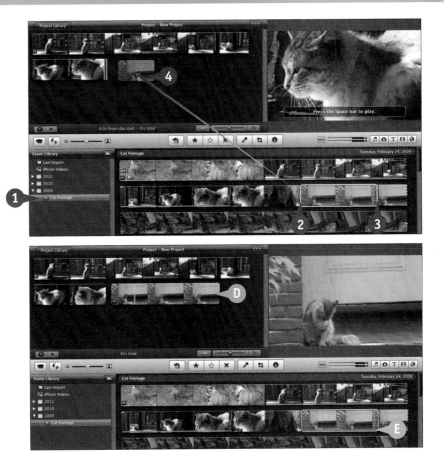

TIPS

Is it possible to play a clip before I add it?
Yes. The easiest way to do this is to click the clip at the point where you want the playback to start and then press Spacebar. iMovie plays the clip in the Viewer in the top right corner of the window. Press Spacebar again to stop the playback. If you want to see only a portion of the clip, follow steps **2** and **3** in the section "Add a Partial Clip" to make your selection, right-click the clip, and then click **Play Selection**.

I added a clip in the wrong place. Can I move it?
Yes. In your project, click the added clip to select it. Use your mouse (k) to click and drag the clip and then drop the clip in the correct location within the project. If you want to delete the clip from the project, click it, click **Edit**, and then click **Delete Entire Clip** (or press Option+Del).

Trim a Clip

If you have a video clip that is too long or contains footage you do not need, you can shorten the clip or remove the extra footage. Removing parts of a video clip is called *trimming* the clip. Trimming a clip is particularly useful if you recorded extra footage before and after the action you were trying to capture. By trimming this unneeded footage, your movie will include only the scenes you really require.

Trim a Clip

1 In your project, click the clip you want to trim.

A iMovie selects the entire clip.

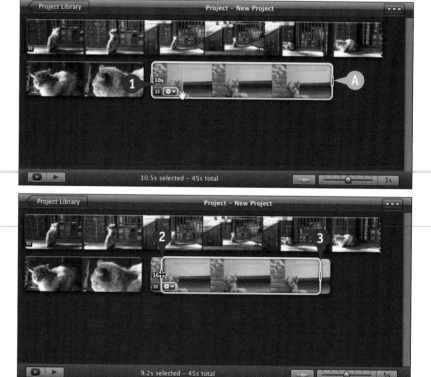

2 Use your mouse (➤) to click and drag the left edge of the selection box to the starting position of the part of the clip you want to keep.

3 Use your mouse (➤) to click and drag the right edge of the selection box to the ending position of the part of the clip you want to keep.

4 Click **Clip**.

5 Click **Trim to Selection**.

Note: You can also press ⌘+B.

B iMovie trims the clip.

Is it possible to trim a certain number of frames from a clip?

Yes, iMovie enables you to trim one frame at a time from either the beginning or the end of the clip. Follow these steps:

1 In your project, click the clip you want to trim.

iMovie selects the entire clip.

2 Click **Clip**.

3 Click **Trim Clip End**.

4 Select the trim direction:

A To trim from the beginning, click **Move Left** (or press Option+←).

B To trim from the end, click **Move Right** (or press Option+→).

iMovie trims the clip.

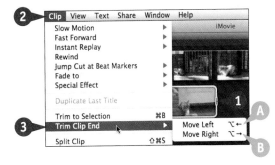

5 Repeat step 4 until you reach the number of frames that you want to trim.

Add a Transition Between Clips

You can use the iMovie application to enhance the visual appeal of your digital movie by inserting transitions between some or all of the project's video clips. By default, iMovie jumps immediately from the end of one clip to the beginning of the next clip, a transition called a *jump cut*. You can add more visual interest to your movie by adding a transition between the two clips.

iMovie offers 24 different transitions, including various fades, wipes, and dissolves. More transitions are available if you applied a theme to your iMovie project.

Add a Transition Between Clips

1 Click the **Transitions Browser** button (⊞), or press ⌘+4.

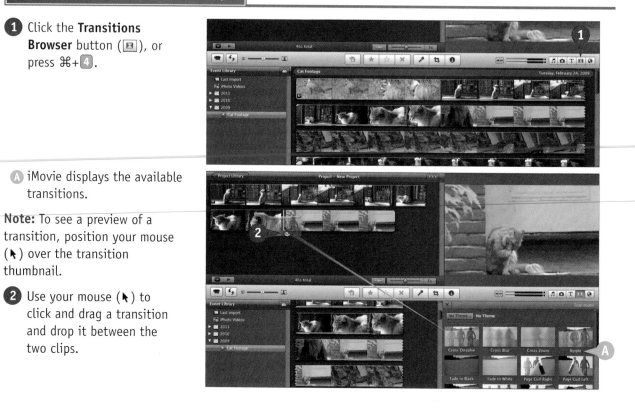

Ⓐ iMovie displays the available transitions.

Note: To see a preview of a transition, position your mouse (▶) over the transition thumbnail.

2 Use your mouse (▶) to click and drag a transition and drop it between the two clips.

B iMovie adds an icon for the transition between the two clips.

3 Position your mouse (⬉) over the beginning of the transition and move the ⬉ to the right.

C iMovie displays a preview of the transition.

TIP

Can I change the duration of the transition?
Yes. The default length is half a second, but you can increase or decrease the duration by following these steps:

1 Double-click the transition icon in your project.

The Inspector appears.

2 Use the Duration text box to set the number of seconds you want the transition to take.

3 If you want to change only the current transition, click **Applies to all transitions** (☑ changes to ☐).

4 Click **Done**.

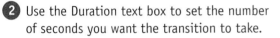

Add a Photo

You can use the iMovie application to enhance your movie projects with still photos. Although most movie projects consist of several video clips, you can also add a photo to your project. By default, iMovie displays the photo for 4 seconds.

You can also specify how the photo fits in the movie frame: You can adjust the size of the photo to fit the frame, you can crop the photo, or you can apply a Ken Burns effect — which automatically pans and zooms the photo — to animate the static photo.

Add a Photo

1. Click the **Photos Browser** button ( ), or press ⌘+2.

   A iMovie displays the available photos.

2. Click the event or album that contains the photo you want to add.

3. Click and drag the photo and drop it inside your project.

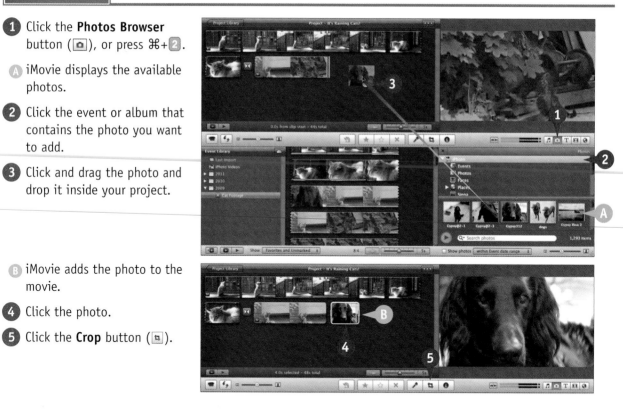

   B iMovie adds the photo to the movie.

4. Click the photo.

5. Click the **Crop** button ( ).

iMovie displays the cropping options for the photo.

6 Click **Ken Burns**.

⊙ You can also click **Fit** to have iMovie adjust the size of the photo to fit the movie frame.

⊙ You can also click **Crop** and then click and drag the cropping rectangle to specify how much of the photo you want to appear in the movie frame.

7 Click and drag the green rectangle to set the start point of the Ken Burns animation.

8 Click and drag the red rectangle to set the end point of the Ken Burns animation.

Note: Click and drag the corners and edges of the rectangle to change the size; click and drag the interior of the rectangles to change the position.

⊙ The arrow shows the direction of motion.

9 Click **Done**.

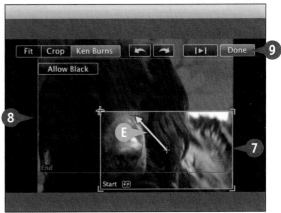

Can I change the length of time that the photo appears in the movie?
Yes. The default length is 4 seconds, but you can increase or decrease the duration by following these steps:

1 Double-click the photo in your project.

2 Click **Clip**.

3 Use the Duration text box to set the number of seconds you want the photo to appear.

4 To change the duration for all the photos in your project, click **Applies to all stills** (☐ changes to ☑).

5 Click **Done**.

Add a Music Track

Using the iMovie application, you can enhance the audio component of your movie by adding one or more songs that play in the background. With iMovie you can also add sound effects and other audio files that you feel would enhance your project's audio track.

To get the best audio experience, you can adjust various sound properties. For example, you can adjust the volume of the music clip or the volume of the video clip. You can also use iMovie to adjust the time it takes for the song clip to fade in and fade out.

Add a Music Track

1. Click the **Music and Sound Effects Browser** button (🎵), or press ⌘+①.

   Ⓐ iMovie displays the available audio files.

2. Click the folder, category, or playlist that contains the track you want to add.

3. Use your mouse (►) to click and drag the song and drop it on a video clip.

   Ⓑ iMovie adds the song to the movie.

Note: iMovie treats the song like a clip, which means you can trim the song as needed, as described earlier in the "Trim a Clip" section.

4. Double-click the music clip.

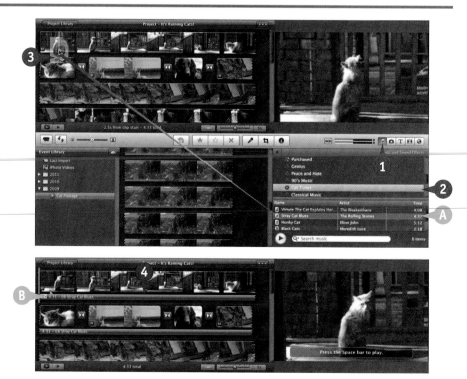

iMovie displays the Inspector.

5 Click the **Audio** tab.

6 Use the **Volume** slider to adjust the volume of the music clip.

7 If you want to reduce the video clip volume, click **Ducking** (☐ changes to ☑) and then click and drag the slider.

8 To adjust the fade-in time, click **Fade In: Manual** (☐ changes to ☑) and then click and drag the slider.

9 To adjust the fade-out time, click **Fade Out: Manual** (☐ changes to ☑) and then click and drag the slider.

10 Click **Done**.

TIP

When I add a video clip before the music clip, the music does not play with the new video clip. How can I work around this?
You need to add your song as a background track instead of a clip. Follow these steps:

1 Click 🎵.

2 Use your mouse (🔺) to click and drag a song.

3 Drop the song on the project background, not on a clip or between two clips.

🄰 The background turns green when you have the song positioned correctly.

Record a Voiceover

You can use the iMovie application to augment the audio portion of your movie with a *voiceover*, a recording that you make using audio equipment attached to your Mac. A voiceover is useful for explaining a video clip, introducing the movie, or giving the viewer background information about the movie. You can also use a voiceover to add custom sound effects.

To record a voiceover, your Mac must have either a built-in microphone, such as the one that comes with the iSight or FaceTime HD camera, or an external microphone connected via an audio jack, USB port, or Bluetooth.

Record a Voiceover

1 If your Mac does not have a built-in microphone, attach a microphone.

Note: You may need to configure the microphone as the sound input device. Click **System Preferences** (▨), click **Sound**, click **Input**, and then click your microphone.

2 Click the **Voiceover** button (▨).

The Voiceover dialog appears.

3 Click the spot in the movie at which you want the voiceover to begin.

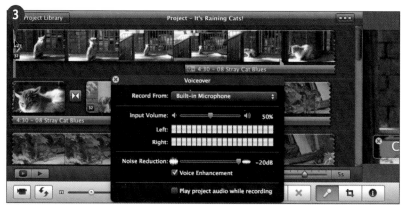

iMovie counts down and then begins the recording.

4 Speak your voiceover text into the microphone.

Ⓐ The progress of the recording appears here.

5 When you are finished, click **Recording**.

Ⓑ iMovie adds the voiceover to the clip.

6 Click **Close** (■).

You can double-click the voiceover to adjust the audio, as described in the previous section, "Add a Music Track."

TIP

Is there a way to tell if my voice is too loud or too soft?

Yes, you can use the controls in the Voiceover dialog. You check your voice level by talking into the microphone and then watching the Left and Right volume meters:

Ⓐ If you see no green bars or just a few green bars, your voice level is too low.

Ⓑ If you see yellow or red bars, your voice level is too high.

Use the Input Volume slider to adjust the voice level up or down, as needed.

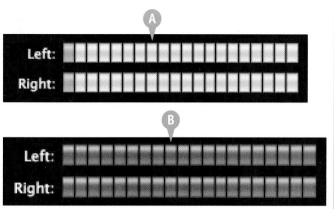

Add Titles and Credits

You can use the iMovie application to enhance your movie project with titles and scrolling credits. You can get your movie off to a proper start by adding a title and a subtitle at or near the beginning of the movie. iMovie offers a number of title styles that you can choose from, and you can also change the title font.

You can also enhance your movie with *scrolling credits*. This is a special type of title that you place at the end of the movie and that scrolls the names of the people responsible for the project.

Add Titles and Credits

1 Click the **Titles Browser** button (T).

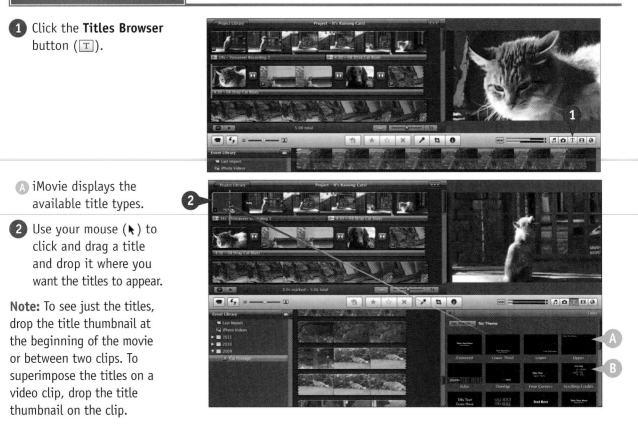

A iMovie displays the available title types.

2 Use your mouse (▶) to click and drag a title and drop it where you want the titles to appear.

Note: To see just the titles, drop the title thumbnail at the beginning of the movie or between two clips. To superimpose the titles on a video clip, drop the title thumbnail on the clip.

B If you want to add credits, click and drag the **Scrolling Credits** thumbnail and drop it at the end of the movie.

C iMovie adds a clip for the title.

3 Replace this text with the movie title.

4 Replace this text with the movie subtitle.

5 Click **Done**.

Note: iMovie treats the title like a clip, which means you can lengthen or shorten the title duration by clicking and dragging the beginning or end, as described earlier in the "Trim a Clip" section.

TIP

How do I change the font of the titles?
The Text menu offers several font-related commands, including Bold, Italic, Bigger, and Smaller. You can also click the **Show Fonts** command to display the Choose Font dialog. If you do not see the Choose Font dialog shown here, you can switch to iMovie's predefined fonts by clicking **iMovie Font Panel**. You can then click a typeface, font color, and type size; click **Done** (**A**) to close the dialog.

Play the Movie

The iMovie application offers the Viewer pane, which you can use to play your movie. While you are building your iMovie project, it is a good idea to occasionally play some or all of the movie to check your progress. For example, you can play the entire movie to make sure the video and audio are working properly and are synchronized correctly. You can also play parts of the movie to ensure that your transitions and titles appear when you want them to.

Play the Movie

Play from the Beginning

1 Click **View**.

2 Click **Play from Beginning**.

Note: You can also press or click the **Play Project from Beginning** button (▶).

Play from a Specific Location

1 Position the mouse (🖰) over the spot where you want to start playing the movie.

2 Press Spacebar.

Play a Selection

1 Select the video clips you want to play.

Note: See the first tip below to learn how to select multiple video clips.

2 Click **View**.

3 Click **Play Selection**.

Note: You can also press .

TIPS

How do I select multiple video clips?
To select multiple video clips, press and hold ⌘ and then click anywhere inside each clip you want to select. If you select a clip by accident, ⌘+click it again to deselect it. If you want to skip just a few clips, first press ⌘+Ⓐ to select all the clips, and then press and hold ⌘ and click the clips you do not want in the selection.

Can I enlarge the size of the playback pane?
Yes, you can play your movie in full-screen mode. To do this, click **View** and then click **Play in Full-Screen Playback Mode**. You can also press ⌘+Ⓖ or click the **Play project in full-screen playback mode** button (▶).

Publish Your Movie to YouTube

You can send your movie to YouTube for viewing on the web. You must have a YouTube account, available from www.youtube.com. You must also know your YouTube username, which you can see by clicking your account icon on YouTube and then clicking **Settings**. Your movie must be no more than 15 minutes long.

Before you can publish your movie, you must select a YouTube category, such as Entertainment or Pets and Animals, provide a title and description, and enter at least one *tag*, which is a word or short phrase that describes some aspect of the movie's content.

Publish Your Movie to YouTube

1. Click **Share**.
2. Click **YouTube**.

3. Click **Add**.

iMovie prompts you for your YouTube username.

4 Type your username.

5 Click **Done** (not shown).

6 Type your YouTube password.

7 Select a category.

8 Type a title.

9 Type a description.

10 Type one or more tags for the video.

11 If you want to allow anyone to view the movie, click **Make this movie personal** (☑ changes to ☐).

12 Click **Next**.

iMovie displays the YouTube terms of service.

13 Click **Publish**.

iMovie prepares the movie and then publishes it to YouTube.

14 Click **OK** (not shown).

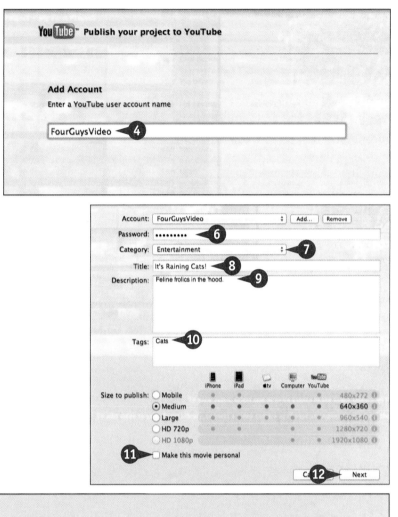

How do I publish my movie to Facebook?

If you have a Facebook account, click **Share** and then click **Facebook**. Click **Add**, type your Facebook email address, and then click **Done**. Type your Facebook password. Use the **Viewable by** pop-up to choose who can see the video, such as Only Friends or Everyone. Type a title and description, select a size, click **Next**, and then click **Publish**. (Facebook converts the movie to the Flash format, so it cannot be viewed on an iPhone, iPad, or iPod touch.)

How do I view my movie outside of iMovie?

Beyond viewing it on YouTube or Facebook, you need to export the movie to a digital video file. Click **Share** and then click **Export Movie** (or press ⌘+E). Type a title, and then click a **Size to Export** option, such as Large or HD 720p (○ changes to ⊙). Click **Export**.

CHAPTER 8

Browsing the Web

The *World Wide Web*, or simply, the web, is a massive storehouse of information that resides on computers, called *web servers*, located all over the world. If your Mac is connected to the Internet, you can use the Safari browser to navigate — or *surf* — websites.

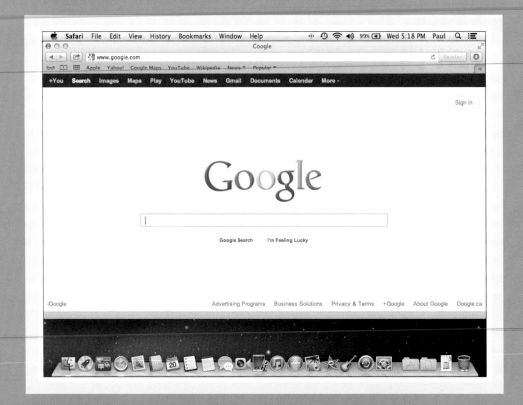

Open and Close Safari

In OS X, the default web browser is Safari, which you can use to surf websites when your Mac is connected to the Internet. The Safari application offers a number of features that make it easier to browse the web. For example, you can open multiple pages in a single Safari window and you can save your favorite sites for easier access.

To use these features, you must know how to start the Safari application. When you have finished surfing the web, you also need to know how to shut down Safari to save system resources on your Mac.

Open and Close Safari

Open Safari

1 In the Dock, click the **Safari** icon (●).

The Safari window appears.

Note: The initial web page you see depends on how your version of Safari has been configured. In most cases, you see the Apple.com Start page.

Close Safari

1 Click **Safari**.

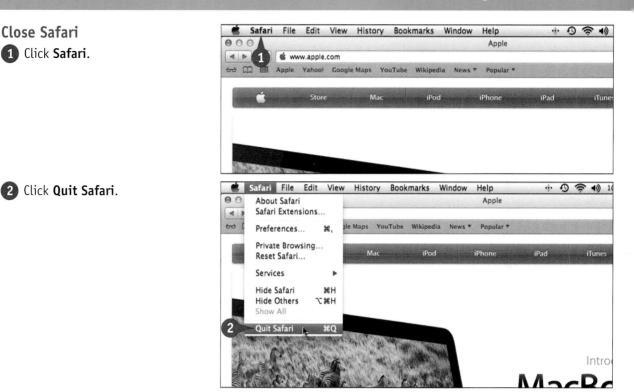

2 Click **Quit Safari**.

Are there other methods I can use to open Safari?

If you have removed the ⬡ icon from the Dock, there are a couple of other quick methods you can use to start Safari. If you have used Safari recently, click ⬡, click **Recent Items**, and then click **Safari**. You can also click **Spotlight** (🔍), type **safari**, and then click **Safari** in the search results.

Select a Link

Most web pages include links to other pages that contain related information. When you select a link, your web browser loads the other page. Web page links come in two forms: text and images. Text links consist of a word or phrase that usually appears underlined and in a different color from the rest of the page text.

However, web page designers can control the look of their links, so text links may not always stand out in this way. The only way to tell for sure is to position the mouse (▶) over the text or image; if the ▶ changes to ⬚, the item is a link.

Select a Link

1 Position ▶ over the link (▶ changes to ⬚).

2 Click the text or image.

A The status bar shows the address of the linked page.

Note: The address shown in the status bar when you point to a link may be different from the one shown when the page is downloading. This occurs when the website "redirects" the link.

Note: If you do not see the status bar, click **View** and then click **Show Status Bar**.

The linked web page appears.

B The web page title and address change after the linked page is loaded.

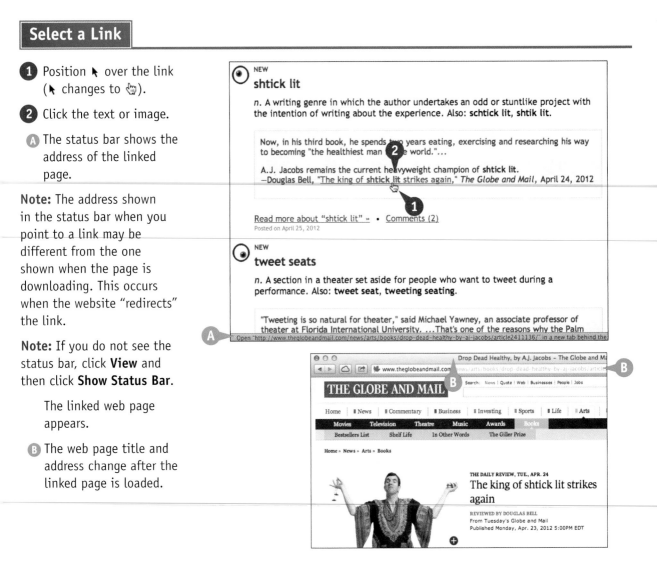

Enter a Web Page Address

If you know the address of a specific web page, you can type it into the web browser to display the page. Every web page is uniquely identified by an address called the Uniform Resource Locator, or URL (pronounced *yoo-ar-ell*). The URL is composed of four basic parts: the *transfer method* (usually HTTP, which stands for Hypertext Transfer Protocol); the website *domain name;* the *directory* where the web page is located on the server; and the *web page filename.*

The website domain name suffix most often used is .com (commercial), but other common suffixes include .gov (government), .org (nonprofit organization), and country domains such as .ca (Canada).

Enter a Web Page Address

1 Click inside the address bar.

2 Press **Del** to delete the existing address.

3 Type the address of the web page you want to visit.

4 Press **Return**.

A You can also click the site if it appears in the list of suggested sites.

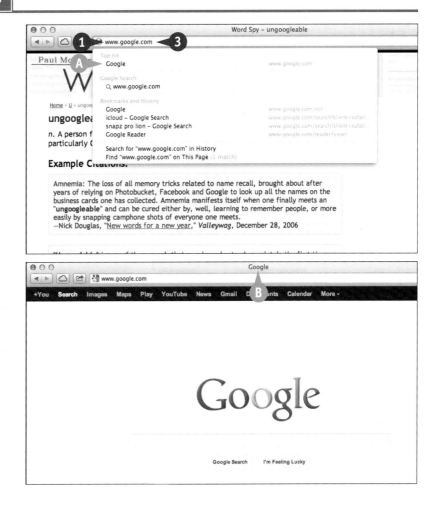

The web page appears.

B The web page title changes after the page is loaded.

Open a Web Page in a Tab

You can make it easier to work with multiple web pages and sites simultaneously by opening each page in its own tab. As you surf the web, you may come upon a page that you want to keep available while you visit other sites. That page may contain important information that you need to reference, or it might be a page that you want to read later on.

Instead of leaving the page and trying to find it again when you need it, Safari lets you leave the page open in a special section of the browser window called a *tab*.

Open a Web Page in a Tab

Open a Link in a New Tab

1 Right-click the link you want to open.

2 Click **Open Link in New Tab**.

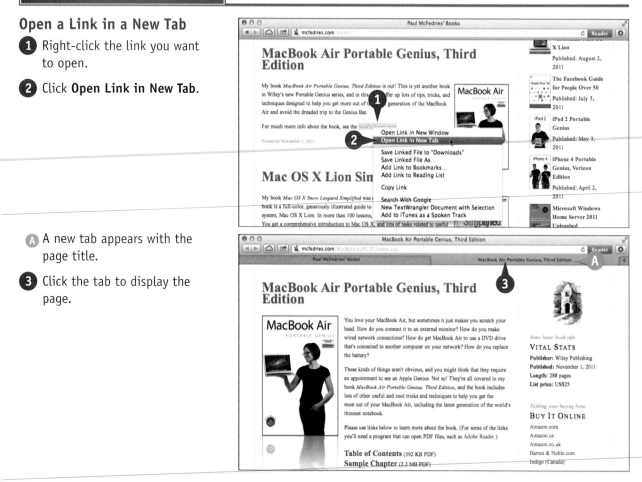

A A new tab appears with the page title.

3 Click the tab to display the page.

Create a New Tab

1 Click **File**.

2 Click **New Tab**.

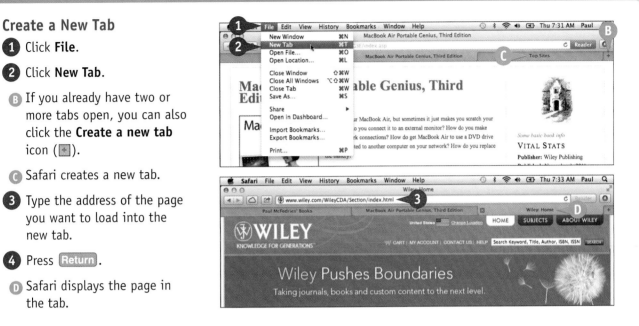

B If you already have two or more tabs open, you can also click the **Create a new tab** icon (![]).

C Safari creates a new tab.

3 Type the address of the page you want to load into the new tab.

4 Press Return.

D Safari displays the page in the tab.

Are there any shortcuts I can use to open web pages in tabs?

Yes, here are a few useful keyboard techniques you can use:

• Press and hold ⌘ and click a link to open the page in a tab.

• Press and hold ⌘+Shift and click a link to open the page in a tab and display the tab.

• Type an address and then press ⌘+Return to open the page in a new tab.

• Type an address and then press Shift+⌘+Return to open the page in a new foreground tab.

• Press Shift+⌘+[ ] or Shift+⌘+[ ] to cycle through the tabs.

• Press ⌘+W to close the current tab.

• Press Option and click ![] to close every tab but the one you clicked.

Navigate Web Pages

After you have visited several pages, you can return to a page you visited earlier. Instead of retyping the address or looking for the link, Safari gives you some easier methods. When you navigate from page to page, you create a kind of "path" through the web. Safari keeps track of this path by maintaining a list of the pages you have visited. You can use that list to go back to a page you have visited.

After you have gone back to a page you have visited, you can also use the same list of pages to go forward through the pages again.

Navigate Web Pages

Go Back One Page

1 Click the **Previous Page** icon (◄).

The previous page you visited appears.

Go Back Several Pages

1 Click and hold down ▶ on ◄.

Note: The list of visited pages is different for each tab that you have open. If you do not see the page you want, you may need to click a different tab.

A list of the pages you have visited appears.

2 Click the page you want to revisit.

The page appears.

Go Forward One Page

1 Click the **Next Page** icon ().

The next page appears.

Note: If you are at the last page viewed up to that point, ▶ is not active.

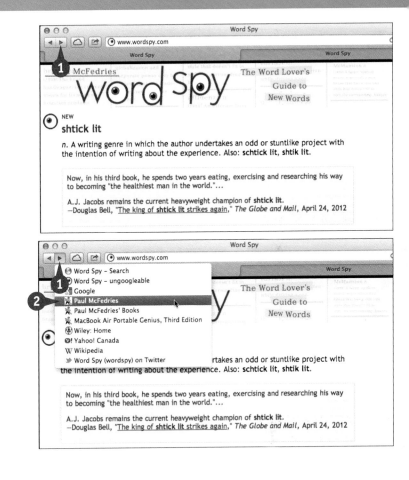

Go Forward Several Pages

1 Click and hold down ▸ on ▶.

A list of the pages you have visited appears.

Note: The list of visited pages is different for each tab that you have open. If you do not see the page you want, you may need to click a different tab.

2 Click the page you want to revisit.

The page appears.

TIP

Are there any shortcuts I can use to navigate web pages?
Yes, there are a few useful keyboard shortcuts you can use:

- Press ⌘+[to go back one page.
- Press ⌘+] to go forward one page.
- Press Shift+⌘+H to return to the Safari home page (the first page you see when you open Safari).

Navigate with the History List

The Previous Page and Next Page buttons (◀ and ▶) enable you to navigate pages in the current browser session. To redisplay sites that you have visited in the past few days or weeks, you need to use the History list, which is a collection of the websites and pages you have visited over the past month.

If you visit sensitive places such as an Internet banking site or your corporate site, you can increase security by clearing the History list so that other people cannot see where you have been.

Navigate with the History List

Load a Page from the History List

1 Click **History**.

2 Click the date when you visited the page.

A submenu of pages that you visited during that day appears.

3 Click the page you want to revisit.

Ⓐ The page appears.

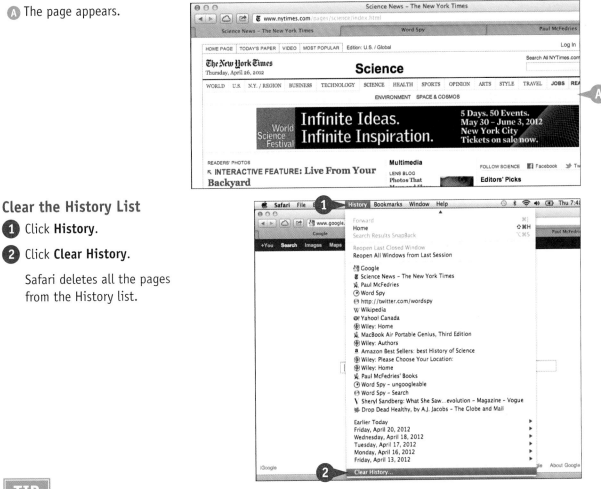

Ⓐ

Clear the History List

1 Click **History**.

2 Click **Clear History**.

Safari deletes all the pages from the History list.

Can I control the length of time that Safari keeps track of the pages I visit?

Yes, by following these steps:

1 In the menu bar, click **Safari**.

2 Click **Preferences**.

3 Click **General**.

4 In the Remove History Items pop-up menu, click ⬍ and then click the amount of time you want Safari to track your history.

5 Click 🔘.

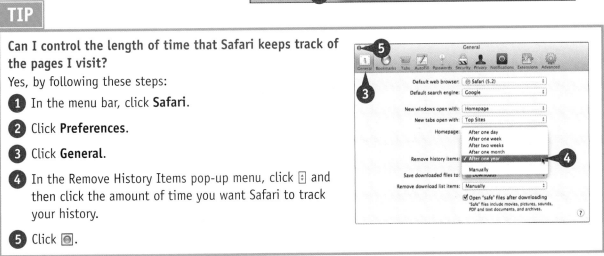

Change Your Home Page

Your home page is the web page that appears when you first start Safari. The default home page is usually the Apple.com Start page, but you can change that to any other page you want, or even to an empty page. This is useful if you do not use the Apple.com Start page, or if there is another page that you always visit at the start of your browsing session. For example, if you have your own website, it might make sense to always begin there.

Safari also comes with a command that enables you to view the home page at any time during your browsing session.

Change Your Home Page

Change the Home Page

1 Display the web page that you want to use as your home page.

2 Click **Safari**.

3 Click **Preferences**.

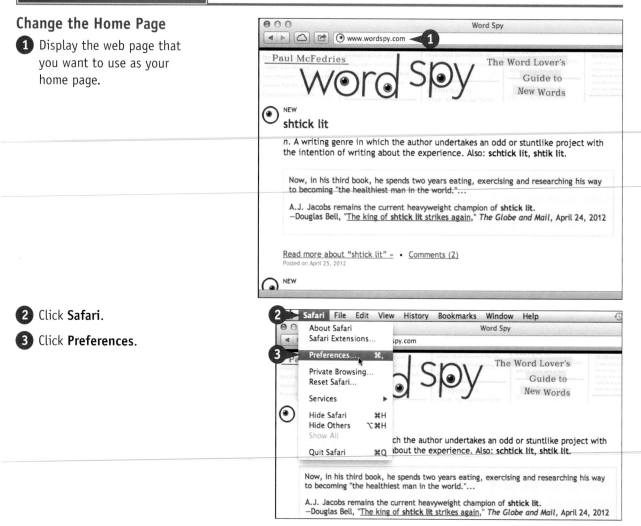

4 Click **General**.

5 Click **Set to Current Page**.

A Safari inserts the address of the current page in the Homepage text box.

Note: If your Mac is not currently connected to the Internet, you can also type the new home page address manually using the Homepage text box.

6 Click 🔘.

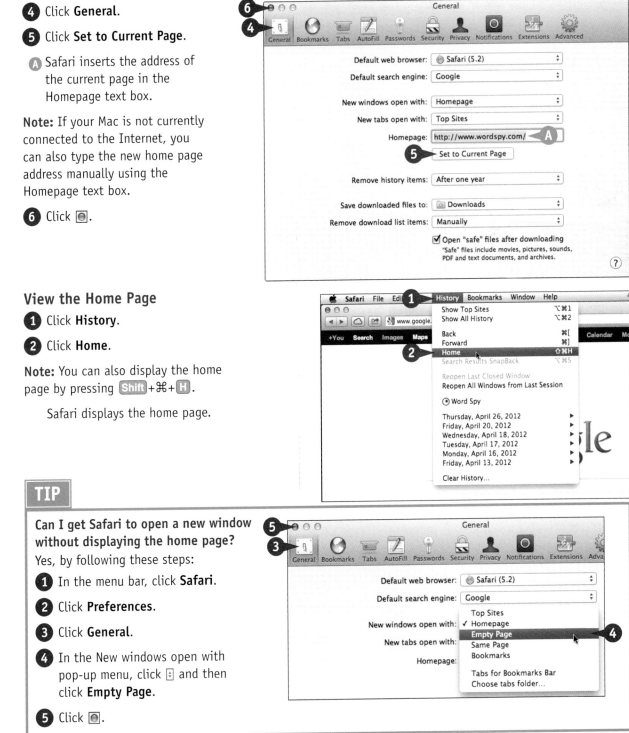

View the Home Page

1 Click **History**.

2 Click **Home**.

Note: You can also display the home page by pressing [Shift]+⌘+[H].

Safari displays the home page.

TIP

Can I get Safari to open a new window without displaying the home page?
Yes, by following these steps:

1 In the menu bar, click **Safari**.

2 Click **Preferences**.

3 Click **General**.

4 In the New windows open with pop-up menu, click 🔽 and then click **Empty Page**.

5 Click 🔘.

Bookmark Web Pages

If you have web pages that you visit frequently, you can save yourself time by storing those pages as bookmarks within Safari. This enables you to display the pages with just a couple of mouse clicks. The bookmark stores the name as well as the address of the page.

Most bookmarks are stored on the Safari Bookmarks menu. However, Safari also offers the Bookmarks bar, which appears just below the address bar. You can put your favorite sites on the Bookmarks bar for easiest access.

Bookmark Web Pages

Bookmark a Web Page

① Display the web page you want to save as a bookmark.

② Click **Bookmarks**.

③ Click **Add Bookmark**.

Ⓐ You can also run the Add Bookmark command by clicking **Share** (⬀) and then clicking **Add Bookmark**.

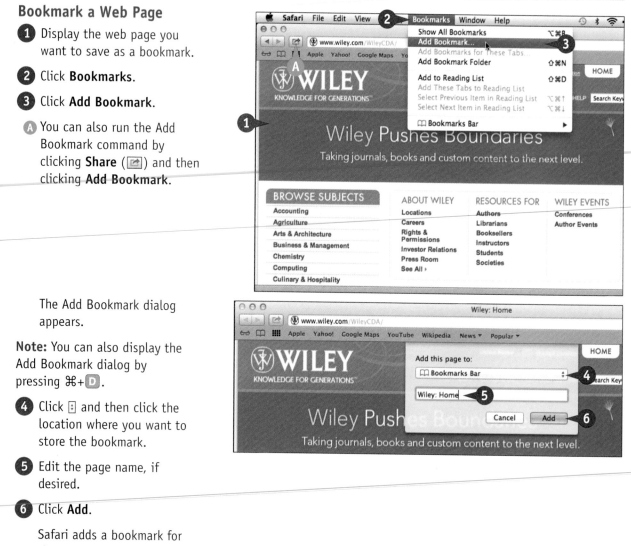

The Add Bookmark dialog appears.

Note: You can also display the Add Bookmark dialog by pressing ⌘+D.

④ Click ⬍ and then click the location where you want to store the bookmark.

⑤ Edit the page name, if desired.

⑥ Click **Add**.

Safari adds a bookmark for the page.

Display a Bookmarked Web Page

1 Click the **Show all bookmarks** button (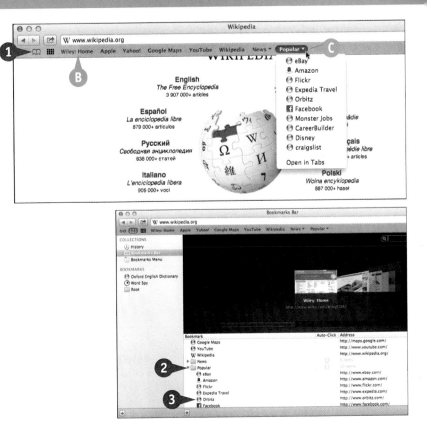).

B If you added the bookmark to the Bookmarks bar, click the page name.

C If you added the bookmark to a folder, click the folder and then click the page name.

The Bookmarks window appears.

2 Click ▶ to open the folder that contains the bookmark you want (▶ changes to ▼).

3 Double-click the bookmark.

The web page appears.

I use my Bookmarks bar a lot. Is there an easier way to display these pages?

Yes. Safari automatically assigns keyboard shortcuts to the first nine bookmarks, counting from left to right and not including folders. For example, you display the leftmost bookmark by pressing ⌘+1. Moving to the right, the shortcuts are ⌘+2, ⌘+3, and so on.

How do I delete a bookmark?

If the site is on the Bookmarks bar, right-click the bookmark and then click **Delete**, or hold down ⌘ and drag it off the bar. For all other bookmarks, click 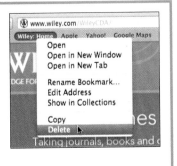 to display the Bookmarks window. Locate the bookmark you want to remove, right-click the bookmark, and then click **Delete**. You can also click the bookmark and then press Del.

Search for Sites

If you need information on a specific topic, Safari has a built-in feature that enables you to quickly search the web for sites that have the information you require. The web has a number of sites called *search engines* that enable you to find what you are looking for. By default, Safari uses the Google search site (www.google.com).

Simple, one-word searches often return tens of thousands of *hits*, or matching sites. To improve your searching, type multiple search terms that define what you are looking for. To search for a phrase, enclose the words in quotation marks.

Search for Sites

1 Click in the address bar.

2 Delete the address.

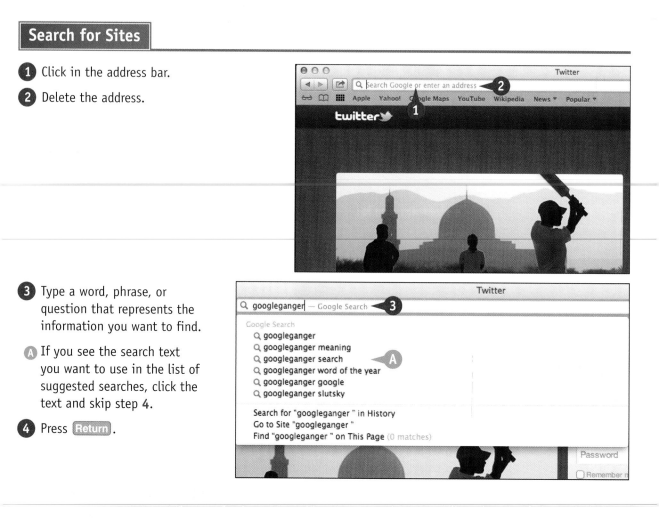

3 Type a word, phrase, or question that represents the information you want to find.

Ⓐ If you see the search text you want to use in the list of suggested searches, click the text and skip step 4.

4 Press Return.

B A list of pages that match
your search text appears.

5 Click a web page.

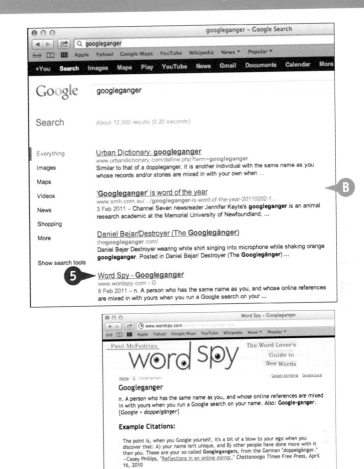

The page appears.

Is there an easy way that I can rerun a recent search?
Yes, Safari remembers your most recent search. Follow these steps
to quickly rerun that search:

1 Click **History**.

2 Click **Search Results SnapBack**.

You can also press Option+⌘+S.

Safari sends the search text to Google again.

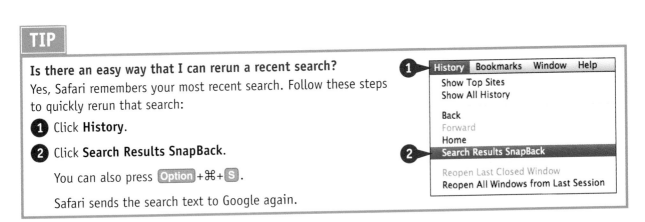

CHAPTER 9

Communicating with Your Mac

Your Mac comes with the Mail application, which you can use to exchange email messages. Your Mac also comes with the Messages application, which you use to exchange instant messages. You can also use the FaceTime application to make video calls to other people. This chapter shows you how to perform these tasks.

Open and Close Mail

Your Mac includes the Mail application to enable you to use an email account to exchange and manage email messages. Email is one of the most popular Internet services because it offers three main advantages: It is universal, fast, and convenient. Email is universal because nearly anyone who can access the Internet has an email address. Email is fast because messages are generally delivered within a few minutes. Email is convenient because you can send messages at any time of day, and your recipient does not need to be at the computer or connected to the Internet.

Before you can send or receive email messages, you must know how to start the Mail application.

Open and Close Mail

Open Mail

1. In the Dock, click the **Mail** icon ().

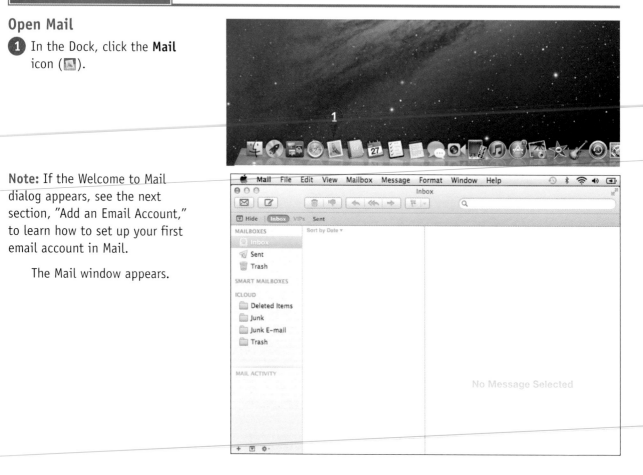

Note: If the Welcome to Mail dialog appears, see the next section, "Add an Email Account," to learn how to set up your first email account in Mail.

The Mail window appears.

Close Mail

1 Click **Mail**.

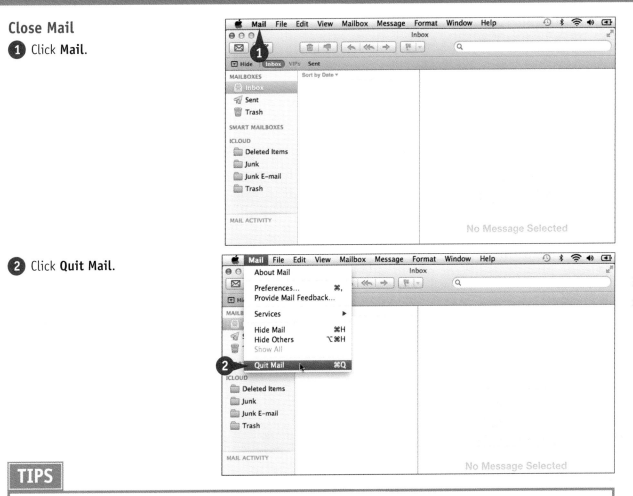

2 Click **Quit Mail**.

Are there other methods I can use to open Mail?

If you have removed the ▣ icon from the Dock, there are a couple of other quick methods you can use to start Mail. If you have used Mail recently, click , click **Recent Items**, and then click **Safari**. You can also click **Spotlight** (Q), type **mail**, and then click **Mail** in the search results.

Are there faster methods I can use to close Mail?

Probably the fastest method you can use to quit Mail is to right-click its icon (▣) in the Dock and then click **Quit**. If your hands are closer to the keyboard than to the mouse, you can quit Mail by switching to the application and then pressing ⌘+Q.

Add an Email Account

Before you can send and receive email messages, you must add your email account to the Mail application. Your email account is usually a POP (Post Office Protocol) account supplied by your Internet service provider, which should have supplied you with the POP account details. You can also set up web-based email accounts with services such as Hotmail and Gmail. A web-based account is convenient because it enables you to send and receive messages from any computer. If you have an Apple ID — that is, an account for use on the Apple iCloud service (http://www.icloud.com) — you can also set up Mail with your Apple account details.

Add an Email Account

Get Started Adding an Account

1 Click **File**.

2 Click **Add Account**.

Note: If you are just starting Mail and the Welcome to Mail dialog is on-screen, you can skip steps **1** and **2**.

The Add Account dialog appears. If you are starting Mail for the first time, the Welcome to Mail dialog is identical.

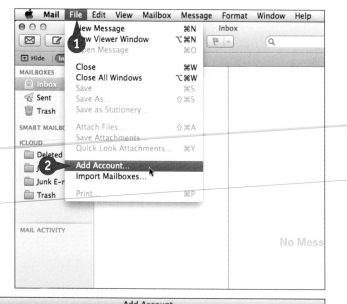

Add an Apple Account

1 Type your name.

2 Type your Apple account address.

3 Type your Apple account password.

4 Click **Create**.

Mail checks your Apple account.

5 Click **Create** (not shown).

Mail adds your Apple account.

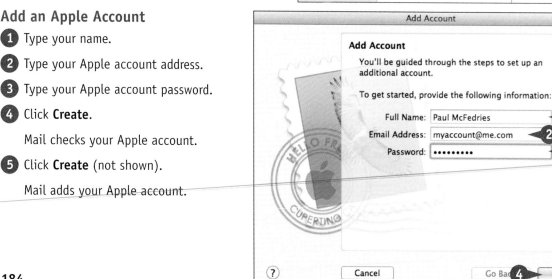

Add a POP Account

1 Type your name.

2 Type your POP account address.

3 Type your POP account password and click **Continue**.

Note: If you see a Verify Certificate dialog, click **Connect**.

4 Click ⊡ and then click **POP**.

5 Type a description of the account.

6 Type the address of the account's incoming mail server.

7 Edit the User Name text as required and click **Continue**.

8 Type a description of the outgoing mail server.

9 Type the address of the outgoing mail server, which is sometimes called the SMTP server.

A If your ISP requires authentication, click **Use Authentication** (☐ changes to ☑).

10 Click **Continue** (not shown).

Note: If you see a Verify Certificate dialog, click **Connect**.

11 Click **Create** (not shown).

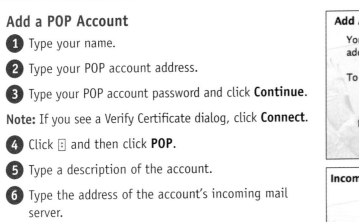

Add Account

You'll be guided through the steps to set up an additional account.

To get started, provide the following information:

Full Name: Paul McFedries **1**

Email Address: myaccount@myisp.com **2**

Password: •••••••• **3**

Incoming Mail Server

Account Type: POP **4**

Description: My POP Server **5**

Incoming Mail Server: pop.myisp.com **6**

User Name: myaccount **7**

Password: ••••••••

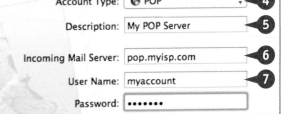

Add Account

Outgoing Mail Server

Description: My SMTP Server **8**

Outgoing Mail Server: smtp.myisp.com **9**

☑ Use only this server

A ☑ Use Authentication

User Name: myaccount

Password: ••••••••

TIP

My email account requires me to use a nonstandard outgoing mail port. How do I set this up?

1 In the menu bar, click **Mail**.

2 Click **Preferences**.

3 Click **Accounts**.

4 In the Outgoing Mail Server (SMTP) list, click ⊡ and then click **Edit SMTP Server List**.

5 Click the outgoing mail server.

6 Click **Advanced**.

7 Click **Use custom port** (○ changes to ⊙).

8 Type the nonstandard port number.

9 Click **OK**.

10 Click ⊚.

11 Click **Save**.

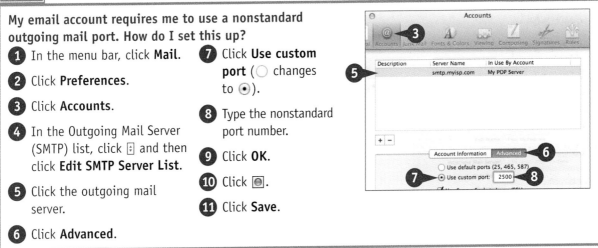

Send an Email Message

If you know the email address of a person or organization, you can send an email message to that address. An email address is a set of characters that uniquely identifies the location of an Internet mailbox. Each email address takes the form *username@domain*, where *username* is the name of the person's account with the ISP or within his or her organization; and *domain* is the Internet name of the company that provides the person's email account.

When you send an email message, it travels through your ISP's outgoing mail server. This server routes the messages to the recipient's incoming mail server, which then stores the message in the recipient's mailbox.

Send an Email Message

1 Click **New Message** (⬚).

Note: You can also start a new message by pressing ⌘+⎕.

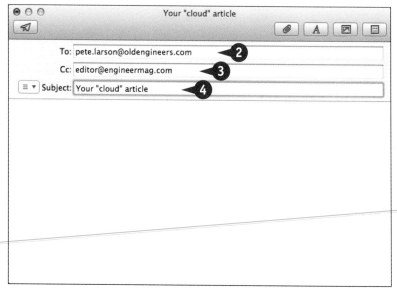

A message window appears.

2 Use the To field to type the email address of the person to whom you are sending the message.

3 To send a copy of the message to another person, use the Cc field to type that person's email address.

Note: You can add multiple email addresses in both the To line and the Cc line. Separate each address with a comma (,).

4 Use the Subject field to type a title or short description for the message.

Type the message.

 To change the message font, click **Fonts** (🅰) to display the Font panel.

Ⓑ To change the overall look of the message, click **Show Stationery** (▣) and then click a theme.

Note: Many people use email programs that cannot process text formatting. Unless you are sure your recipient's program supports formatting, it is best to send plain-text messages. To do this, click **Format** and then click **Make Plain Text**.

⑥ Click **Send** (✈).

Mail sends your message.

Note: Mail stores a copy of your message in the Sent folder.

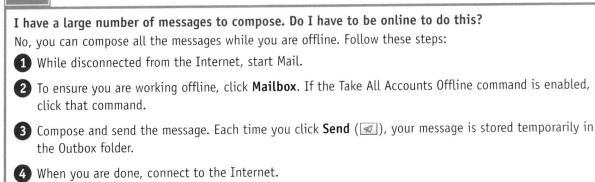

TIP

I have a large number of messages to compose. Do I have to be online to do this?

No, you can compose all the messages while you are offline. Follow these steps:

❶ While disconnected from the Internet, start Mail.

❷ To ensure you are working offline, click **Mailbox**. If the Take All Accounts Offline command is enabled, click that command.

❸ Compose and send the message. Each time you click **Send** (✈), your message is stored temporarily in the Outbox folder.

❹ When you are done, connect to the Internet.

After a few moments, Mail automatically sends all the messages in the Outbox folder.

Add a File Attachment

If you have a document that you want to send to another person, you can attach the document to an email message. A typical email message is fine for short notes, but you may have something more complex to communicate, such as budget numbers or a slide show, or some form of media that you want to share, such as an image or a song.

Because these more complex types of data usually come in a separate file — such as a spreadsheet, presentation file, or picture file — it makes sense to send that file to your recipient. You do this by attaching the file to an email message.

Add a File Attachment

1 Click **New Message** (▨).

A message window appears.

2 Fill in the recipients, subject, and message text as described in the previous section, "Send an Email Message."

3 Press Return two or three times to move the cursor a few lines below your message.

4 Click **Attach** (📎).

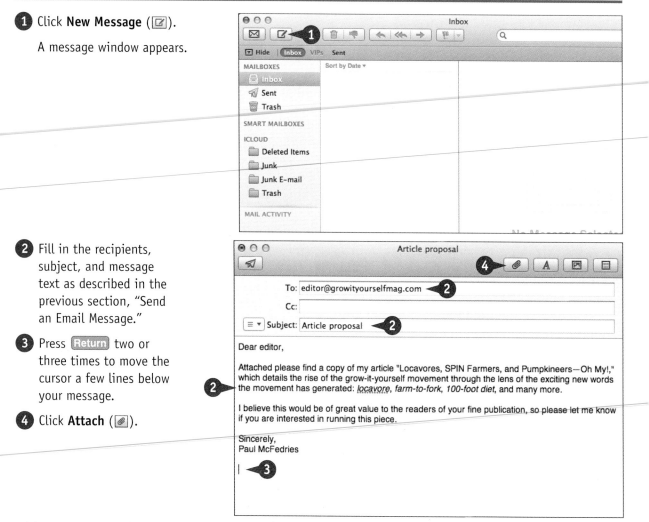

A file selection dialog appears.

5 Click the file you want to attach.

6 Click **Choose File**.

A Mail attaches the file to the message.

Note: Another way to attach a file to a message is to click and drag the file from Finder and drop it inside the message.

7 Repeat steps **4** to **6** to attach additional files to the message.

8 Click **Send** ( ).

Mail sends your message.

DOCX	XLS	XLSX
Loan Approval.docx	Loan Payment.xls	Loan Worksheets.xlsx
XLSX	DOCX	
Loans.xlsx	Locavores, SPIN Farmers,...Oh My!	Logophiia – 2013 Sales Plan.pptx
DOCX	RTF	DOCX
Logophilia Limited Annual...012.docx	Logophilia Ltd Account.rtf	Logophilia Newslett...er.docx

☑ Send Windows-Friendly Attachments

Cancel   Choose File

Article proposal

To: editor@growityourselfmag.com

Cc:

Subject: Article proposal

Dear editor,

Attached please find a copy of my article "Locavores, SPIN Farmers, and Pumpkineers—Oh My!," which details the rise of the grow-it-yourself movement through the lens of the exciting new words the movement has generated: *locavore*, *farm-to-fork*, *100-foot diet*, and many more.

I believe this would be of great value to the readers of your fine publication, so please let me know if you are interested in running this piece.

Sincerely,
Paul McFedries

Locavores, S...y! (178 KB)

TIP

Is there a limit to the number of files I can attach to a message?

The number of files you can attach to the message has no practical limit. However, you should be careful with the total *size* of the files you send to someone. If either of you have a slow Internet connection, sending or receiving the message can take an extremely long time. Also, many ISPs place a limit on the size of a message's attachments, which is usually between 2MB and 5MB. In general, use email to send only a few small files at a time.

Add a Signature

In an email message, a *signature* is a small amount of text that appears at the bottom of the message. Instead of typing this information in each message, you can save the signature in your Mail preferences and click a button to have Mail add the signature to your outgoing message.

Signatures usually contain personal contact information, such as your phone numbers, business address, and email and website addresses. Mail supports multiple signatures, which is useful if you use Mail with multiple accounts or for different purposes such as business and personal.

Add a Signature

Create a Signature

1 Click **Mail**.

2 Click **Preferences**.

The Mail preferences appear.

3 Click **Signatures**.

4 Click the account for which you want to use the signature.

5 Click **Create a signature** (⊞).

Mail adds a new signature.

6 Type a name for the signature.

7 Type the signature text.

8 Repeat steps **4** to **7** to add other signatures, if required.

Note: You can add as many signatures as you want. For example, you may want to have one signature for business use and another for personal use.

9 Click 🔘.

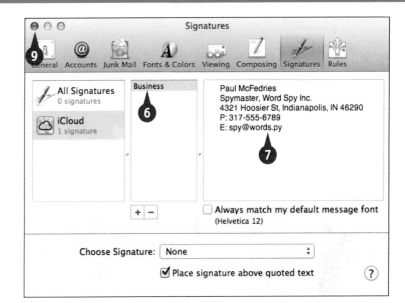

Insert the Signature

1 Click **New Message** (📝) to start a new message.

Note: To start a new message, see the section "Send an Email Message."

2 In the message text area, move the insertion point to the location where you want the signature to appear.

3 Click the **Signature** 🔾 and then click the signature you want to insert.

Ⓐ The signature appears in the message.

TIP

When I have multiple signatures, how can I choose which of them Mail adds automatically?

1 Follow steps **1** to **4** to display the signature preferences and choose an account.

2 Click 🔾 and then click the signature you want to insert automatically into each message.

Ⓐ If you prefer to add a signature manually, click **None** instead of a signature.

3 Click 🔘.

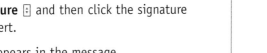
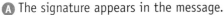
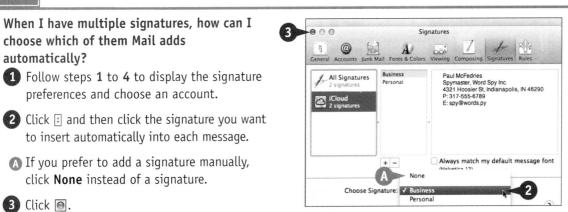

Receive and Read Email Messages

You must connect to your mail provider's incoming mail server to retrieve and read messages sent to you. When another person sends you an email message, that message ends up in your email account's mailbox on the incoming mail server maintained by your ISP or email provider. However, that company does not automatically pass along that message to you. Instead, you must use Mail to connect to your mailbox on the incoming mail server and then retrieve any messages waiting for you.

By default, Mail automatically checks for new messages every 5 minutes while you are online, but you can also check for new messages at any time.

Receive and Read Email Messages

Receive Email Messages

1 Click **Get Mail** (✉).

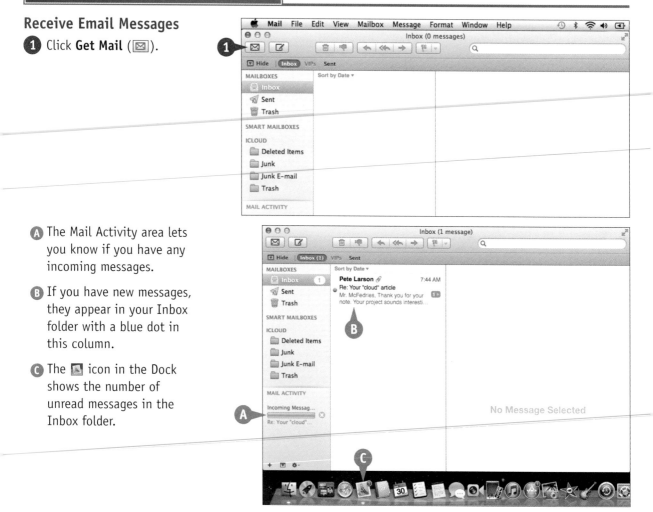

Ⓐ The Mail Activity area lets you know if you have any incoming messages.

Ⓑ If you have new messages, they appear in your Inbox folder with a blue dot in this column.

Ⓒ The 🖼 icon in the Dock shows the number of unread messages in the Inbox folder.

Read a Message

1 Click the message.

2 If you do not see the full message, click **See More**.

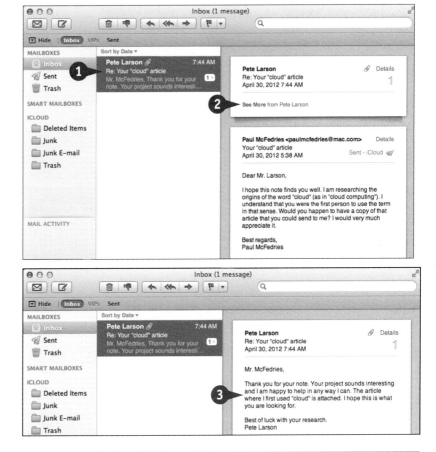

3 Read the message text in the preview pane.

Note: If you want to open the message in its own window, double-click the message.

Can I change how often Mail automatically checks for messages?

Yes, by following these steps:

1 Click **Mail**.

2 Click **Preferences**.

The Mail preferences appear.

3 Click the **General** tab.

4 In the Check for new messages pop-up menu, click 🔽 and then click the time interval that you want Mail to use when checking for new messages automatically.

A If you do not want Mail to check for messages automatically, click **Manually** instead.

5 Click 🔘.

Reply to a Message

When a message you receive requires some kind of response — whether it is answering a question, supplying information, or providing comments — you can reply to that message. Most replies go only to the person who sent the original message. However, it is also possible to send the reply to all the people who were included in the original message's To and Cc lines.

Mail includes the text of the original message in the reply, but you should edit the original message text to include only enough of the original message to put your reply into context.

Reply to a Message

1 Click the message to which you want to reply.

2 Click the reply type you want to use.

Click **Reply** (⬑) to respond only to the person who sent the message.

Click **Reply All** (⬑) to respond to all the addresses in the message's From, To, and Cc lines.

A message window appears.

Ⓐ Mail automatically inserts the recipient addresses.

Ⓑ Mail also inserts the subject line, preceded by Re:.

Ⓒ Mail includes the original message text at the bottom of the reply.

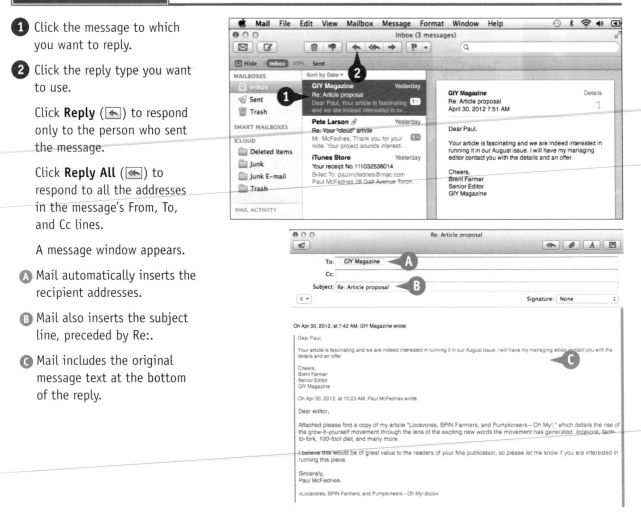

③ Edit the original message to include only the text that is relevant to your reply.

④ Click the area above the original message text and type your reply.

⑤ Click **Send** (✈).

Mail sends your reply.

Note: Mail stores a copy of your reply in the Sent folder.

TIPS

I received a message inadvertently. Is there a way that I can pass it along to the correct recipient?

Yes. Mail comes with a feature that enables you to pass along inadvertent messages to the correct recipient. Click the message that you received inadvertently, click **Message**, and then click **Redirect** (or press Shift+⌘+E). Type the recipient's address and then click **Send**. Replies to this message will be sent to the original sender, not to you.

How much of the original message should I include in my reply?

If the original message is fairly short, you usually do not need to edit the text. However, if the original message is long, and your response deals only with part of that message, you will save the recipient time and confusion by deleting everything except the relevant portion of the text. Also, instead of editing the original text within the reply, first select the text you want to keep and then click **Reply** (or **Reply All**), which tells Mail to include only the selected text in the reply.

Forward a Message

If a message has information relevant to or that concerns another person, you can forward a copy of the message to that person. You can also include your own comments in the forward.

In the body of the forward, Mail includes the original message's addresses, date, and subject line. Below this information Mail also includes the text of the original message. In most cases you will leave the entire message intact so your recipient can see it. However, if only part of the message is relevant to the recipient, you should edit the original message accordingly.

Forward a Message

1 Click the message that you want to forward.

2 Click **Forward** (➡).

Note: You can also press [Shift] + ⌘ + [F].

A message window appears.

A Mail inserts the subject line, preceded by Fwd:.

B The original message's addressees (To and From), date, subject, and text are included at the top of the forward.

3 Type the email address of the person to whom you are forwarding the message.

4 To send a copy of the forward to another person, type that person's email address in the Cc line.

5 Edit the original message to include only the text relevant to your forward.

6 Click the area above the original message text and type your comments.

7 Click **Send** ().

Mail sends your forward.

Note: Mail stores a copy of your forward in the Sent folder.

Note: You can forward someone a copy of the actual message instead of just a copy of the message text. Click the message, click **Message**, and then click **Forward As Attachment**. Mail creates a new message and includes the original message as an attachment.

TIP

Mail always formats my replies as rich text, even when the original message is plain text. How can I fix this problem?
You can configure Mail to always reply using the same format as the original message. Follow these steps:

1 Click **Mail**.

2 Click **Preferences**.

The Mail preferences appear.

3 Click the **Composing** tab.

4 Click the **Use the same message format as the original message** check box (☐ changes to ☑).

5 Click .

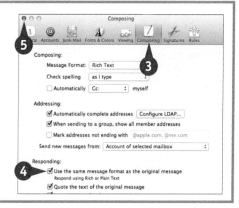

Open and Save an Attachment

If you receive a message that has a file attached, you can open the attachment to view the contents of the file. You can also save the attachment as a file on your Mac. Some files that you receive as email attachments require only a quick viewing, so you can open these files and then close them when you are done. Other attachments may contain information that you want to keep, so you should save these files to your Mac's hard drive so that you can open them later without having to launch Mail.

Be careful when dealing with attached files. Computer viruses and other malicious files are often transmitted by email attachments.

Open and Save an Attachment

Open an Attachment

1 Click the message that has the attachment, as indicated by the Attachment symbol (📎).

A An icon appears for each message attachment.

2 Double-click the attachment you want to open.

The file opens in the associated application.

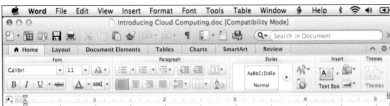

Save an Attachment

1 Click the message that has the attachment, as indicated by the Attachment symbol (⬚).

2 Right-click the attachment you want to save.

3 Click **Save Attachment**.

Mail prompts you to save the file.

4 Use the Save As text box to edit the filename, if desired.

5 Select the folder into which you want the file saved.

6 Click **Save**.

Mail saves the attachment.

TIP

Can I open an attachment using a different application?

In most cases, yes. Your Mac usually has a default application that it uses when you double-click a file attachment. However, it also usually defines one or more other applications capable of opening the file. To check this out, right-click the icon of the attachment you want to open and then click **Open With**. In the menu that appears, click the application that you prefer to use to open the file.

Configure Messages

OS X Mountain Lion includes the Messages application to enable you to exchange instant messages with other people who are online. The first time you open Messages, you must run through a short configuration process to set up your account. This process involves signing in with your Apple ID and deciding whether you want Messages to send out notifications that tell people when you have read the messages they send to you.

Configure Messages

1 Click **Messages** (◻).

The Welcome to Messages dialog appears.

2 Click **Continue**.

Messages

Welcome to Messages

Messages brings iMessage to Mac and lets you send unlimited messages to iPhone, iPad, iPod touch, or Mac right from your Mac.

Send unlimited messages, photos, videos, documents, and contacts – even send messages to a group of people. If you have more than one Mac or iOS device, iMessage keeps the conversation going across all of them. iMessages are securely encrypted so your messages stay safe and private.

To get started, click Continue.

Go Back   **2** ▶ Continue

The iMessage Setup dialog appears.

3 Type your Apple ID.

4 Type your Apple ID password.

5 Click **Sign In**.

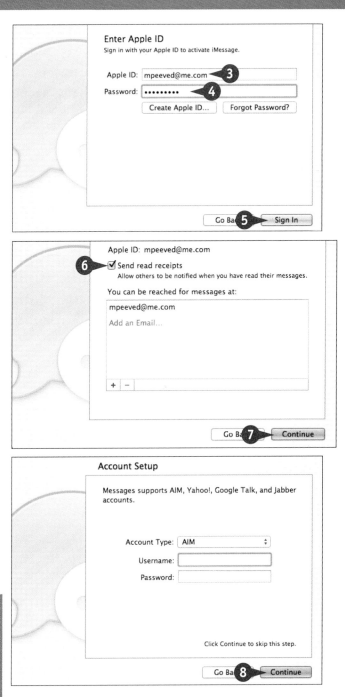

6 If you want other people to know when you have read their messages, click **Send read receipts** (○ changes to ⊙).

7 Click **Continue**.

The Account Setup dialog appears.

8 Click **Continue**.

9 Click **Done** (not shown).

Messages is now ready to use.

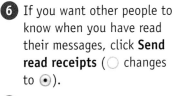

What if I do not have an Apple ID?
You can create a new Apple ID during the configuration process. Follow steps **1** and **2** to open the iMessage Setup dialog, and then click **Create Apple ID**. In the dialog that appears, type your name, the email address you want to use as your Apple ID, and the password you want to use. You must also choose a secret question and specify your birthday. Click **Create Apple ID** to complete the operation.

201

Send a Message

In the Messages application, an instant-messaging conversation is most often the exchange of text messages between two or more people who are online and available to chat. An instant-messaging conversation begins by one person inviting another person to exchange messages. In Messages, this means sending an initial instant message, and the recipient either accepts or rejects the invitation.

Send a Message

1 Click **Compose new message** (☑).

Note: You can also click **File** and then click **New Message**, or press ⌘+N.

Messages begins a new conversation.

2 Use the To field to specify the message recipient using one of the following:

The person's email address.

The person's mobile phone number.

The person's name, if that person is in your Contacts list.

A You can also click **Add Contact** (◎) to select a name from your Contacts list.

③ Type your message.

ⓑ You can also click here if you want to insert a smiley symbol into your message.

④ Press **Return**.

Messages sends the text to the recipient.

ⓒ The recipient's response appears in the transcript window.

ⓓ You see the ellipsis symbol () when the other person is typing.

⑤ Repeat steps **3** and **4** to continue the conversation.

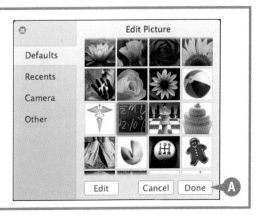

Sign In to FaceTime

To use FaceTime to conduct video chats, you must each first sign in using your Apple ID. This could be an iCloud account that uses the Apple me.com address, or it could be your existing email address. Once you have created your Apple ID, you can use it to sign in to FaceTime. Note that you have to do this only once. In subsequent sessions, FaceTime automatically signs you in.

Sign In to FaceTime

1 In the Dock, click **FaceTime** (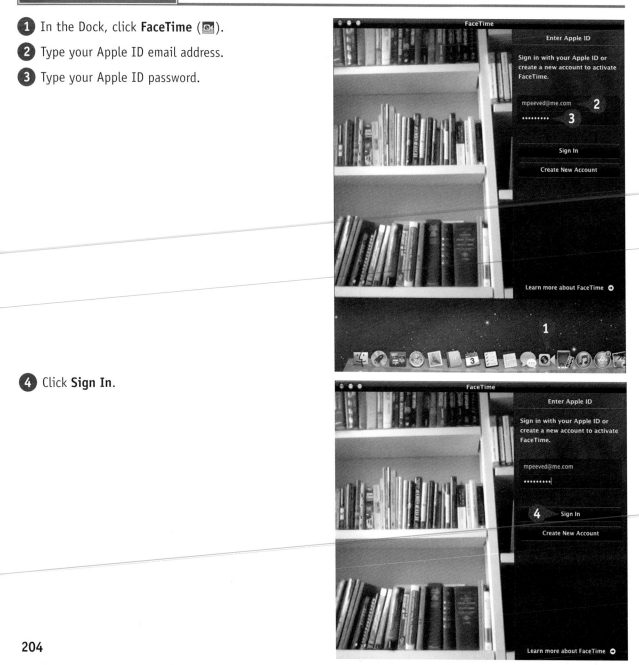).

2 Type your Apple ID email address.

3 Type your Apple ID password.

4 Click **Sign In**.

FaceTime prompts you to specify an email address that people can use to contact you via FaceTime.

5 If the address you prefer to use is different than your Apple ID, type the address you want to use.

6 Click **Next**.

FaceTime verifies your Apple ID and then displays a list of contacts.

TIP

Which devices support FaceTime?

You can use the FaceTime application on any Mac running OS X 10.6.6 or later. For OS X Snow Leopard (10.6.6), FaceTime is available through the App Store for 99 cents. For OS X Mountain Lion (10.8) and OS X Lion (10.7), FaceTime is installed by default. The FaceTime software is also available as an app that runs on the iPhone 4 and later, the iPad 2 and later, and the iPod touch fourth generation and later.

Connect Through FaceTime

Once you have signed in with your Apple ID, you can use the FaceTime application to connect with another person and conduct a video chat. How you connect with the other person depends on what device he or she is using for FaceTime. If the person is using a Mac, an iPad, or an iPod touch, you can use whatever email address the person has designated as his or her FaceTime contact address, as described in the previous section, "Sign In to FaceTime." If the person is using an iPhone 4 or later, you can use that person's mobile number to make the connection.

Connect Through FaceTime

1 Click **Contacts**.

2 Click the contact you want to call.

FaceTime displays the contact's data.

3 Click the phone number (for an iPhone) or email address (for a Mac, iPad, or iPod touch) that you want to use to connect to the contact.

FaceTime sends a message to the contact asking if he or she would like a FaceTime connection.

④ The other person must click or tap **Accept** to complete the connection.

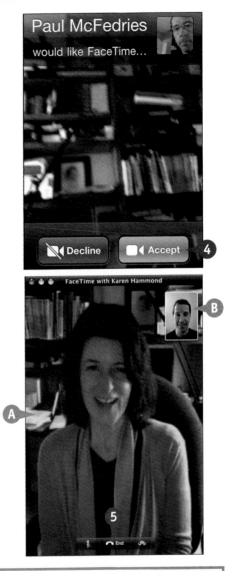

FaceTime connects with the other person.

Ⓐ The other person's video takes up the bulk of the FaceTime screen.

Ⓑ Your video appears in the picture-in-picture (PiP) window.

Note: You can click and drag the PiP to a different location within the FaceTime window.

⑤ When you have finished your FaceTime call, click **End**.

TIP

Are there easier ways to connect to someone through FaceTime?
Yes, FaceTime offers a couple of methods that you might find faster. If you have connected with a person through FaceTime recently, that person may appear in the FaceTime Recents list. In the FaceTime window, click **Recents** and then click the person you want to contact.

Alternatively, if you connect with someone frequently, you can add that person to the FaceTime Favorites list. Use the Contacts list to click the person, and then click **Add to Favorites**. To connect with a favorite, click **Favorites** and then click the person.

CHAPTER 10

Working with Contacts and Events

To help you manage your busy life, you can use the Contacts application to maintain your address book, and you can use the Calendar application to enter and track events.

Open and Close Contacts

OS X includes the Contacts application to help you manage information about the people you know, whether they are colleagues, friends, or family members. The Contacts app refers to these people as *contacts*, and you store each person's data in an object called a *card*.

Before you can add or work with your contacts, you must know how to start the Contacts application. When you are finished with Contacts, you should close it to reduce desktop clutter and save system resources.

Open and Close Contacts

Open Contacts

1 In the Dock, click **Contacts** (🗐).

The Contacts window appears.

Close Contacts

1 Click **Contacts**.

2 Click **Quit Contacts**.

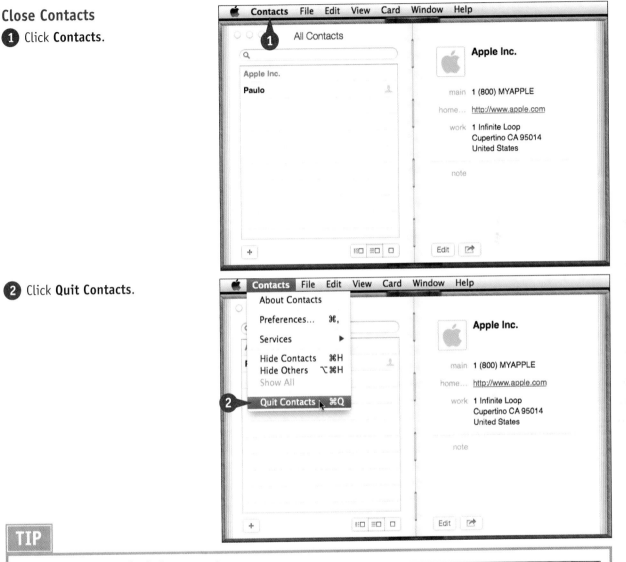

TIP

Are there other methods I can use to open Contacts?

Yes. If you have removed the 🔲 icon from the Dock, you can use a couple of other quick methods to start Contacts. If you have used Contacts recently, a reasonably fast method is to click 🍎, click **Recent Items**, and then click **Contacts**. You can also click **Spotlight** (🔍), type **contacts**, and then click **Contacts** in the search results.

Add a New Contact

To store contact information for a particular person, you first need to create a new contact within Contacts. You do that by creating a new card, which is a Contacts item that stores data about a person or company. Each card can store a wide variety of information. For example, you can store a person's name, company name, phone numbers, email address, instant messaging data, street address, notes, and much more.

Although you will mostly use Contacts cards to store data about people, you can also use a card to keep information about companies.

Add a New Contact

1 Click **File**.

2 Click **New Card**.

A You can also begin a new contact by clicking ⊞.

Note: You can also invoke the New Card command by pressing ⌘+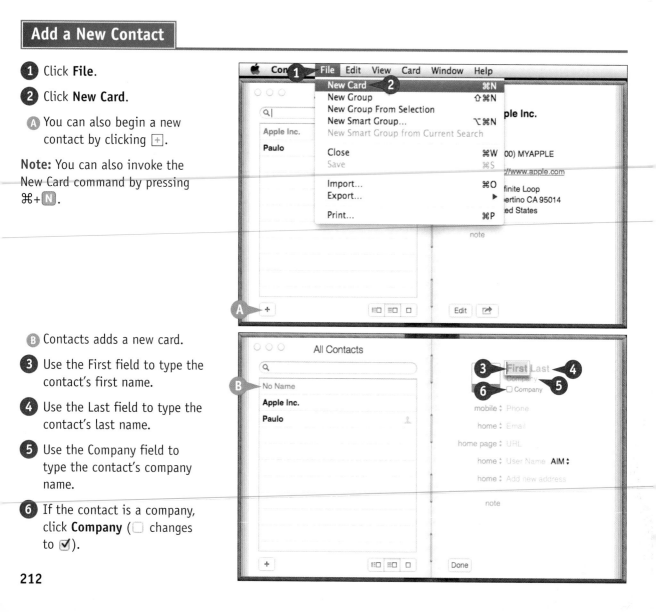N.

B Contacts adds a new card.

3 Use the First field to type the contact's first name.

4 Use the Last field to type the contact's last name.

5 Use the Company field to type the contact's company name.

6 If the contact is a company, click **Company** (☐ changes to ☑).

7 In the first Phone field, click ⚏ and then click the category you want to use.

8 Type the phone number.

9 Repeat steps **7** and **8** to enter data in some or all of the other fields.

Note: See the next section, "Edit a Contact," to learn how to add more fields to the card.

10 Click **Done**.

Contacts saves the new card.

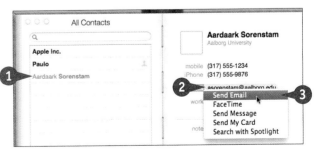

If I include a contact's email address, is there a way to send that person a message without having to type the address?

1 Click the contact's card.

2 Click the email address category.

3 Click **Send Email**.

Apple Mail displays a new email message with the contact already added in the To line.

4 Fill in the rest of the message as required.

5 Click **Send**.

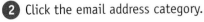
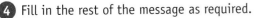

Edit a Contact

If you need to make changes to the information already in a contact's card, or if you need to add new information to a card, you can edit the card from within Contacts.

The default fields you see in a card are not the only types of data you can store for a contact. Contacts offers a large number of extra fields. These include useful fields such as Middle Name, Nickname, Job Title, Department, URL (web address), and Birthday. You can also add extra fields for common data items such as phone numbers, email addresses, and dates.

Edit a Contact

1 Click the card you want to edit.

2 Click **Edit**.

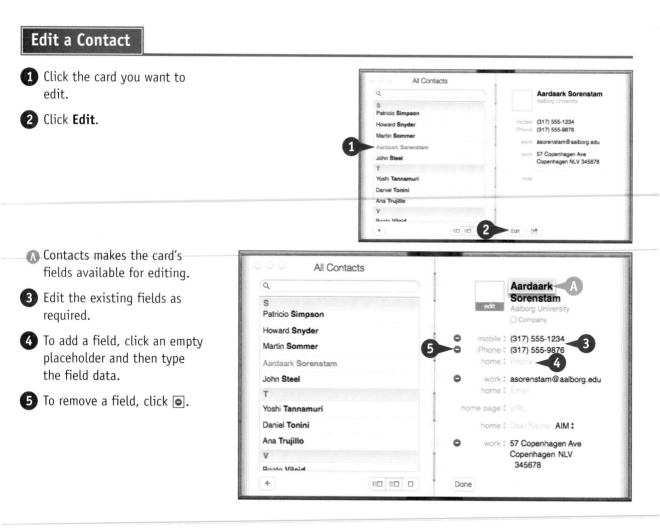

A Contacts makes the card's fields available for editing.

3 Edit the existing fields as required.

4 To add a field, click an empty placeholder and then type the field data.

5 To remove a field, click [○].

6 To add a new field type, click **Card**.

7 Click **Add Field**.

8 Click the type of field you want.

B Contacts adds the field to the card.

9 When you have completed your edits, click **Done**.

Contacts saves the edited card.

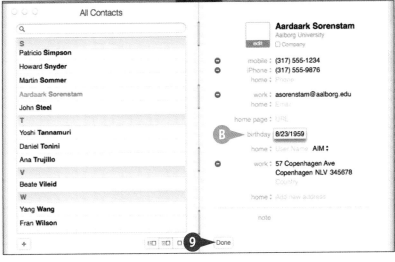

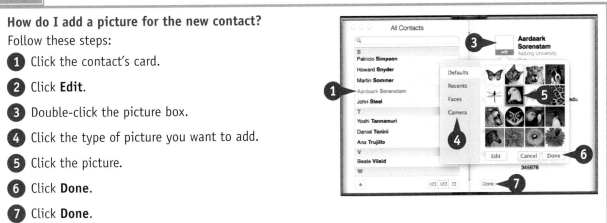

TIP

How do I add a picture for the new contact?
Follow these steps:

1 Click the contact's card.

2 Click **Edit**.

3 Double-click the picture box.

4 Click the type of picture you want to add.

5 Click the picture.

6 Click **Done**.

7 Click **Done**.

Create a Contact Group

You can organize your contacts into one or more groups, which is useful if you want to view just a subset of your contacts. For example, you could create separate groups for friends, family members, work colleagues, or business clients.

Groups are particularly handy if you have a large number of contacts in your address book. By creating and maintaining groups, you can navigate your contacts more easily. You can also perform groupwide tasks, such as sending a single email message to everyone in the group. You can create a group first and then add members, or you can select members in advance and then create the group.

Create a Contact Group

Create a Contact Group

1 Click **File**.

2 Click **New Group**.

Note: You can also run the New Group command by pressing Shift+⌘+N.

A Contacts adds a new group.

3 Type a name for the group.

4 Press Return.

5 Click and drag a contact to the group.

Contacts adds the contact to the group.

6 Repeat step **5** for the other contacts you want to add to the group.

Create a Group of Selected Contacts

1. Select the contacts you want to include in the new group.

Note: To select multiple contacts, press and hold ⌘ and click each card.

2. Click **File**.

3. Click **New Group From Selection**.

B. Contacts adds a new group.

C. Contacts adds the selected contacts as group members.

4. Type a name for the group.

5. Press Return.

TIPS

Can I send an email message to the group?

Yes, this is one of the best reasons to create a group. Normally, sending an email message to multiple contacts involves typing or selecting multiple addresses. With a group, however, you send a single message to the group, and Mail automatically sends a copy to each member. Right-click the group and then click **Send Email to "Group"**, where *Group* is the name of the group.

What is a Smart Group?

A *Smart Group* is a special group where each member has one or more fields in common, such as the company name, department name, city, or state. When you create the smart group, you specify one or more criteria, and then Contacts automatically adds members to the group if they meet those criteria. To create a Smart Group, click **File**, click **New Smart Group**, and then enter your group criteria.

Open and Close Calendar

Your Mac comes with the Calendar application to enable you to manage your schedule. Calendar enables you to create and work with events, which are either scheduled appointments such as meetings, lunches, and visits to the dentist, or all-day activities, such as birthdays, anniversaries, or vacations. You can also use Calendar to send event invitations and to accept or decline any event invitations that you receive.

Before you can add or work with events (appointments, meetings, all-day activities, and so on), and before you can send or accept event invitations, you must know how to start the Calendar application.

Open and Close Calendar

Open Calendar

1 In the Dock, click **Calendar** (📅).

The Calendar window appears.

Close Calendar

1 Click **Calendar**.

2 Click **Quit Calendar**.

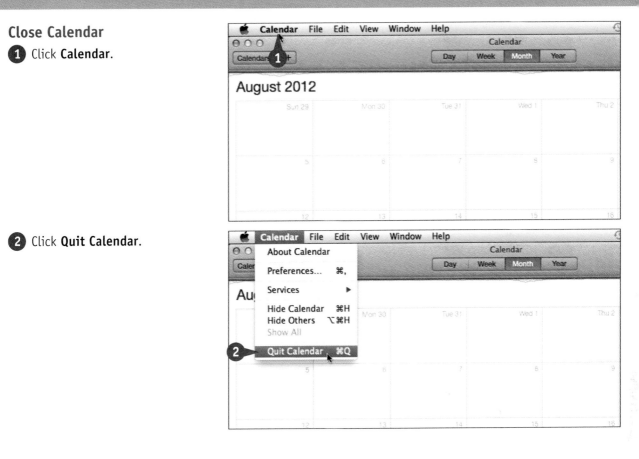

Are there other methods I can use to open Calendar?

Yes. If you have removed the ▣ icon from the Dock, you can use a couple of other quick methods to start Calendar. If you have used Calendar recently, a reasonably fast method is to click ▣, click **Recent Items**, and then click **Calendar**. You can also click **Spotlight** (ℚ), type **cal**, and then click **Calendar** in the search results.

Navigate the Calendar

Before you create an event such as an appointment or meeting, or an all-day event such as a conference or trip, you must first select the date on which the event occurs. You do that in Calendar by navigating the built-in calendar or by specifying the date you want.

Calendar also lets you change the calendar view to suit your needs. For example, you can show just a single day's worth of events if you want to concentrate on that day's activities. Similarly, you can view a week's worth of events if you want to get a larger sense of what your overall schedule looks like.

Navigate the Calendar

Use the Calendar

1 Click **Month**.

2 Click the **Next Month** button (▶) until the month of your event appears.

Ⓐ If you go too far, click the **Previous Month** button (◀) to move back to the month you want.

Ⓑ To see a specific date, click the day and then click **Day** (or press ⌘+1).

Ⓒ To see a specific week, click any day within the week and then click **Week** (or press ⌘+2).

Ⓓ To return to viewing the entire month, click **Month** (or press ⌘+3).

Ⓔ If you want to return to today's date, click **Today** (or press ⌘+T).

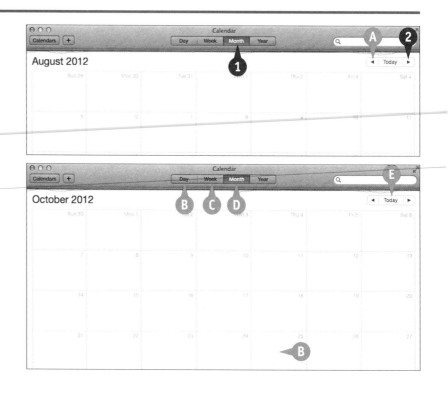

Go to a Specific Date

1 Click **View**.

2 Click **Go to Date**.

Note: You can also select the Go to Date command by pressing `Shift`+`⌘`+`T`.

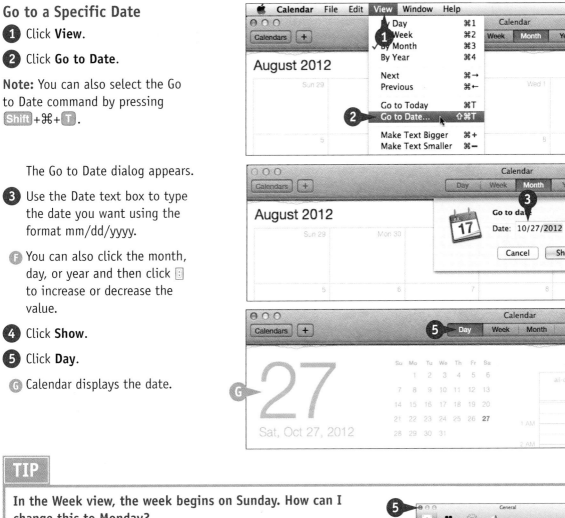

The Go to Date dialog appears.

3 Use the Date text box to type the date you want using the format mm/dd/yyyy.

F You can also click the month, day, or year and then click to increase or decrease the value.

4 Click **Show**.

5 Click **Day**.

G Calendar displays the date.

TIP

In the Week view, the week begins on Sunday. How can I change this to Monday?

Calendar's default Week view has Sunday on the left and Saturday on the right. Many people prefer to display the weekend days together, with Monday on the left signaling the start of the week. To set this up, follow these steps:

1 Click **Calendar** in the menu bar.

2 Click **Preferences**.

3 Click the **General** tab.

4 In the Start week on pop-up menu, click and then click **Monday**.

5 Click .

Create an Event

You can help organize your life by using Calendar to record your events — such as appointments, meetings, phone calls, and dates — on the date and time they occur.

If the event has a set time and duration — for example, a meeting or a lunch date — you add the event directly to the calendar as a regular appointment. If the event has no set time — for example, a birthday, anniversary, or multiple-day event such as a convention or vacation — you can create an all-day event.

Create an Event

Create a Regular Event

1 Navigate to the date when the event occurs.

2 Click **Calendars**.

3 Click the calendar you want to use.

4 Double-click the time when the event starts.

Ⓐ Calendar adds a one-hour event.

Note: If the event is less than or more than an hour, you can also click and drag the mouse (➤) over the full event period.

5 Type the name of the event.

6 Press Return.

Create an All-Day Event

1 Click **Week**.

2 Navigate to the week that includes the date when the event occurs.

3 Click **Calendars**.

4 Click the calendar you want to use.

5 Double-click anywhere inside the event date's all-day section.

B Calendar adds a new all-day event.

6 Type the name of the event.

7 Press **Return**.

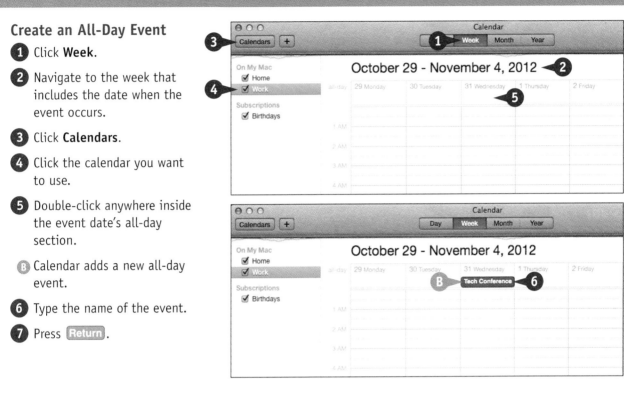

How can I specify event details such as the location and a reminder message?

1 Follow the steps in this section to create an event.

2 Double-click the event.

3 Click **Edit**.

4 Use the location text box to type the location of the event.

5 Use the alert pop-up menu to choose **Message**.

6 Choose the amount of time before the event that you want to receive the reminder.

7 Click **Done**.

Calendar saves the new event configuration.

Karen's Birthday Lunch

location	McGugan's Fine Scottish Fare
all-day	☐
from	10/27/2012 12:00 PM
to	10/27/2012 01:00 PM
repeat	None
show as	Busy
calendar	■ Home
alert	Message
	15 minutes before
alert	None
invitees	Add Invitees...
attachments	Add File...
url	None
note	None

Done

Create a Repeating Event

If you have an activity or event that recurs at a regular interval, you can create an event and configure it to automatically repeat in Calendar. This saves you from having to repeatedly add the future events yourself because Calendar adds them for you automatically.

You can repeat an event daily, weekly, monthly, or yearly. For even greater flexibility, you can set up a custom interval. For example, you could have an event repeat every five days, every second Friday, on the first Monday of every month, and so on.

Create a Repeating Event

1 Follow the steps in the previous section, "Create an Event," to create an event.

2 Double-click the event.

Calendar displays information for the event.

3 Click **Edit**.

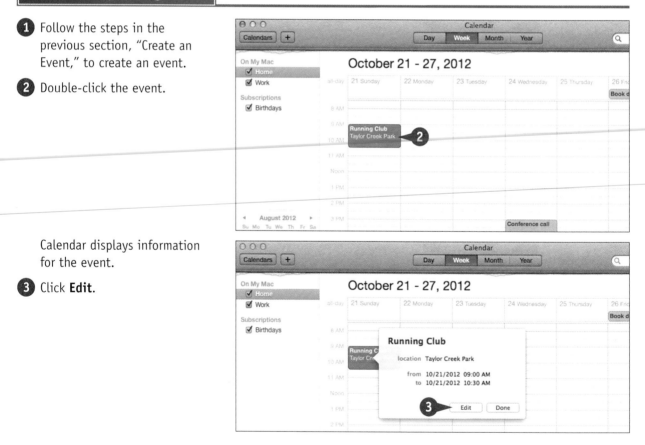

Calendar opens the event for editing.

4 Beside the repeat label, click **None**.

5 Click the interval you want to use.

A If you want to specify a custom interval such as every two weeks or the first Monday of every month, click **Custom** and configure your interval in the dialog that appears.

6 Click **Done**.

Calendar adds the repeating events to the calendar.

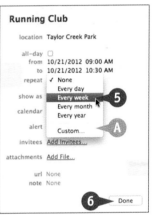

TIPS

How do I configure an event to stop after a certain number of occurrences?

Follow these steps:

1 Follow steps **1** to **5** to select a recurrence interval.

2 Beside the end label, click **None** and then click **After**.

3 Type the number of occurrences you want.

4 Click **Done**.

Is it possible to delete just a single occurrence out of a recurring series of events?

Yes, you can delete one occurrence from the calendar without affecting the rest of the series. Click the occurrence you want to delete, and then press Del. Calendar asks whether you want to delete all the occurrences or just the selected occurrence. Click **Delete Only This Event**.

CHAPTER 11

Learning Useful Mac Tasks

Your Mac comes with many tools that help you accomplish everyday tasks. In this chapter you learn how to work with notes and reminders, post to Twitter, share data, work with notifications, and view the Mac screen on a TV.

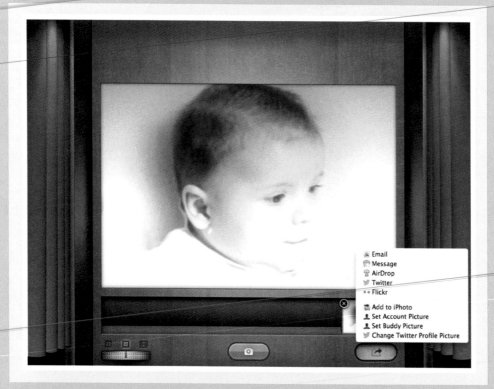

Install a Program Using the App Store

You can enhance and extend your Mac by installing new programs from the App Store. Your Mac comes with an impressive collection of applications — or *apps* — particularly because your Mac comes with the iLife suite preinstalled.

However, your Mac does not offer a complete collection of apps. For example, your Mac lacks apps in categories such as productivity, personal finance, and business tools. To fill in these gaps, you can use the App Store to locate, purchase, and install new programs, or look for apps that go beyond what the default Mac programs can do.

Install a Program Using the App Store

1 In the Dock, click **App Store** (🔵).

The App Store window appears.

2 Locate the app you want to install.

3 Click the price button.

Note: If the app is free, click the Free button instead.

The price button changes to a Buy App button, or the Free button changes to an Install button.

④ Click **Buy App** (or **Install**).

AirAttack

AirAttack - is Award Winning next-generation top do
3D graphics alongside great audio, effects and awes○

Unity Awards 2010 - Grand Prix

*** AirAttack is also available for iPad and iPhone. **
AirAttack HD was #1 paid game on iPad in more than

Features:...

The App Store prompts you to log in with your Apple ID.

⑤ Type your Apple ID.

⑥ Type your password.

⑦ Click **Sign In**.

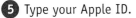

Sign in to download from the App Store.

If you have an Apple ID, sign in with it here. If you have used the iTunes Store or iCloud, for example, you have an Apple ID. If you don't have an Apple ID, click Create Apple ID.

Apple ID

myaccount@me.com ◄⑤

Password   Forgot?

•••••••••| ◄⑥

(?)   Create Apple ID

Cancel   Sign In ◄⑦

Ⓐ The App Store opens Launchpad and begins downloading the app.

When the progress meter disappears, your app is installed. Click the app to run it.

TextWrangler   Web Fo...er Lite   Downloading

TIP

How do I use an App Store gift card to purchase apps?

If you have an App Store or iTunes gift card, you can redeem the card to give yourself store credit in the amount shown on the card. Scratch off the sticker on the back to reveal the code. Click 🅐 to open the App Store, click **Redeem** (Ⓐ), type the code, and then click **Redeem**.

In the App Store window, the Account item (Ⓑ) shows your current store credit balance.

Quick Links

Welcome Paul
Account $48.88 ◄Ⓑ
Redeem
Support

Write a Note

You can use the Notes app to create simple text documents for things such as to-do lists and meeting notes. Word processing programs such as Word and Pages are useful for creating complex and lengthy documents. However, these powerful tools feel like overkill when all you want to do is jot down a few notes. For these simpler text tasks, the Notes app that comes with OS X Mountain Lion is perfect because it offers a simple interface that keeps all your notes together.

As you see in the next section, you can also pin a note to the Mac desktop for easy access.

Write a Note

Create a New Note

1 In the Dock, click **Notes** (▢).

The Notes window appears.

2 Click **New Note** (⊞).

Note: You can also click **File** and then click **New Note**, or press ⌘+N.

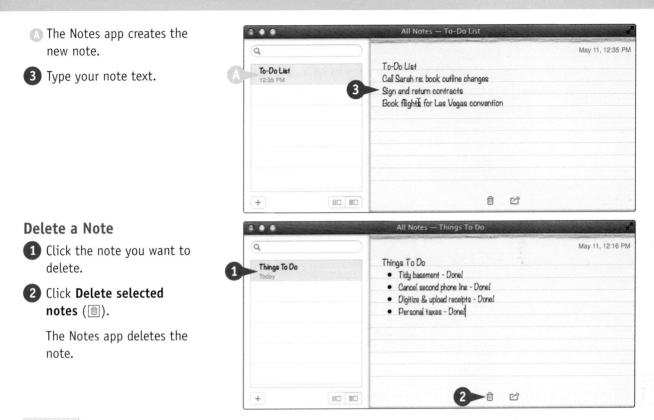

Ⓐ The Notes app creates the new note.

③ Type your note text.

Delete a Note

① Click the note you want to delete.

② Click **Delete selected notes** (🗑).

The Notes app deletes the note.

Can I synchronize my notes with my iPod touch, iPhone, or iPad?

Yes, as long as you have an iCloud account and you have set up that account in your Mac, as described in Chapter 14, "Networking with Your Mac." To create a new note using iCloud, click **View**, click **View Folders List**, and then click **Notes** under the iCloud folder.

How do I create a bulleted or numbered list?

Position the cursor where you want the list to begin, click **Format**, and then click **Lists**. In the menu that appears, click **Insert Bulleted List**, **Insert Dashed List**, or **Insert Numbered List**.

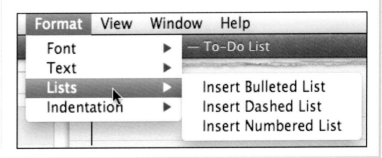

Pin a Note to the Desktop

Y ou can ensure that you always see the content of a note by pinning that note to the Mac desktop. The Notes app is useful for setting up to-do lists, jotting down things to remember, and creating similar documents that contain text that you need to refer to while you work. Instead of constantly switching back and forth between Notes and your working application, you can pin a note to the desktop, which forces the note to stay visible, even when you switch to another application.

Pin a Note to the Desktop

1 Double-click the note you want to pin.

The Notes app opens the note in its own window.

2 Click and drag the note title to the position you want.

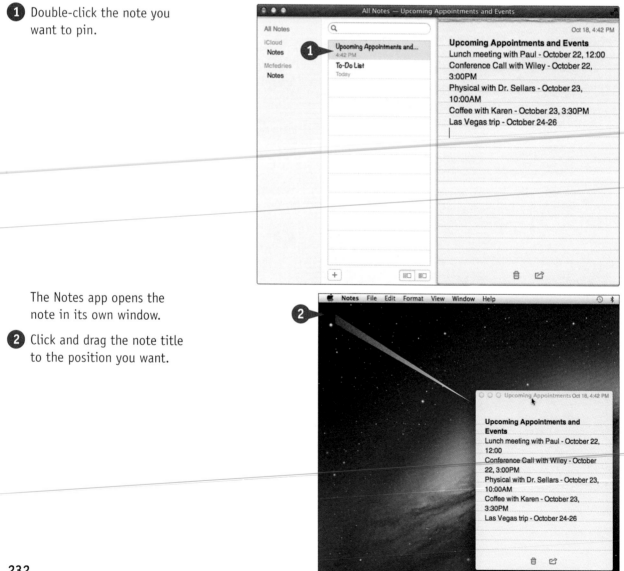

3 Click **Window**.

4 Click **Float on Top**.

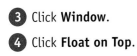

A The Notes app keeps each opened note on top of any other window you open.

Is it possible to pin the Notes app window to the desktop so that it always remains in view?

No, your Mac does not allow you to keep the Notes window on top of other windows on your desktop. The pinning technique described in this section applies only to open note windows.

Am I only able to pin one note at a time to the desktop?

No, the Notes app enables you to pin multiple notes to the Mac desktop. This is useful if you have different notes that apply to the same task that you are working on in another application. However, you need to exercise some caution because the pinned notes take up space on the desktop, so you need to leave enough room to work in your other applications.

Create a Reminder

You can use the Reminders app to have your Mac display a notification when you need to perform a task. You can use the Calendar app to schedule important events, but you likely have many tasks during the day that cannot be considered full-fledged events: returning a call, taking clothes out of the dryer, turning off the sprinkler. If you need to be reminded to perform such tasks, the Calendar app is overkill, but your Mac offers a better solution: the Reminders app. You use this app to create reminders, which are notifications that tell you to do something or to be somewhere.

Create a Reminder

1 In the Dock, click **Reminders** ().

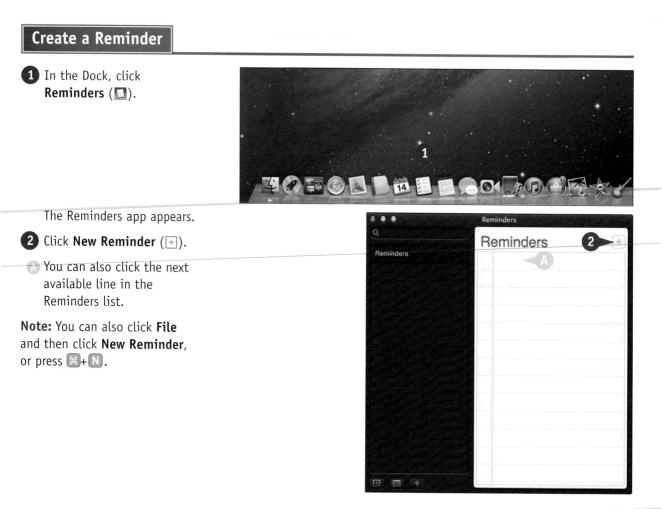

The Reminders app appears.

2 Click **New Reminder** ().

Ⓐ You can also click the next available line in the Reminders list.

Note: You can also click **File** and then click **New Reminder**, or press ⌘+N.

3 Type the reminder title.

4 Click the **Show Info** icon ().

The Reminders app displays the reminder details.

5 Click **On a Day** (changes to).

6 Specify the date and time you want to be reminded.

7 Click **Done**.

The Reminders app adds the reminder to the list.

Ⓑ When you have completed the reminder, click its check box (changes to).

What does the At a Location option do?

The At a Location option allows the Reminders app to display a notification for a task when you arrive at or leave a location and you have your Mac notebook with you. To set this up, follow steps **1** to **4**, click **At a Location** (changes to), and then type the address or choose a contact that has a defined address. Click either **Leaving** or **Arriving** (changes to), and then click **Done**.

Create a New Reminder List

You can organize your reminders and make them easier to locate by creating new reminder lists. By default, the Reminders app comes with a single list called Reminders. However, if you use reminders frequently, the Reminders list can become cluttered, making it difficult to locate reminders. To solve this problem, you can organize your reminders by creating new lists. For example, you could have one list for personal tasks and another for business tasks. After you have created one or more new lists, you can move some or all of your existing reminders to the appropriate lists.

Create a New Reminder List

Create a Reminder List

1. Click **New List** (➕).

Note: You can also click **File** and then click **New List**, or press ⌘+L.

A. The Reminders app adds the new list to the sidebar.

2. Type the list name.

3. Press Return.

Move a Reminder to a Different List

1 Click the list that contains the reminder you want to move.

2 Click and drag the reminder and drop it on the destination list.

3 Click the destination list.

B The reminder now appears in the destination list.

Note: You can also right-click the reminder, click **Move to List**, and then click the destination list.

Why does my Reminders app not have a Completed list?
The Reminders app does not show the Completed list when you first start using the program. When you mark a reminder as complete by clicking its check box (☐ changes to ☑), Reminders creates the Completed list and moves the task to that list.

Can I change the order of the lists in the sidebar?
Yes. By default, the Reminders app displays the new lists in the order you create them. However, if you have several lists, you might find them easier to use if you place them in, say, alphabetical order. To move a list to a new position, click and drag the list up or down in the sidebar. When the horizontal blue bar shows the list to be in the position you want, release the mouse button.

I f you have a Twitter account, you can use it to share information with your followers directly from OS X Mountain Lion. OS X Mountain Lion comes with built-in support for Twitter. This enables you to send tweets directly from many Mac apps. For example, you can send a link to a web page from Safari or tweet a photo from Photo Booth. OS X also displays notifications if you are mentioned on Twitter or if a Twitter user sends you a direct message. Before you can tweet or see Twitter notifications, you must sign in to your Twitter account.

Sign In to Your Twitter Account

1 Click **System Preferences** (⬚).

Note: You can also click ⬚ and then click **System Preferences**.

The System Preferences window appears.

2 Click **Mail, Contacts & Calendars**.

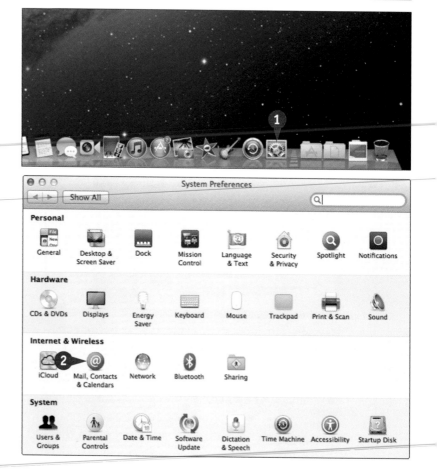

The Mail, Contacts & Calendars window appears.

3 Click the Twitter logo.

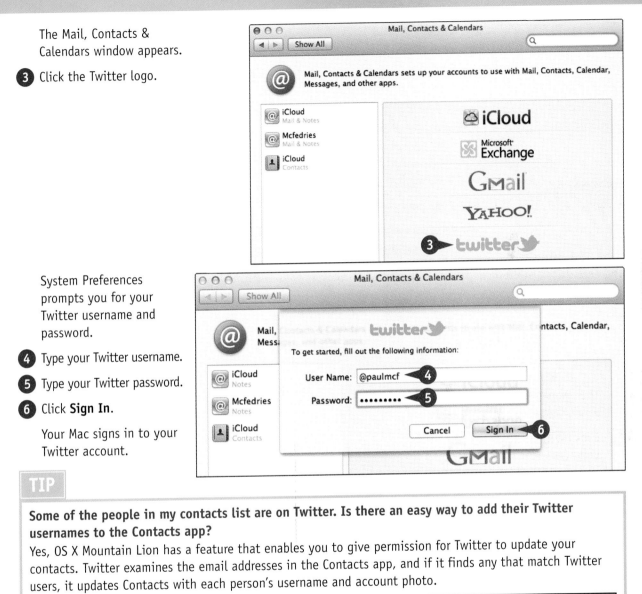

System Preferences prompts you for your Twitter username and password.

4 Type your Twitter username.

5 Type your Twitter password.

6 Click **Sign In**.

Your Mac signs in to your Twitter account.

TIP

Some of the people in my contacts list are on Twitter. Is there an easy way to add their Twitter usernames to the Contacts app?

Yes, OS X Mountain Lion has a feature that enables you to give permission for Twitter to update your contacts. Twitter examines the email addresses in the Contacts app, and if it finds any that match Twitter users, it updates Contacts with each person's username and account photo.

Follow steps **1** and **2** to open the Mail, Contacts & Calendars window, click your Twitter account, and then click **Update Contacts**. When your Mac asks you to confirm, click **Update Contacts**.

Send a Tweet

After you sign in to your Twitter account in OS X Mountain Lion, you can send tweets from various Mac apps. Although signing in to your Twitter account is useful for seeing notifications that tell you about mentions and direct messages, you will mostly use it for sending tweets to your followers. For example, if you come across a web page that you want to share, you can tweet a link to that page. You can also take a picture using Photo Booth and tweet that picture to your followers.

Send a Tweet

Tweet a Web Page

1 Use Safari to navigate to the web page you want to share.

2 Click **Share** (⬆).

3 Click **Twitter**.

Your Mac displays the Twitter share sheet.

Ⓐ The attachment appears as a link inside the tweet.

4 Type your tweet text.

Ⓑ This value tells you how many characters you have remaining.

5 Click **Send**.

Tweet a Photo Booth Photo

1 Use Photo Booth to take a picture.

2 Click the picture you want to share.

3 Click **Share** (🔁).

4 Click **Twitter**.

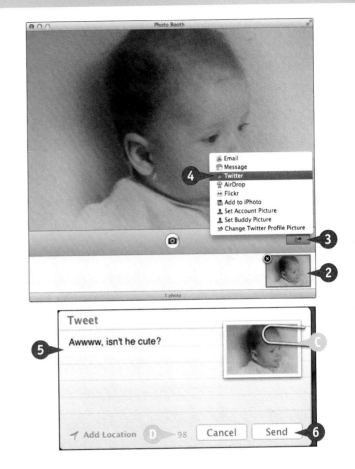

Your Mac displays the Twitter share sheet.

C The attachment appears as a link inside the tweet.

5 Type your tweet text.

D This value tells you how many characters you have remaining.

6 Click **Send**.

 TIP

Are there other apps I can use to send tweets?

Yes. If you open a photo using Quick Look (click the photo in Finder and then press **Spacebar**), you can click **Share** (🔁) and then click **Twitter**. Similarly, you can open a photo in Preview, click 🔁, and then click **Twitter**. Also, with your permission, many third-party apps are able to use your sign-in information to send tweets from the apps without requiring separate Twitter logins for each program.

Share Information with Other People

Y ou can use OS X Mountain Lion to share information with other people, including web pages, notes, pictures, videos, and photos. OS X Mountain Lion was built with sharing in mind. In previous versions of OS X, it was often difficult or tedious to share information such as web pages, images, and videos. OS X Mountain Lion implements a feature called the *share sheet*, which makes it easy to share data using multiple methods, such as email, instant messaging, and Twitter.

Share Information with Other People

Share a Web Page

1. Use Safari to navigate to the web page you want to share.

2. Click **Share** (🖼️).

3. Click the method you want to use to share the web page.

Share a Note

1. In the Notes app, click the note you want to share.

2. Click **Share** (🖼️).

3. Click the method you want to use to share the note.

Share a Picture

1. In iPhoto, click the picture you want to share.

2. Click **Share** (⤴).

3. Click the method you want to use to share the picture.

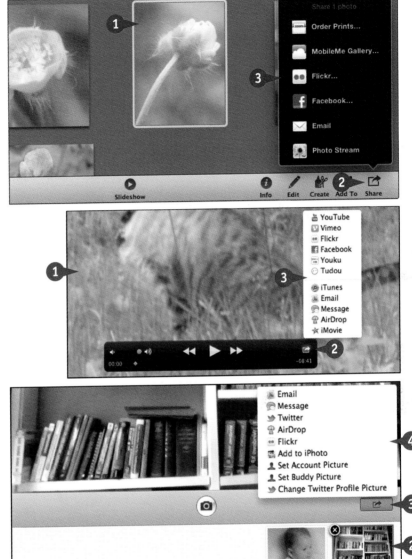

Share a Video

1. In QuickTime Player, open the video you want to share.

2. Click **Share** (⤴).

3. Click the method you want to use to share the video.

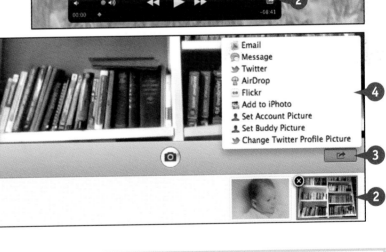

Share a Photo

1. Use Photo Booth to snap a photo.

2. Click the photo.

3. Click **Share** (⤴).

4. Click the method you want to use to share the photo.

Do I need to configure my Mac to use some of the sharing methods?

Yes, in most cases. For example, you cannot use the Email method unless you configure Mail with an email account, and you cannot use the Message method until you configure Messages with an account. Other services such as Flickr and Vimeo must be configured in System Preferences. Click ⚙ in the Dock, click **Mail, Contacts & Calendars**, and then click the type of account you want to add.

Work with the Notification Center

You can keep on top of what is happening while you are using your Mac by taking advantage of the Notification Center. Several OS X Mountain Lion apps take advantage of a feature called notifications, which enables them to send messages and alerts to your Mac about events that are happening on your Mac. For example, the App Store uses the Notification Center to let you know when OS X updates are available. There are two types of notifications: a banner that appears on the desktop temporarily, and an alert that stays on the desktop until you dismiss it. You can also open the Notification Center to view your recent notifications.

Work with the Notification Center

Handle Alert Notifications

Ⓐ An alert notification displays one or more buttons.

① Click a button to dismiss the notification.

Ⓑ For example, in a notification about new OS X updates, click **Details** to open the App Store and see the updates.

Ⓒ If you want to install the updates right away, click **Update** instead.

Handle Banner Notifications

Ⓓ A banner notification does not display any buttons.

Note: The banner notification stays on-screen for about 5 seconds and then disappears.

View Recent Notifications

1 Click **Notification Center** (▤).

Note: If your Mac has a trackpad, you can also open the Notification Center by using two fingers to swipe left from the right edge of the trackpad.

E Your Mac displays your recent notifications.

2 Click a notification to view the item in the original application.

TIP

Can I control which apps use the Notification Center and how they use it?

Yes. Click **System Preferences** (⚙) in the Dock and then click **Notifications**. Click an app on the left side of the window, and then click a notification style: **Alerts**, **Banners**, or **None**. To control the maximum number of items the app can display in the Notification Center, click the **Show in Notification Center** pop-up and then click a number. To remove an app from the Notification Center, click the **Show in Notification Center** check box (☑ changes to ☐).

View the Mac Screen on Your TV

If you have an Apple TV, you can use it to view your Mac screen on your TV. Demonstrating something on your Mac to a group of people is often difficult because most Mac screens are too small to see from a distance. However, if you have a TV or a projector nearby and you have an Apple TV device connected to that display, you can connect your Mac to the same wireless network and then send the Mac screen to the TV or projector. This is called AirPlay mirroring.

View the Mac Screen on Your TV

Mirror via System Preferences

1 Click **System Preferences** (⬛) in the Dock.

The System Preferences window appears.

2 Click **Displays**.

The display preferences appear.

3 Click the **AirPlay mirroring** ⬍ and then click your Apple TV.

OS X displays your Mac's screen on your TV.

Mirror via the Menu Bar

1 Follow steps **1** and **2** to open the display preferences.

2 Click the **Show mirroring options in the menu bar when available** check box (☐ changes to ☑).

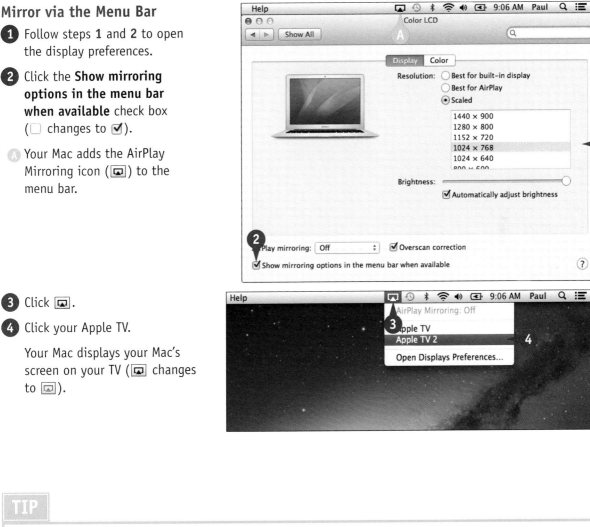

A Your Mac adds the AirPlay Mirroring icon (▣) to the menu bar.

3 Click ▣.

4 Click your Apple TV.

Your Mac displays your Mac's screen on your TV (▣ changes to ▣).

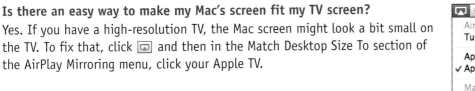

TIP

Is there an easy way to make my Mac's screen fit my TV screen?
Yes. If you have a high-resolution TV, the Mac screen might look a bit small on the TV. To fix that, click ▣ and then in the Match Desktop Size To section of the AirPlay Mirroring menu, click your Apple TV.

CHAPTER 12

Working with Your iCloud Account

You can get a free iCloud account, which is a web-based service that gives you email, an address book, and a calendar. You can also use iCloud to automatically synchronize data between iCloud and your Mac.

Create an Apple ID

To use iCloud, you need to create a free Apple ID, which you use to sign in to iCloud on the web and to synchronize your Mac and other devices. An Apple ID is an email address. You can use an existing email address for your Apple ID, or you can sign up for a new iCloud email address, which uses the icloud.com domain name. If you use an existing email address, you will be required to verify via email that the address is legitimate.

Create an Apple ID

1 Click **System Preferences** ( ).

The System Preferences window appears.

2 Click **iCloud**.

The iCloud preferences appear.

3 Click **Create an Apple ID**.

The Create an Apple ID dialog appears.

4 Use the **Location** pop-up menu to choose your country.

5 Use the three **Birthday** pop-up menus to choose your month, day, and year of birth.

6 Click **Next**.

Create an Apple ID   Step 1 of 2

An Apple ID lets you set up iCloud, the Mac App Store, the iTunes Store, FaceTime, and more.

Location: United States ◆ **4**

Birthday: August ◆ 23 ◆ 1959 ◆ **5**

Your birthday is used to determine appropriate services and retrieve your password if you forget it.

Not all services are available in all areas.

Ca **6** Next

7 Select **Get a free iCloud email address** (○ changes to ◉).

A If you prefer to use an existing address, select **Use an existing email address** (○ changes to ◉), instead.

8 Type the address.

9 Type your name.

10 Type the password.

11 Select and answer a secret question.

12 Click **Next**.

Create an Apple A   Step 2 of 2

Apple ID: ○ Use an existing email address
7 ◉ Get a free iCloud email address

Email: tyvmacs **8** @icloud.com
This will be your new Apple ID.

Name: Paul   McFedries **9**

Password: •••••••••
•••••••• **10**

Password must be at least 8 characters and include a number, an uppercase letter, and a lowercase letter.

Secret Question: Favorite teacher? ◆ **11**
Mrs. Petrie

This information is used to help retrieve your password if you forget it.

Ba **12** Next

TIP

If I do not want to create a new iCloud address, can I use any email address?
Yes, as long as the address belongs to you. Also, you need to be able to retrieve and read messages sent to that address because this is part of the verification process. To learn how to verify an existing address that you entered in step **8**, see the tip at the end of this section.

continued ▶

As part of the sign-up process for an Apple ID, you must specify which iCloud services you want to use. First, you must decide whether you want to synchronize data such as contacts, calendars, and bookmarks with iCloud. If you are not sure, you can turn this feature off for now, and decide later (see the "Set Up iCloud Synchronization" section, later in this chapter). Second, you must decide whether you want to use Find My Mac, which enables you to use iCloud to locate your Mac if it is lost or stolen. Again, if you are not sure what to do, you can decide later (see the "Locate a Lost Mac, iPod touch, iPhone, or iPad" section, later in this chapter).

Create an Apple ID (continued)

13 Select the **I have read and agree to the iCloud Terms of Service** check box (☐ changes to ☑).

14 Click **Continue**.

Your Mac asks you to confirm the change.

15 Type your OS X administrator password.

16 Click **OK**.

Your Mac prompts you to choose which iCloud services you want to use.

17 If you do not want to sync your data to iCloud, click **Use iCloud for contacts, calendars, and bookmarks** (☑ changes to ☐).

18 If you do not want to use iCloud to locate your Mac, click **Use Find My Mac** (☑ changes to ☐).

19 Click **Next**.

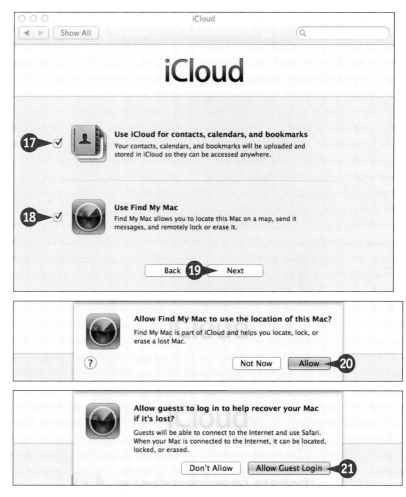

If you elected to use Find My Mac, your Mac asks you to confirm.

20 Click **Allow**.

Your Mac asks if you want to allow guest users to help recover your Mac.

21 Click **Allow Guest Login**.

Your Mac sets up your iCloud account on your Mac.

Note: If you have trouble enabling Find My Mac, see the first tip in the "Locate a Lost Mac, iPod touch, iPhone, or iPad" section.

TIP

What happens after I create my Apple ID from an existing address?
After you agree to the terms of service, Apple sends an email message to the address you typed in step **8**. When that message arrives, open it and click the verification link. In the web page that appears, type your Apple ID (that is, the email address from step **8**), type your password, and then click **Verify Address**. Return to the iCloud preferences, click **Next**, and then follow steps **15** to **21**.

Sign In to iCloud

Before you can use any of the features associated with your iCloud account, you must sign in to the service. iCloud is a web-based service, so you access it using a web browser. Most modern browsers should work fine with iCloud, but Apple recommends that you use at least Safari 5, Firefox 5, Internet Explorer 8, or Chrome 12.

You can also sign in to iCloud using a Mac, and for that you must be using OS X Lion 10.7.2 or later. You can also access iCloud using a Windows PC, and in this case the PC must be running Windows 8, Windows 7, or Windows Vista with Service Pack 2 or later.

Sign In to iCloud

1 In your web browser, type **www.icloud.com**.

2 Press **Return**.

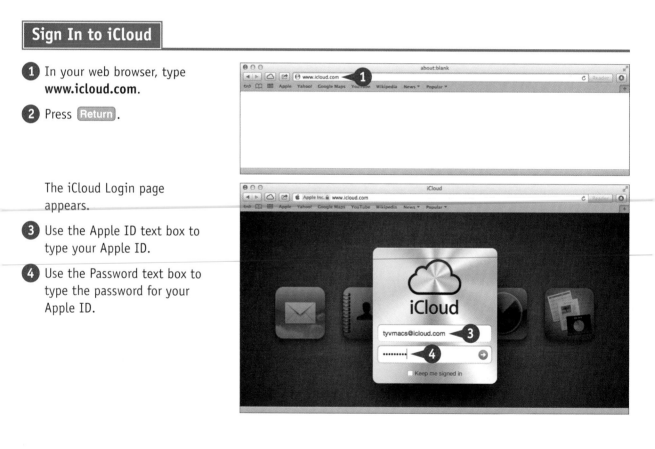

The iCloud Login page appears.

3 Use the Apple ID text box to type your Apple ID.

4 Use the Password text box to type the password for your Apple ID.

A If you want iCloud to sign you in automatically in the future, click **Keep me signed in** (☐ changes to ☑).

5 Click **Sign In** (⊙).

The first time you sign in, iCloud prompts you to configure some settings.

6 Click **Add Photo**, drop a photo on the dialog that appears, and then click **Done**.

7 Click **Language** and then click the language you prefer to use.

8 Click **Time Zone** and then click your time zone.

9 Click **Done**.

TIPS

Can I sign in from my Mac?

Yes. Click **System Preferences** (◻) in the Dock (or click ◻ and then click **System Preferences**) and then click **iCloud**. Type your Apple ID and password and then click **Sign In**.

Use iCloud with your Apple ID:

tyvmacs@icloud.com   ••••••••   Sign In

Create an Apple ID...   Forgot password?

How do I sign out from iCloud?

When you are done working with your iCloud account, if you prefer not to remain signed in to your account, click the **Sign Out** link beside your account name in the upper right corner of the iCloud page.

Set Up iCloud Synchronization

You can ensure that your Mac and your iCloud account have the same data by synchronizing the two. The main items you will want to synchronize are Mail email accounts, contacts, calendars, reminders, and notes. However, you may want to synchronize many other types of data to iCloud, including Safari bookmarks, photos, and documents.

If you have a second Mac, a Windows PC, or an iPhone, iPad, or iPod touch, you can also synchronize it with the same iCloud account, which ensures that your Mac and the device use the same data.

Set Up iCloud Synchronization

1 Click the **Apple** icon ().

2 Click **System Preferences**.

Note: You can also open System Preferences by clicking its icon () on the Dock.

The System Preferences window appears.

3 Click **iCloud**.

The iCloud preferences appear.

④ Select the check box beside a type of data you want to sync (☐ changes to ☑).

Ⓐ Your Mac sets up the sync.

⑤ Repeat step 4 for each type of data you want to sync.

⑥ If you do not want to sync a type of data, click its check box (☑ changes to ☐).

Your Mac asks if you want to keep or delete the iCloud data that you are no longer syncing.

⑦ Click here to keep the data on your Mac.

Ⓑ If you do not want to keep the data, click **Delete from Mac** instead.

Your Mac synchronizes the data with your iCloud account.

TIP

What happens if I modify an appointment, contact, bookmark, or other data in iCloud?
The synchronization process works both ways. That is, all the Mac data you selected to synchronize is sent to your iCloud account. However, the data on your iCloud account is also sent to your Mac. This means that if you modify, add, or delete data on your iCloud account, your Mac data also reflects those changes.

Send and Receive iCloud Mail

You can use the iCloud Mail feature to work with your iCloud email account online. Using either your Mac or any computer or device that has web access and is compatible with iCloud, you can access iCloud using a web browser and then perform your email tasks. These include checking for incoming messages, replying to messages you receive, forwarding a received message, and composing and sending a new message.

You can also configure iCloud Mail to send blind courtesy copies and to automatically send vacation messages.

Send and Receive iCloud Mail

Display iCloud Mail

1 Sign in to your iCloud account.

Note: See the "Sign In to iCloud" section, earlier in this chapter.

2 If you are using another section of iCloud, click **Switch Apps** (🔲).

3 Click **Mail** (🔳).

Get Incoming Messages

1 Click **Get Mail** (🔁).

Ⓐ iCloud Mail checks for incoming messages and, if there are any, displays them in the Inbox folder.

Reply to a Message

1 Click the message.

2 Click **Reply, Reply All, Forward** ().

3 Click **Reply**.

B To reply to the sender and all the recipients of the original message, click **Reply All** instead.

C To pass the message to another person, click **Forward** instead.

4 In the message window that appears (not shown), type your message and then click **Send**.

Send a New Message

1 Click **Compose new message** (🖼).

The New Message window appears.

2 Use the To text box to type the recipient's email address.

D If you want another person to see a copy of the message, type that person's address in the Cc text box.

3 Use the Subject text box to type the subject of the message.

4 Type your message.

5 Click **Send**.

TIP

Can I use iCloud to send a message to a person without other recipients knowing?

Yes, you can send that person a blind courtesy copy (Bcc), which means that he or she receives a copy of the message, but the other message recipients do not see that person's name or address in the recipient fields. To activate this feature, open iCloud Mail, click **Actions** (⚙), click **Preferences**, and then click the **Composing** tab. Click **Show Bcc field** (☐ changes to ☑) and then click **Done**.

Work with iCloud Contacts

You can use iCloud to store information about your friends, family, colleagues, and clients. Using the Contacts app, you can store data such as the person's name, company name, phone numbers, email address, and street address. The Contacts app also enables you to write notes about a contact, store extra data such as the person's job title and birthday, and assign a picture to a contact.

If you already have contacts in your Mac's Contacts app, you can synchronize them with iCloud. See the "Set Up iCloud Synchronization" section, earlier in this chapter.

Work with iCloud Contacts

Display iCloud Contacts

1. Sign in to your iCloud account.

Note: See the "Sign In to iCloud" section, earlier in this chapter.

2. Click **Switch Apps** (⬜).

3. Click **Contacts** (🖼).

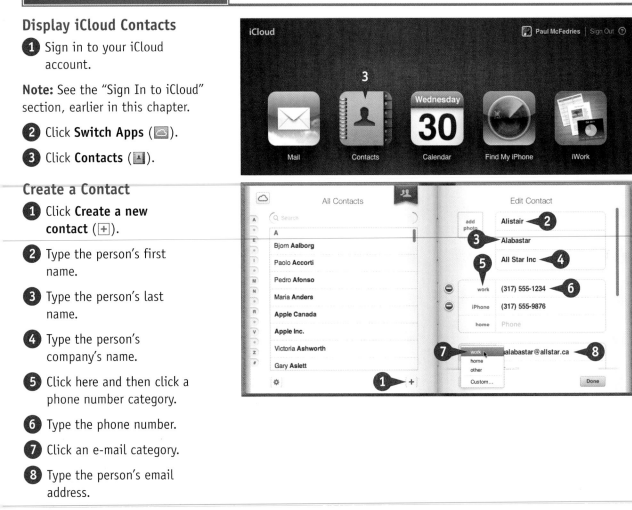

Create a Contact

1. Click **Create a new contact** (⊞).

2. Type the person's first name.

3. Type the person's last name.

4. Type the person's company's name.

5. Click here and then click a phone number category.

6. Type the phone number.

7. Click an e-mail category.

8. Type the person's email address.

9 Click **Add Field** (⊕) beside **add new address** (not shown).

10 Click a street address category.

11 Use the text boxes in this section to type the person's street address.

12 Type a note about the person.

13 Click **Done**.

iCloud saves the contact.

Display a Contact

1 Use the scroll bar to locate the contact.

2 Click the contact.

A iCloud displays the contact's details.

B You can also type part of the contact's name in the Search box.

C To email the contact, click the address.

D To make changes to the contact, click **Edit**.

To remove the contact, click **Edit** and then click **Delete Contact**.

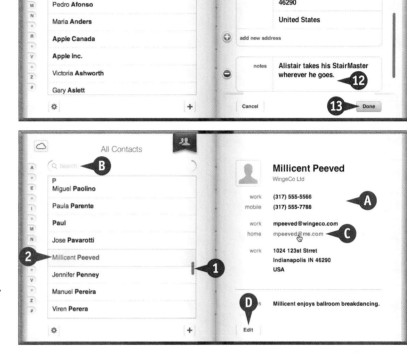

TIPS

How do I add a photo for a contact?
To add a photo to an existing contact, click the contact and then click **Edit**. Click **add photo** and then drag a photo to the dialog that appears. Alternatively, click **Choose**, click the photo you want to use, and then click **Choose**. Click **Done**. Note that you can use only GIF, JPEG, or PNG files that are no larger than 1MB.

Is there any way to store data such as the person's birthday or job title?
Yes, the Contacts app offers a number of other fields, including Birthday, Job Title, Nickname, Prefix, and Suffix. To add a field to an existing contact, click the contact and then click **Edit**. Click **Add Field**, click the field you want, and then edit the field data. Note, too, that you can also add more instances of some fields by clicking the **Add Field** icon (⊕) to the left of a field.

Manage Your Schedule with iCloud

You can use iCloud to manage your schedule. Using the Calendar application, you can add events (appointments and all-day activities) and reminders. For events, you can specify the date and time they occur, the event name and location, and notes related to the event. You can also use the Calendar application to display your schedule by day, by week, or by month.

If you already have events in your OS X Calendar application, you can synchronize them with iCloud. See the "Set Up iCloud Synchronization" section, earlier in this chapter.

Manage Your Schedule with iCloud

Display iCloud Calendar

1 Sign in to your iCloud account.

Note: See the "Sign In to iCloud" section, earlier in this chapter.

2 Click **Switch Apps** (⬆).

3 Click **Calendar** (📅).

Navigate Calendar

1 Click **Month**.

2 Click the month you want.

A You can also click **Next Month** (▶) and **Previous Month** (◀) to select the month you want.

3 Click the date.

B To see just that date, click **Day**.

C To see the date in the context of its week, click **Week**.

D To return to today's date, click **Today**.

Create an Event

1 Navigate to the date when the event occurs.

2 Click the calendar you want to use.

3 Click **Week**.

4 Position the ⬈ at the time when the event starts.

5 Click and drag the ⬈ down to the time when the event ends.

Ⓔ Calendar adds the event.

6 Type the event name.

7 Type the event location.

Ⓕ If the event lasts all day, click **all-day** (☐ changes to ☑).

8 Adjust the start time, if necessary.

9 Adjust the end time, if necessary.

10 Fill in the other event details as needed.

11 Click **OK**.

Note: To edit the event, double-click it.

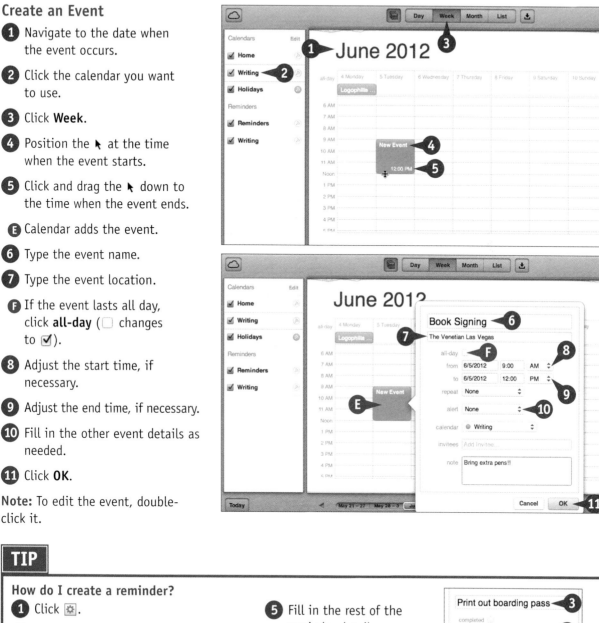

TIP

How do I create a reminder?

1 Click ⚙.

2 Click **New Reminder**.

3 Type the reminder name.

4 Click the **priority** 🔽 and then click **None**, **Low**, **Medium**, or **High**.

5 Fill in the rest of the reminder details as needed.

6 Click **OK**.

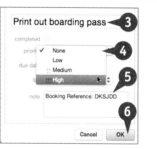

Locate a Lost Mac, iPod touch, iPhone, or iPad

You can use iCloud to locate a lost or stolen Mac, iPod touch, iPhone, or iPad. Depending on how you use your Mac, iPod touch, iPhone, or iPad, you can end up with many details of your life residing on the device. That is generally a good thing, but if you happen to lose your device, you have also lost those details, plus you have created a large privacy problem because anyone can now see your data.

You can locate your device and even send a message to the device using an iCloud feature called Find My iPhone, which also works for Macs, iPod touches, and iPads.

Locate a Lost Mac, iPod touch, iPhone, or iPad

Locate a Device on a Map

1 Sign in to your iCloud account.

Note: See the "Sign In to iCloud" section, earlier in this chapter.

2 Click **Switch Apps** (⬚).

3 Click **Find My iPhone** (⬚).

Note: If iCloud asks you to sign in to your account, type your password and click **OK**.

4 In the My Devices list, click the device you want to locate.

Ⓐ iCloud displays the device location on a map.

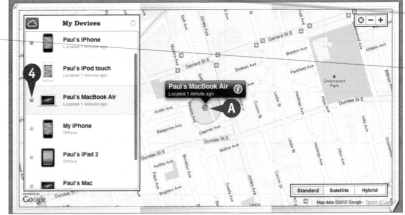

Send a Message to a Device

1 Click the device in the My Devices list.

2 Click the **Info** icon ().

iCloud displays the Info dialog.

3 Click **Play Sound or Send Message**.

iCloud displays the Send Message dialog.

4 Type your message.

5 Click **Send**.

iCloud sends the message, which then appears on the device screen.

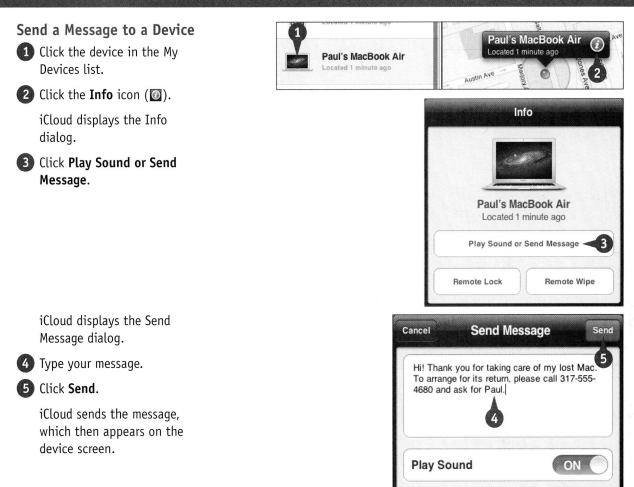

TIPS

I tried to enable Find My Mac, but OS X would not allow it. How can I enable Find My Mac?
You first need to enable location services. To do this, click **System Preferences** (⬚) in the Dock. Click **Security & Privacy**, click the **Lock** icon (🔒), type your OS X administrator password, and then click **OK** (🔒 changes to 🔓). Click **Location Services** and then click **Enable Location Services** (☐ changes to ☑).

Is there a way to ensure that someone who finds my lost device cannot view my files or change any settings?
Yes, you can use iCloud's Find My iPhone application to lock the device. Follow steps **1** and **2** to locate the device on a map, and then click **Remote Lock**. In the Remote Lock dialog that appears, type a four-digit passcode, retype the passcode, type a message that will appear on the device, and then click **Lock**.

CHAPTER 13

Customizing Your Mac

Your Mac comes with a number of features that enable you to customize your Mac. For example, you might not like the default desktop background or the layout of the Dock. Not only can you change the appearance of your Mac to suit your taste, but you can also change the way your Mac works to make it easier and more efficient for you to use.

Display System Preferences

You can find many of the Mac customization features in System Preferences, a collection of settings and options that control the overall look and operation of your Mac. You can use System Preferences to change the desktop background, specify a screen saver, set your Mac's sleep options, add user accounts, and customize the Dock, to name some of the tasks that you learn about in this chapter. To use these settings, you must know how to display the System Preferences window.

Display System Preferences

Open System Preferences

1 In the Dock, click **System Preferences** (🖼️).

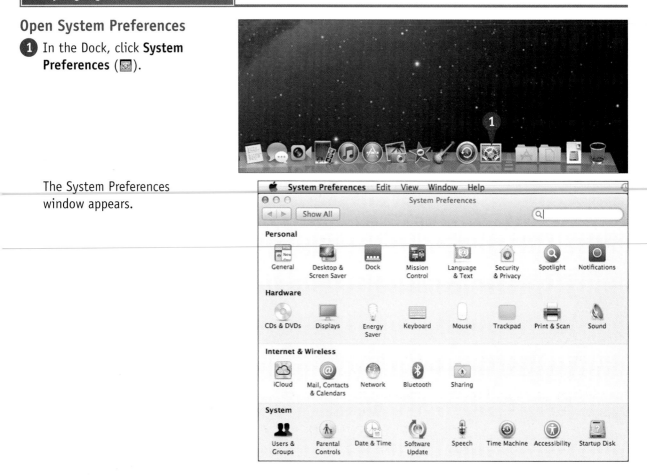

The System Preferences window appears.

Close System Preferences

1 Click **System Preferences**.

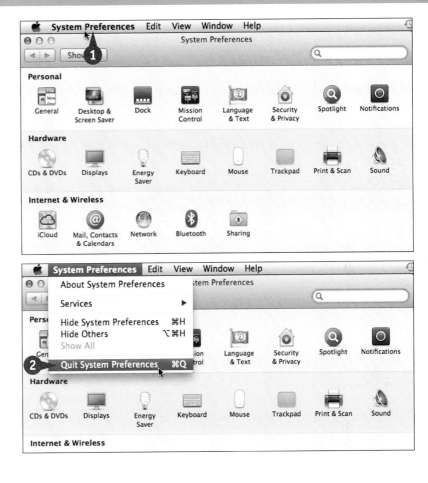

2 Click **Quit System Preferences**.

Are there other methods I can use to open System Preferences?

If you have hidden the Dock (as described later in the "Hide the Dock" section) or removed the System Preferences icon from the Dock, you can click and then click **System Preferences**.

Sometimes when I open System Preferences, I do not see all the icons. How can I restore the original icons?

When you click an icon in System Preferences, the window changes to show just the options and settings associated with that icon. To return to the main System Preferences window, click **View** and then click **Show All Preferences** (or press ⌘+🇱) or use either of the following techniques:

Ⓐ Click ◀ until the main window appears.

Ⓑ Click **Show All**.

Change the Desktop Background

To give your Mac a different look, you can change the default desktop background. Your Mac offers a wide variety of desktop background options. For example, your Mac comes with several dozen images you can use, from abstract patterns to photos of plants and other natural images.

You can also choose a solid color as the desktop background, or you can use one of your own photos. You can change the desktop background to show either a fixed image or a series of images that change periodically.

Change the Desktop Background

Set a Fixed Background Image

1 Open System Preferences.

Note: See the "Display System Preferences" section, earlier in this chapter.

2 Click **Desktop & Screen Saver**.

Note: You can also right-click the desktop and then click **Change Desktop Background**.

The desktop and screen saver preferences appear.

3 Click **Desktop**.

4 Click the image category you want to use.

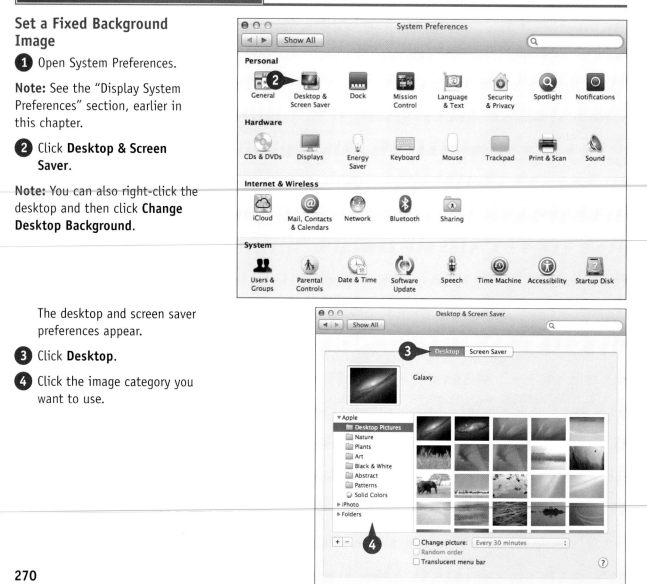

Click the image you want to use as the desktop background.

Your Mac changes the desktop background.

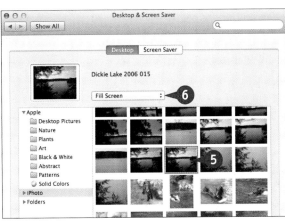

6 If you chose a photo in step **5**, click ⬙ and then click an option to determine how your Mac displays the photo.

Note: Another way to set a fixed background image is to select a photo in iPhoto, click **Share**, and then click **Set Desktop**.

Set a Changing Background Image

1 Click **Change picture** (☐ changes to ☑).

2 Click ⬙ in the pop-up menu and then click how often you want the background image to change.

3 If you want your Mac to choose the periodic image randomly, click **Random order** (☐ changes to ☑).

Your Mac changes the desktop background periodically based on your chosen interval.

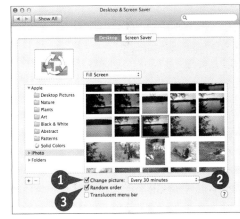

TIP

When I choose a photo, how do the various options differ for displaying the photo?
Your Mac gives you five options for displaying the photo:

- **Fill Screen:** This option expands the photo by the same amount in all four directions until it fills the entire desktop. This option can cause some edges of the photo to be cropped out.
- **Fit to Screen:** This option expands the photo in all four directions until the photo is either the same height as the desktop or the same width as the desktop.
- **Stretch to Fill Screen:** This option expands the photo in all four directions until it fills the entire desktop. Because the photo is usually expanded more either vertically or horizontally, this option can cause the photo to appear distorted.
- **Center:** This option displays the photo at its actual size and places the photo in the center of the desktop.
- **Tile:** This option repeats your photo multiple times to fill the entire desktop.

Activate the Screen Saver

You can set up your Mac to display a *screen saver*, a moving pattern or series of pictures. The screen saver appears after your computer has been idle for a while. If you leave your monitor on for long stretches while your computer is idle, a faint version of the unmoving image can endure for a while on the screen, a phenomenon known as *persistence*. A screen saver prevents this by displaying a moving image. However, persistence is not a major problem for modern screens, so for the most part you use a screen saver for visual interest.

Activate the Screen Saver

1 Open System Preferences.

Note: See the "Display System Preferences" section, earlier in this chapter.

2 Click **Desktop & Screen Saver**.

The desktop and screen saver preferences appear.

3 Click **Screen Saver**.

4 Click the screen saver you want to use.

Ⓐ A preview of the screen saver appears here.

5 Click the **Start after** 🔽 and then click a time delay until the screen saver begins.

Note: The interval you choose is the number of minutes or hours that your Mac must be idle before the screen saver starts.

Ⓑ If the screen saver is customizable, click **Screen Saver Options** to configure it.

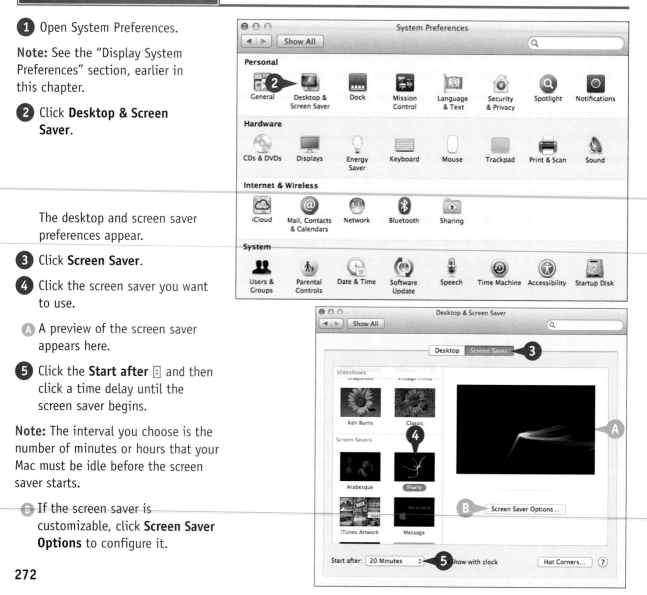

C If you chose a slide show instead of a screen saver, click the **Source** ⬍ to select an image collection.

D If you also want to see the current time when the screen saver is active, click **Show with clock** (☐ changes to ☑).

TIP

What are hot corners and how do I configure them?

A *hot corner* is a corner of your Mac's screen that you have set up to perform some action when you move the mouse (▶) to that corner. To configure hot corners, follow these steps:

1 Follow steps **1** to **4** to select a screen saver.

2 Click **Hot Corners**.

  System Preferences displays the Active Screen Corners dialog.

3 In the top left pop-up menu, click ⬍ and then click the action you want to perform when you move ▶ to the top left corner of the screen.

4 Click ⬍ and then click the action you want to perform when you move ▶ to the top right corner of the screen.

5 Click ⬍ and then click the action you want to perform when you move ▶ to the bottom left corner of the screen.

6 Click ⬍ and then click the action you want to perform when you move ▶ to the bottom right corner of the screen.

7 Click **OK**.

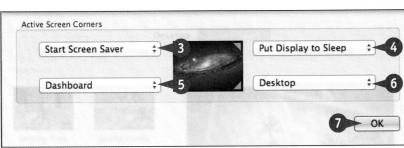

Set Your Mac's Sleep Options

You can make your Mac more energy efficient by configuring parts of your Mac to go into sleep mode automatically when you are not using them. *Sleep mode* means that your display or your Mac is in a temporary low-power mode. This saves energy on all Macs, and also saves battery power on a notebook Mac. For example, you can set up your Mac to put the display to sleep automatically after a period of inactivity. Similarly, you can configure your Mac to put your entire Mac to sleep after you have not used it for a specified amount of time.

Set Your Mac's Sleep Options

Open the Energy Saver Preferences

1 Open System Preferences.

Note: See the "Display System Preferences" section, earlier in this chapter.

2 Click **Energy Saver**.

The Energy Saver preferences appear.

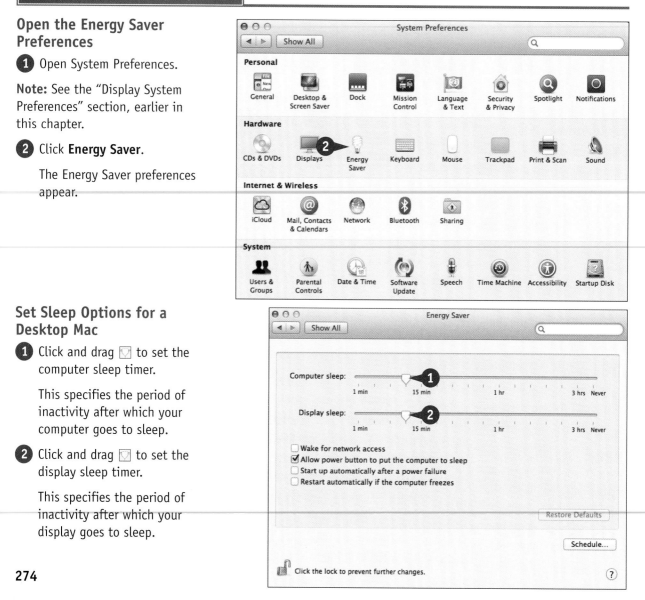

Set Sleep Options for a Desktop Mac

1 Click and drag ⬇ to set the computer sleep timer.

This specifies the period of inactivity after which your computer goes to sleep.

2 Click and drag ⬇ to set the display sleep timer.

This specifies the period of inactivity after which your display goes to sleep.

Set Sleep Options for a Notebook Mac

1 Click **Battery**.

2 Click and drag ⊡ to set the computer sleep timer for when your Mac is on battery power.

3 Click and drag ⊡ to set the display sleep timer for when your Mac is on battery power.

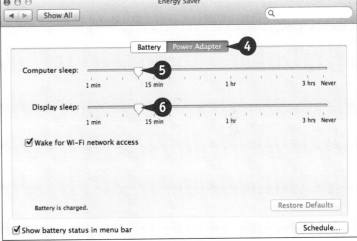

4 Click **Power Adapter**.

5 Click and drag ⊡ to set the computer sleep timer for when your Mac is plugged in.

6 Click and drag ⊡ to set the display sleep timer for when your Mac is plugged in.

TIPS

How do I wake up a sleeping display or computer?

If your Mac's display is in sleep mode, you can wake up the display by moving your mouse or sliding your finger on the trackpad. You can also wake up the display or your entire Mac by pressing a key such as ⌘, Control, Option, or Shift on your keyboard.

I changed the display sleep timer, and now I never see my screen saver. Why?

You have set the display sleep timer to a time that is less than your screen saver timer. Suppose you have configured your Mac to switch on the screen saver after 15 minutes. If you then set the display sleep timer to a shorter interval, such as 10 minutes, your Mac will always put the display to sleep before the screen saver appears.

Change the Display Resolution

You can change the resolution of your Mac's display. This enables you to adjust the display for best viewing or for maximum compatibility with whatever application you are using. Increasing the display resolution is an easy way to create more space on the screen for applications and windows because the objects on the screen appear smaller. Conversely, if you are having trouble reading text on the screen, decreasing the display resolution can help because the screen objects appear larger. You can change the Mac display resolution using either the System Preferences window or the menu bar.

Change the Display Resolution

Change Resolution via the Display Preferences

1 Open System Preferences.

Note: See the "Display System Preferences" section, earlier in this chapter.

2 Click **Displays**.

The Displays preferences appear.

3 Click **Display**.

4 Click the resolution you want to use.

Your Mac adjusts the screen to the new resolution.

A To change the resolution using your Mac's menu bar, as described next, click **Show mirroring options in menu bar when available** (☐ changes to ☑).

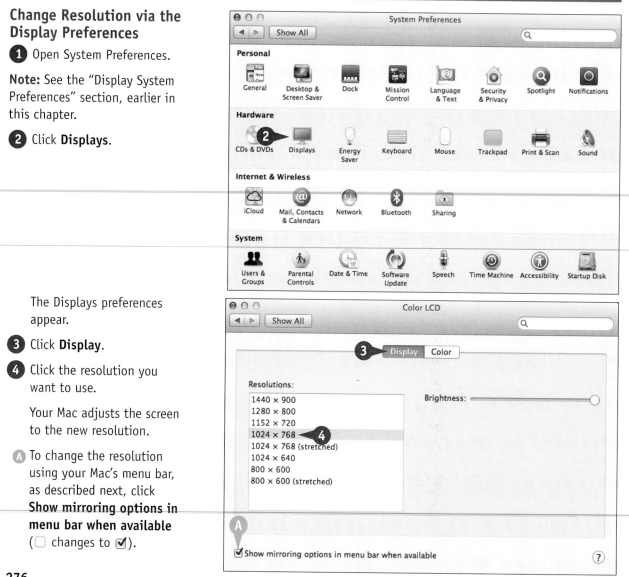

Change Resolution via the Menu Bar

1 Click the **Mirroring Options** icon (▣).

Your Mac opens a menu that shows the most commonly or recently used resolutions.

B The resolution with the check mark (☑) is the current resolution.

2 Click the resolution you want to use.

Your Mac adjusts the screen to the new resolution.

TIPS

What do the resolution numbers mean?
The resolution numbers are expressed in *pixels*, which are the individual dots that make up your Mac's screen. The pixels are arranged in rows and columns, so a resolution of 1024 × 768 means that the display is using 1,024 pixels in each row and 768 pixels in each column.

Why do some resolutions also include the word *stretched*?
Most older displays are made with the ratio of the width to the height — this is called the *aspect ratio* — set at 4:3. However, most new Mac displays are made with an aspect ratio of 16:10, which is called *widescreen*. Resolutions designed for 4:3 displays — such as 800 × 600 and 1024 × 768 — take up only part of a widescreen display. To make them take up the entire display, choose the *stretched* version of the resolution.

Create an App Folder in Launchpad

You can make Launchpad easier to work with by combining two or more icons into a single storage area called an *app folder*. Your Mac displays the Launchpad icons in up to 5 rows per screen, with up to 7 icons in each row, so you can have as many as 35 icons in each Launchpad screen. Also, if you have configured your Mac with a relatively low display resolution, you might see only partial app names in the Launchpad screens.

All of this can make it difficult to locate the app you want. However, by creating app folders, you can organize similar apps and reduce the clutter on the Launchpad screens.

Create an App Folder in Launchpad

1 Click **Launchpad** ( ).

Ⓐ Launchpad displays icons for each installed application.

2 Click the dot for the Launchpad screen you want to work with.

3 Use the mouse ( ) to click and drag an icon that you want to include in the folder, and drop it on another icon that you want to include in the same folder.

B Launchpad creates the app folder.

C Launchpad applies a name to the folder based on the type of applications in the folder.

D Launchpad adds the icons to the app folder.

④ To specify a different name, click the name and then type the one you prefer.

⑤ Click the Launchpad screen, outside of the app folder.

E Launchpad displays the app folder.

⑥ To add more icons to the new app folder, use the mouse (▶) to click and drag each icon and drop it on the folder.

Note: To launch a program from an app folder, click ☑, click the app folder to open it, and then click the program's icon.

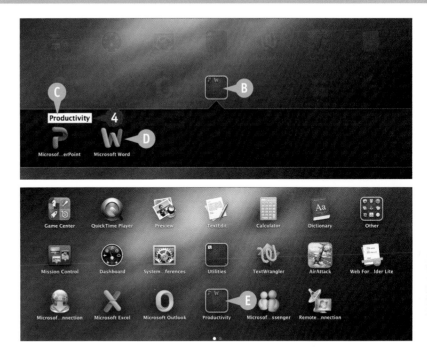

TIPS

Can I make changes to an app folder after it has been created?
Yes, you can rename the folder or rearrange the icons within the folder. Open Launchpad and then click the app folder to open it. To rename the app folder, click the current name, type the new name, and then press `Return`. To rearrange the icons, use the mouse (▶) to drag and drop the apps within the folder. Click outside the app folder to close it.

Can I remove an icon from an app folder?
Yes. To begin, click ☑ to open Launchpad, and then click the app folder to open it. To remove an app from a folder, use the mouse (▶) to click and drag the app out of the folder. Launchpad closes the folder, and you can then drop the icon within the Launchpad screen. Note that if you remove all the icons from an app folder, Launchpad deletes the folder.

Add a User Account

You can share your Mac with another person by creating a user account for that person. This enables the person to log on to your Mac and use the system. The new user account is completely separate from your own account. This means that the other person can change settings, create documents, and perform other Mac tasks without interfering with your own settings or data. For maximum privacy for all users, you should set up each user account with a password.

Add a User Account

1 Open System Preferences.

Note: See the "Display System Preferences" section, earlier in this chapter.

2 Click **Users & Groups**.

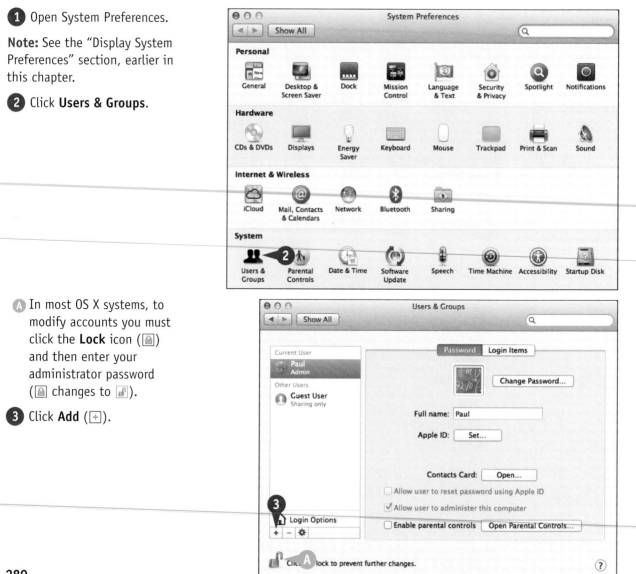

A In most OS X systems, to modify accounts you must click the **Lock** icon (🔒) and then enter your administrator password (🔒 changes to 🔓).

3 Click **Add** (⊞).

The New Account dialog appears.

4 Click  and then click an account type.

5 Type the user's name.

6 Edit the short username that your Mac creates.

7 Type a password for the user.

8 Retype the user's password.

9 As an option, type a hint that your Mac will display if the user forgets the password.

10 Click **Create User**.

B Your Mac adds the user account to the Users & Groups preferences window.

New Account: Standard — 4
Full Name: Karen — 5
Account name: karen — 6
Password: •••••••• — 7
Verify: •••••••• — 8
Password hint: Mom's maiden name and year of birth — 9
(Recommended)
Cancel   Create User — 10

Users & Groups
Show All

Current User
Paul — Admin
Other Users
Karen — Standard — B
Guest User — Sharing only

Reset Password...
Full name: Karen
Apple ID: Set...

☐ Allow user to reset password using Apple ID
☐ Allow user to administer this computer
☐ Enable parental controls   Open Parental Controls...

Login Options
+ − ⚙

🔒 Click the lock to prevent further changes.

Which account type should I use for the new account?
The Standard account type is a good choice because it can make changes only to its own account settings. Avoid the Administrator option because it is a powerful account type that enables the user to make major changes to the system. For a child, consider the Managed with Parental Controls account type, which enables you to place restrictions on the user's actions and content.

How do I change the user's picture?
In the Users & Groups preferences, click the user and then click the picture. Your Mac displays a list of the available images. If you see one you like, click it. If your Mac has a camera attached and the user is nearby, you can click Camera and then click the Camera icon to take the user's picture. Click **Done** to set the picture.

Customize the Dock

You can customize various aspects of the Dock by using System Preferences to modify a few Dock options. For example, you can make the Dock take up less room on the screen by adjusting its size. You can also make the Dock a bit easier to use by turning on the Magnification feature, which enlarges Dock icons when you position the mouse pointer over them. You can also make the Dock easier to access and use by moving it to either side of the screen.

Customize the Dock

1 Open System Preferences.

Note: See the "Display System Preferences" section, earlier in this chapter.

2 Click **Dock**.

Note: You can also open the Dock preferences by clicking , clicking **Dock**, and then clicking **Dock Preferences**.

The Dock preferences appear.

3 Click and drag the **Size** to make the Dock smaller or larger.

A You can also click and drag the Dock divider: Drag up to increase the Dock size, and drag down to decrease the Dock size.

B System Preferences adjusts the size of the Dock.

Note: If your Dock is already as wide as the screen, dragging the Size slider to the right (toward the Large value) has no effect.

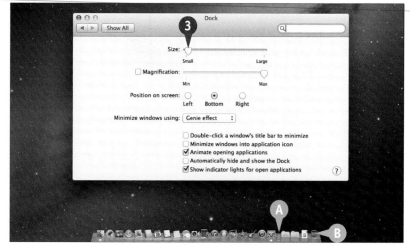

4 Click **Magnification**
(☐ changes to ☑).

5 Click and drag the
Magnification ☑ to set the
magnification level.

C When you position the mouse
(↖) over a Dock icon, your
Mac magnifies the icon.

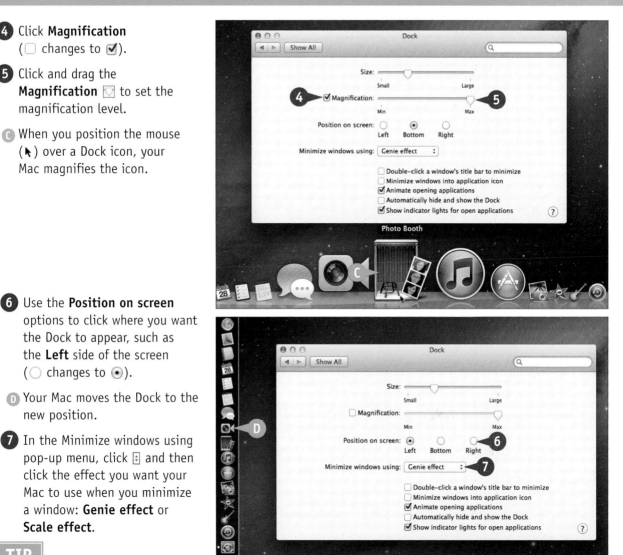

6 Use the **Position on screen**
options to click where you want
the Dock to appear, such as
the **Left** side of the screen
(○ changes to ◉).

D Your Mac moves the Dock to the
new position.

7 In the Minimize windows using
pop-up menu, click ⬚ and then
click the effect you want your
Mac to use when you minimize
a window: **Genie effect** or
Scale effect.

TIP

Is there an easier method I can use to control some of these preferences?

Yes, you can control these preferences directly from the Dock. To set the Dock size, click and drag the Dock divider (Ⓐ) left or right. For the other preferences, right-click the Dock divider. Click **Turn Magnification On** to enable the magnification feature; click **Turn Magnification Off** to disable this feature. To change the Dock position, click **Position on Screen** and then click **Left**, **Bottom**, or

Right. To set the minimize effect, click **Minimize Using** and then click either **Genie Effect** or **Scale Effect**. Finally, you can also click **Dock Preferences** to open the Dock pane in System Preferences.

Add an Icon to the Dock

The icons on the Dock are convenient because you can open them with just a single click. You can enhance the convenience of the Dock by adding an icon for an application you use frequently.

The icon remains in the Dock even when the application is closed, so you can always open the application with a single click. You can add an icon to the Dock even if the program is not currently running.

Add an Icon to the Dock

Add an Icon for a Nonrunning Application

1 Click **Finder** ().

2 Click **Applications**.

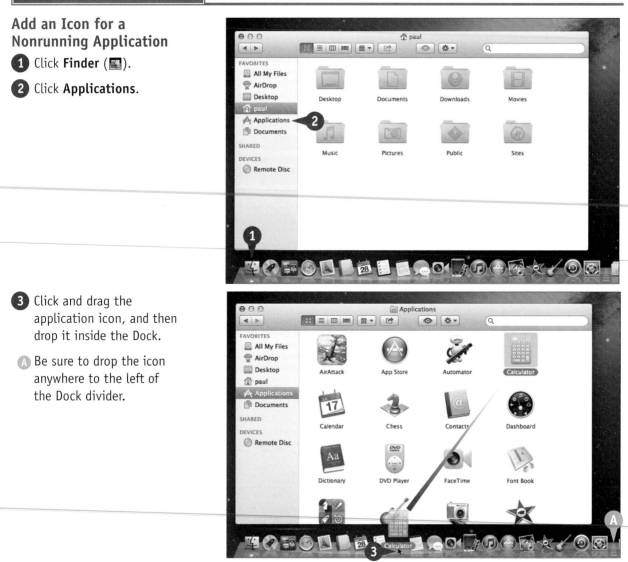

3 Click and drag the application icon, and then drop it inside the Dock.

Ⓐ Be sure to drop the icon anywhere to the left of the Dock divider.

B Your Mac adds the application's icon to the Dock.

Add an Icon for a Running Application

1 Right-click the application icon in the Dock.

2 Click **Options**.

3 Click **Keep in Dock**.

The application's icon remains in the Dock even after you close the program.

TIPS

Is there a way to get my Mac to start the application automatically each time I log in to the computer?

Yes. Your Mac maintains a list of *login items*, which are applications that run automatically after you log in. You can configure your application as a login item, and your Mac opens it automatically each time you log in. Right-click the application's Dock icon, click **Options**, and then click **Open at Login**.

How do I remove an icon from the Dock?

Right-click the application's Dock icon, click **Options**, and then click **Remove from Dock**. If the application is currently running, your Mac removes the icon from the Dock when you quit the program. Note that you can remove any application icon except Finder (▣) and Launchpad (◉). Removing an application's Dock icon does not delete the actual application.

Hide the Dock

If you would like more room on the Mac screen to display your applications, you can hide the Dock to free up some screen space. When you are working in an application, you might find that you need to maximize the amount of vertical space the application window takes up on-screen. This might come up, for example, when you are reading or editing a long document or viewing a large photo. In such cases, you can size the window to maximum height, but your Mac will not let you go past the Dock. You can work around this by hiding the Dock. When the Dock is hidden, you can still easily access it whenever you need to use it.

Hide the Dock

Turn On Dock Hiding

1 Click 🍎.

2 Click **Dock**.

3 Click **Turn Hiding On**.

Ⓐ You can also right-click the Dock divider and then click **Turn Hiding On**.

Ⓑ Your Mac removes the Dock from the desktop.

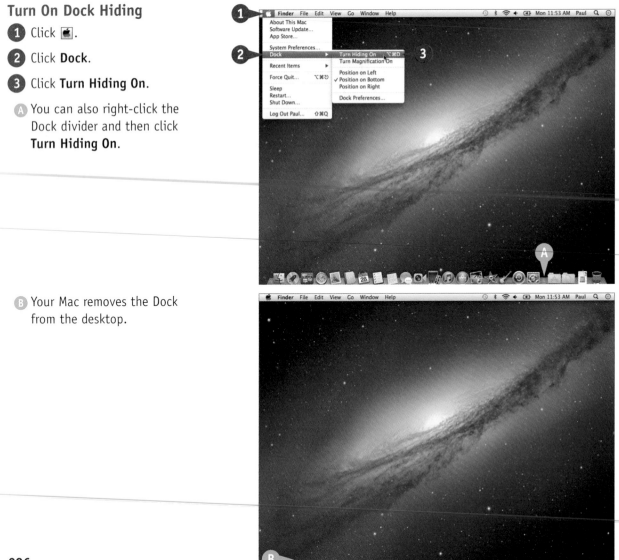

Display the Dock Temporarily

1 Move the mouse ( ) to the bottom of the screen.

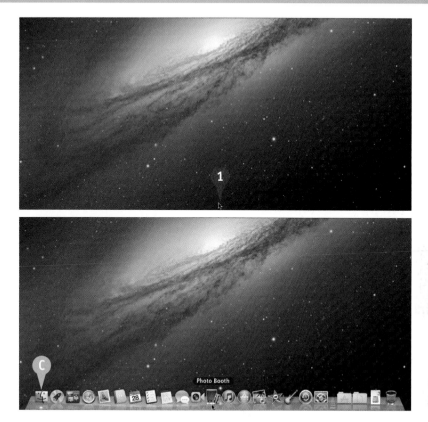

C Your Mac temporarily displays the Dock.

Note: To hide the Dock again, move the mouse ( ) away from the bottom of the screen.

Is there a faster way to hide the Dock?
Yes. You can quickly hide the Dock by pressing Option+⌘+D. This keyboard shortcut is a toggle, which means that you can also turn off Dock hiding by pressing Option+⌘+D. When the Dock is hidden, you can display it temporarily by pressing Control+F3 (on some keyboards you must press Fn+Control+F3).

How do I bring the Dock back into view?
When you no longer need the extra screen space for your applications, you can turn off Dock hiding to bring the Dock back into view. Click , click **Dock**, and then click **Turn Hiding Off**. Alternatively, display the Dock, right-click the Dock divider, and then click **Turn Hiding Off**.

CHAPTER 14

Networking with Your Mac

If you have multiple computers in your home or office, you can set up these computers as a network to share information and equipment. This chapter gives an overview of networking concepts and shows you how to connect to a network, how to work with the other computers on your network, and how to share your Mac's resources with other network users.

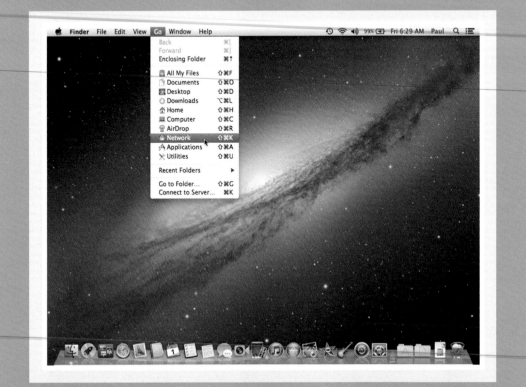

Understanding Networking

A *network* is a collection of connected computers and other devices. You can create a network using cable hookups, wireless hookups, or a combination of the two. In both cases, you need special networking equipment to make the connections.

A network gives you a number of advantages. For example, once you have two or more computers connected on a network, those computers can share documents, photos, and other files. You can also use a network to share equipment, such as printers and optical drives.

Share Files

Networked computers are connected to each other, and so they can exchange files with each other along the connection. This enables people to share information and to collaborate on projects. Your Mac includes built-in security, so that you can control what files you share with other people.

On	Service
☐	Screen Sharing
☑	File Sharing
☐	Printer Sharing
☐	Scanner Sharing
☐	Remote Login
☐	Remote Management
☐	Remote Apple Events
☐	Internet Sharing
☐	Bluetooth Sharing

File Sharing: On

Other users can access shared folders on this computer, and administrators all volumes, at afp://10.0.1.13/ or "Paul's MacBook Air".

Options...

Shared Folders:
- Karen's Public Folder
- Paul's Public Folder

Users:
Karen	Read & Write
Staff	Read Only
Everyone	Read Only

Share Equipment

Computers connected over a network can share some types of equipment. For example, one computer can share its printer, which enables other network users to send their documents to that printer. Networked computers can also share hard drives, optical drives, and document scanners.

On	Service
☐	Screen Sharing
☐	File Sharing
☑	Printer Sharing
☑	Scanner Sharing
☐	Remote Login
☐	Remote Management
☐	Remote Apple Events
☐	Internet Sharing
☐	Bluetooth Sharing

Printer Sharing: On

Printer Sharing allows others on your network to use printers connected to this computer.

Open Print & Scan Preferences...

Printers:
- ☑ EPSON Artisan 837

Users:
Everyone	Can Print

Wired Networking

Network Cable

A *network cable* is a special cable designed for exchanging information. One end of the cable plugs into the Mac's network port. The other end plugs into a network connection point, which is usually the network's router

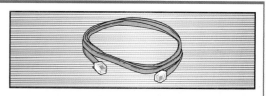

(discussed next), but it could also be a switch, hub, or even another Mac. Information, shared files, and other network data travel through the network cables.

Router

A *router* is a central connection point for all the computers on the wired portion of the network. For each computer, you run a network cable from the Mac's network port to a port in the router.

When network data travels from computer A to computer B, it first goes out through computer A's network port, along its network cable, and into the router. Then the router passes the data along computer B's network cable and into its network port.

Wireless Networking

Wireless Connections

A *wireless network* is a collection of two or more computers that communicate with each other using radio signals instead of cable. The most common wireless technology is Wi-Fi (rhymes with hi-fi) or 802.11. There are three main types — 802.11b, 802.11g, and 802.11n — each of

which has its own range and speed limits. The other common wireless technology is Bluetooth, which enables devices to communicate directly with each other.

Wireless Access Point

A *wireless access point* (WAP) is a device that receives and transmits signals from wireless computers to form a wireless network. Many WAPs also accept wired connections, which enables both wired and wireless computers to form a network.

If your network has a broadband modem, you can connect the modem to a type of WAP called a *wireless gateway,* which includes a built-in router that extends Internet access to all the computers on the network.

Connect to a Wireless Network

Your Mac has built-in wireless networking capabilities that you can use to connect to a wireless network that is within range. This could be a network in your home, your office, or a public location such as a coffee shop. In most cases, this also gives you access to the wireless network's Internet connection.

Most wireless networks have security turned on, which means you must know the correct password to connect to the network. However, after you have connected to the network once, your Mac remembers the password, and connects again automatically the next time the network comes within range.

Connect to a Wireless Network

1 Click the **Wi-Fi status** icon (📶) in the menu bar.

Your Mac locates the wireless networks within range of your Mac.

Ⓐ The available networks appear in the menu.

Ⓑ Networks with a Lock icon (🔒) require a password to join.

2 Click the wireless network you want to join.

If the wireless network is secure, your Mac prompts you for the password.

3 Use the Password text box to type the network password.

C If the password is very long and you are sure no one can see your screen, you can click **Show password** (☐ changes to ☑) to see the actual characters instead of dots. This helps to ensure you type the password correctly.

4 Click **Join**.

Your Mac connects to the wireless network.

D The Wi-Fi status icon changes from 📶 to 📶 to indicate the connection.

The Wi-Fi network "Galt Ave" requires a WPA password.

Password: ••••••••••

☐ Show password
☑ Remember this network

Cancel   Join

🕐 📶 🔊 99% 🔋 Thu 10:00 AM   Paul   🔍   ◎

TIPS

I know a particular network is within range, but I do not see it in the list. Why not?

As a security precaution, some wireless networks do not broadcast their availability. However, you can still connect to such a network, assuming you know its name and the password, if one is required. Click 📶 and then click **Join Other Network**. Use the Network Name text box to type the name of the network, click the **Security** ⬚, and then click the network's security type. Follow steps **3** and **4** to join the network.

I do not see the Wi-Fi status icon on my menu bar. How do I display the icon?

You can do this using System Preferences. Click the System Preferences icon (▣) in the Dock (or click ⬛ and then click **System Preferences**) to open the System Preferences window. Click **Network**, click **Wi-Fi,** and then click the **Show Wi-Fi status in menu bar** check box (☐ changes to ☑).

Connect to a Network Resource

To see what other network users have shared on the network, you can use the Network folder to view the other computers and then connect to them to see their shared resources. To get full access to a Mac's shared resources, you must connect with a username and password for an administrator account on that Mac. To get access to the resources that a particular user has shared, you must connect with that user's name and password.

Note, too, that your Mac can also connect to the resources shared by Windows computers.

Connect to a Network Resource

1 Click the desktop.

2 Click **Go**.

3 Click **Network**.

Note: Another way to run the Network command is to press Shift + ⌘ + K.

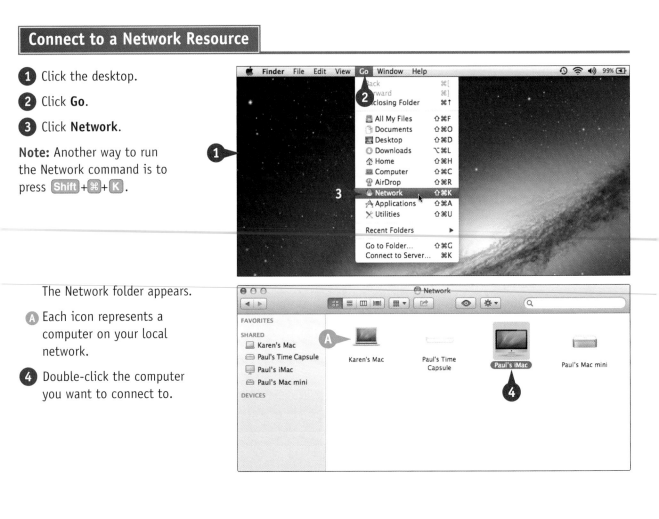

The Network folder appears.

Ⓐ Each icon represents a computer on your local network.

4 Double-click the computer you want to connect to.

Your Mac connects to the network computer using the Guest account.

Note: The Guest account has only limited access to the network computer.

⑤ Click **Connect As**.

Your Mac prompts you to connect to the network computer.

⑥ Click **Registered User** (○ changes to ⊙).

⑦ Use the Name text box to type the username of an account on the network computer.

⑧ Use the Password text box to type the password of the account.

⑨ To store the account data, click **Remember this password in my keychain** (☐ changes to ☑).

⑩ Click **Connect**.

Your Mac connects to the computer and shows the shared resources that you can access.

⑪ When you are done, click **Disconnect**.

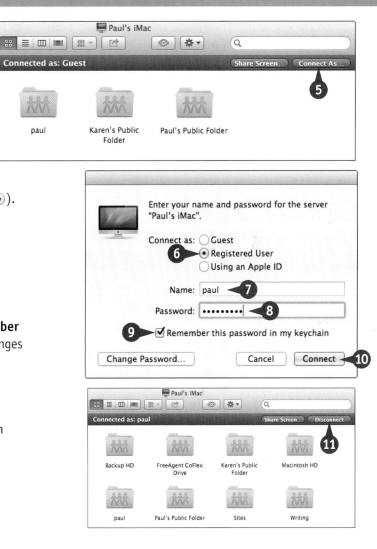

TIPS

Is there a faster way to connect to a network computer?
Yes. In the Shared section of Finder's sidebar area, click the computer you want to connect with (Ⓐ) and then follow steps **5** to **10** to connect as a registered user.

How can I connect to a computer that does not appear in the Network folder?
Right-click **Finder** (🖥), click **Connect to Server**, and then type the address: For a Mac, type the Mac's network name followed by **.local**; for a Windows PC, type **smb://** followed by the PC's name; for any computer, type its IP address. Click **Connect**.

Turn On File and Printer Sharing

You can share your files with other network users. This enables those users to access your files over the network. Before you can share these resources, you must turn on your Mac's file-sharing feature.

To learn how to share a particular folder, see the next section, "Share a Folder." You can also share your printer with other network users. This enables those users to send print jobs to your printer over the network. Before this can happen, you must turn on your Mac's printer-sharing feature. To learn how to share a particular printer, see the section "Share a Printer," later in this chapter.

Turn On File and Printer Sharing

1 Click .

2 Click **System Preferences**.

The System Preferences window appears.

3 Click **Sharing**.

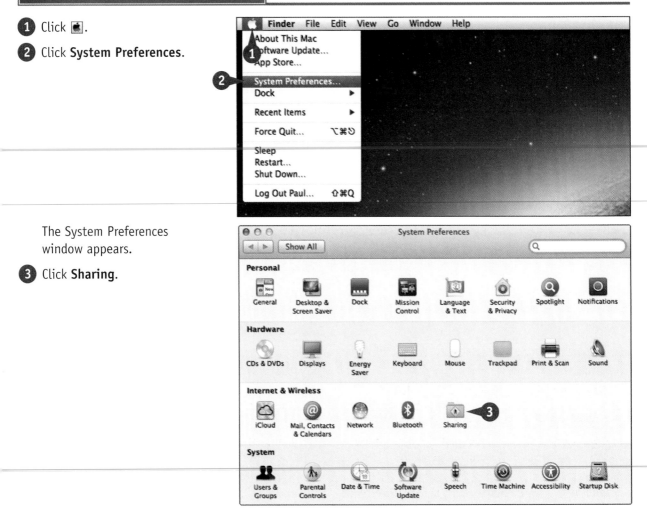

The Sharing preferences appear.

④ Click the **File Sharing** check box (☐ changes to ☑).

You can now share your folders, as described in the next section, "Share a Folder."

⑤ Click the **Printer Sharing** check box (☐ changes to ☑).

You can now share your printers, as described in the section "Share a Printer," later in this chapter.

TIPS

Another user has asked me for my Mac's IP address. How do I look that up?

Your Mac gives you a couple of ways to do this. Follow steps **1** to **3** in this section, and then click **File Sharing** (click the name, not the check box); the series of digits after afp:// is your IP address (such as 10.0.1.13). Alternatively, open System Preferences, click **Network**, click **Ethernet** (or click **Wi-Fi** if you have a wireless network connection), and then read the IP Address value.

What is the Public folder and how do I access it?

Your user account's Public folder is a special folder that you use to share files with other people on the network or on your Mac. If someone connects to your Mac using your username and password, he or she has full access to the Public folder. Everyone else can only read the contents of the folder or add files to the Drop Box folder. To access the folder, click **Finder** (⊞), click your username, and then open the Public folder.

Share a Folder

You can share one of your folders on the network, enabling other network users to view and optionally edit the files you place in that folder. Your Mac automatically shares your user account's Public folder, but you can share other folders. Sharing a folder enables you to work on a file with other people without having to send them a copy of the file.

Your Mac gives you complete control over how people access your shared folder. For example, you can allow users to make changes to the folder, or you can prevent changes.

Share a Folder

1 Open the Sharing preferences.

Note: See the section "Turn On File and Printer Sharing" earlier in this chapter to learn how to display the Sharing preferences.

2 Click **File Sharing**.

Note: Be sure to click the **File Sharing** text, not the check box. This ensures that you do not accidentally uncheck the check box.

3 Under Shared Folders, click +.

An Open dialog appears.

④ Click the folder you want to share.

⑤ Click **Add**.

Your Mac begins sharing the folder.

Note: You can also click and drag a folder from a Finder window and drop it on the list of shared folders.

Ⓐ The folder appears in the Shared Folders list.

⑥ Click the folder.

⑦ For the Everyone user, click the current permission and then click the permission you want to assign.

Ⓑ The current permission is indicated with a check mark (☑).

Your Mac assigns the permission to the user.

Ⓒ You can also click ⊞ under the Users list to add more users.

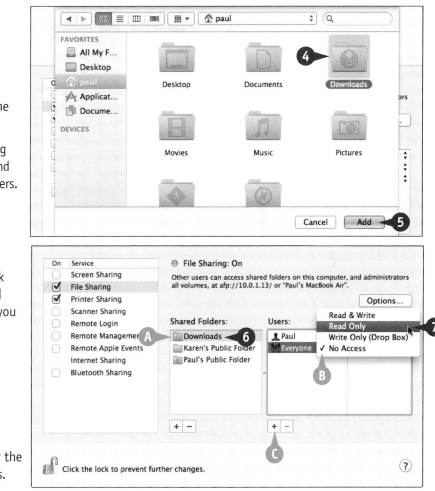

What are the differences between the various types of permissions I can assign to users?

Permissions define what users can and cannot do with the shared folder:

• **Read & Write:** Users can open files, add new files, rename or delete existing files, and edit file contents.

• **Read Only:** Users can open files, but cannot add, delete, rename, or edit files.

• **Write Only (Drop Box):** Users can add files to the folder as a Drop Box, but cannot open the folder.

• **No Access:** Users cannot open (or even see) the folder.

Can I share folders with Windows users?

Yes. In the Sharing window, click **Options** and then click the **Share files and folders using SMB (Windows)** check box (☐ changes to ☑). Click your user account (☐ changes to ☑), use the Password text box to type your account password, click **OK**, and then click **Done**. Windows users must enter your username and password to see your shared folders.

Share a Printer

If you have a printer connected to your Mac, you can share the printer with the network. This enables other network users to send their documents to your printer. Sharing a printer saves you money because you only have to purchase one printer for all the computers on your network. Sharing a printer also saves you time because you only have to install, configure, and maintain a single printer for everyone on your network.

See the next section, "Add a Shared Printer," to learn how to configure your Mac to use a shared network printer.

Share a Printer

① Click .

② Click **System Preferences**.

Note: You can also click
System Preferences ( )
in the Dock.

The System Preferences
window appears.

③ Click **Sharing**.

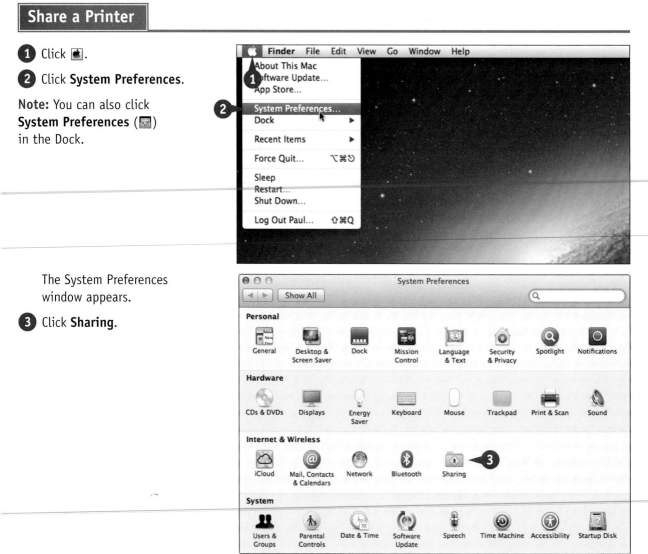

4 Click **Printer Sharing**.

Note: Be sure to click the **Printer Sharing** text, not the check box. This ensures that you do not accidentally uncheck the check box.

5 Click the check box beside the printer you want to share (☐ changes to ☑).

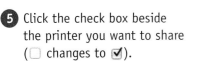

TIP

Is there another method I can use to share a printer?

1 Click .

2 Click **System Preferences**.

3 Click **Print & Scan**.

4 Click the printer you want to share.

5 Click the **Share this printer on the network** check box (☐ changes to ☑).

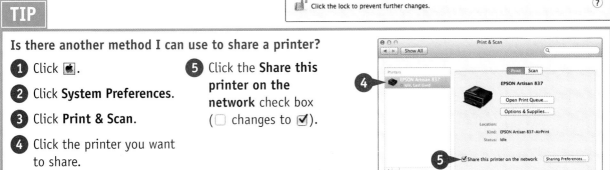

Add a Shared Printer

If another computer on your network has an attached printer that has been shared with the network, as described in the previous section, you can add that shared printer to your Mac. This enables you to send a document from your Mac to that shared printer, which means you can print your documents without having a printer attached directly to your Mac.

Before you can print to a shared network printer, you must add the shared printer to your Mac.

Add a Shared Printer

1 Click **System Preferences** (⬚) in the Dock.

The System Preferences window appears.

2 Click **Print & Scan**.

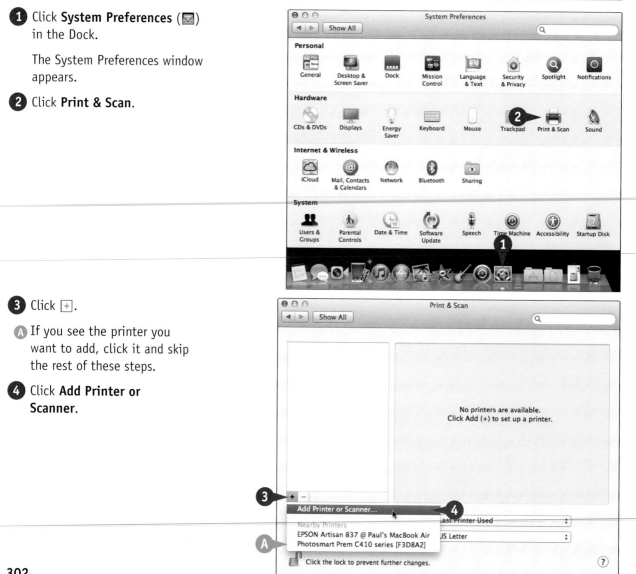

3 Click ⊞.

A If you see the printer you want to add, click it and skip the rest of these steps.

4 Click **Add Printer or Scanner**.

5 Click **Default**.

6 Click the shared printer.

B Look for the word *Shared* in the printer description.

7 Click **Add**.

Note: If your Mac alerts you that it must install software for the printer, click **Install**.

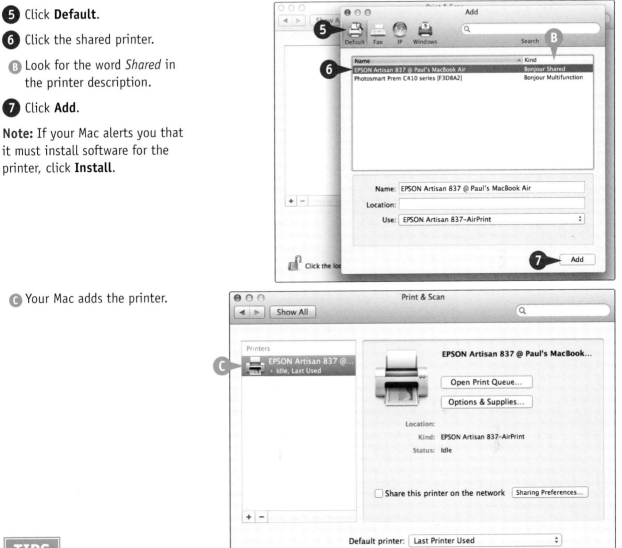

C Your Mac adds the printer.

Can I add a shared Windows printer?

Yes, if you have Windows computers on your network, you can connect to any printers that they share. Follow steps **1** to **4** and then click the **Windows** tab. Click the Windows workgroup, click the computer with the shared printer, log on to the Windows computer, and then click the shared printer you want to use. In the Print Using list, click ⊞, click **Other**, and then click the printer in the list that appears. Click **Add**.

How do I print to the shared network printer that I added?

In any application that supports printing, click **File** and then click **Print**. You can also press ⌘+P. In the Print dialog, use the Printer pop-up menu to click ⊞ and then click the shared printer you added in this section. Choose any other printing options you require, and then click **Print**.

CHAPTER 15

Maintaining Your Mac

To keep your Mac running smoothly, maintain top performance, and reduce the risk of computer problems, you need to perform some routine maintenance chores. This chapter shows you how to empty the Trash, delete unnecessary files, uninstall applications, update applications, back up your files, recondition your notebook battery, and more.

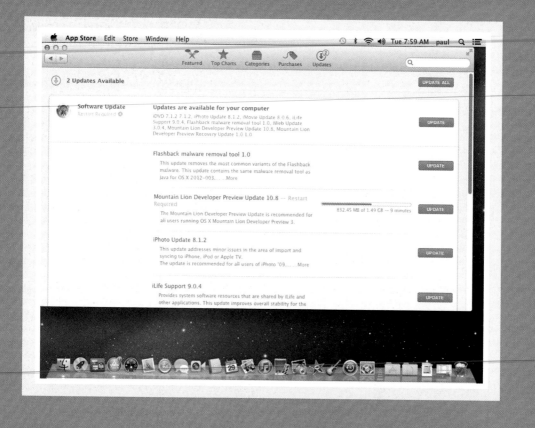

Empty the Trash

You can free up drive space on your Mac by periodically emptying the Trash. When you delete a file or folder, your Mac does not immediately remove the file from your Mac's hard drive. Instead, your Mac moves the file or folder to the Trash. This is useful if you accidentally delete an item because it means you can open the Trash and restore the item. However, all those deleted files and folders take up drive space, so you need to empty the Trash periodically to regain that space.

You should empty the Trash at least once a week.

Empty the Trash

1. Click the desktop.

2. Click **Finder** from the menu.

3. Click **Empty Trash**.

Ⓐ You can also right-click the **Trash** icon (🗑) and then click **Empty Trash**.

Note: Another way to select the Empty Trash command is to press `Shift`+`⌘`+`Del`.

Your Mac asks you to confirm the deletion.

4. Click **Empty Trash**.

Your Mac empties the Trash (🗑 changes to 🗑).

Are you sure you want to permanently erase the items in the Trash?

You can't undo this action.

Cancel   ④ ➤ Empty Trash

Organize Your Desktop

You can make your Mac desktop easier to scan and navigate by organizing the icons. The Mac desktop automatically displays icons for objects such as inserted CDs and DVDs, disk images, and attached iPods. The desktop is also a handy place to store files, file aliases, copies of documents, and more. However, the more you use your desktop as a storage area, the more the desktop can become disarrayed, making it hard to find the icon you want. You can fix this by organizing the icons.

Organize Your Desktop

1 Click the desktop.

2 Click **View**.

3 Click **Clean Up By**.

4 Click **Name**.

You can also right-click the desktop, click **Clean Up By**, and then click **Name**, or press Option + ⌘ + 1.

A Your Mac organizes the icons alphabetically and arranges them in columns from right to left.

Check Hard Drive Free Space

To ensure that your Mac's hard drive does not become full, you should periodically check how much free space it has left. If you run out of room on your Mac's hard drive, you will not be able to install more applications or create more documents, and your Mac's performance will suffer. To ensure your free space does not become too low — say, less than about 20 or 25GB — you can check how much free space your hard drive has left.

You should check your Mac's hard drive free space about once a month. If you frequently install programs, create large files, or download media, you should check your free space every couple of weeks.

Check Hard Drive Free Space

Check Free Space Using Finder

1 Click **Finder** (🖼️).

2 Click your user account.

Note: You can also click any folder on your Mac's hard drive.

3 Press ⌘+/.

Ⓐ Your Mac displays the status bar.

4 Read the "available" value, which tells you the amount of free space left on the hard drive.

Display Free Space on the Desktop

1 Display your Mac's HD (hard drive) icon on the desktop, as described in the first tip on the next page.

2 Click the desktop.

3 Click **View**.

4 Click **Show View Options**.

Note: You can also run the Show View Options command by pressing ⌘+J.

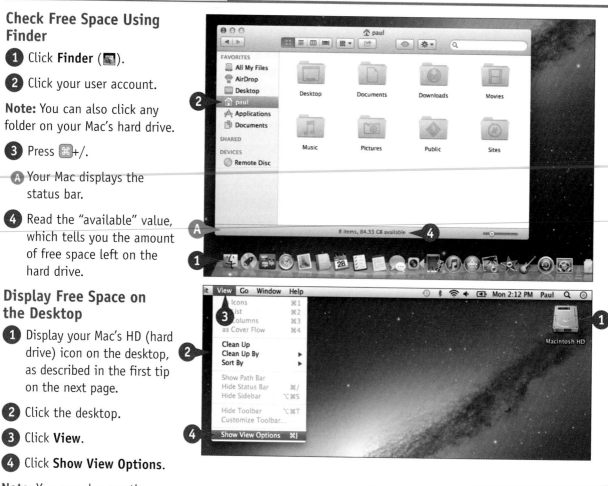

308

The Desktop dialog appears.

5 Click **Show item info** (☐ changes to ☑).

B Your Mac displays the amount of free hard drive space under the Macintosh HD icon.

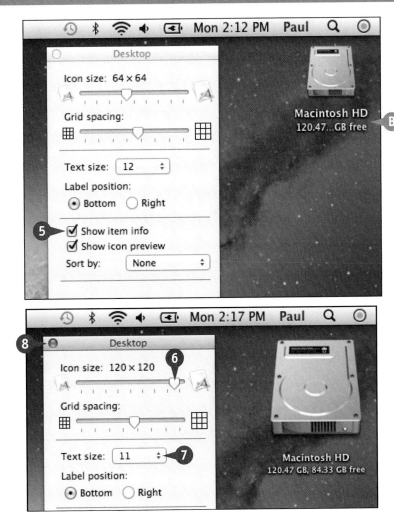

6 Drag the Icon size ☐ until you can read all the icon text.

7 If you still cannot read all the text, click the **Text size** ⊕ and then click a larger size.

8 Click **Close** (⊚).

TIPS

My Mac's hard drive icon does not appear on the desktop. How do I display it?

If you do not see the Macintosh HD icon on your desktop, click the desktop, click **Finder** in the menu bar, and then click **Preferences**. Click the **General** tab, click **Hard disks** (☐ changes to ☑), and then click **Close** (⊚).

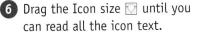

Show these items on the desktop:
☑ Hard disks
☑ External disks
☑ CDs, DVDs, and iPods
☐ Connected servers

What should I do if my Mac's hard drive space is getting low?

First, empty the Trash, as described earlier in this chapter in the section, "Empty the Trash." Next, uninstall applications that you no longer use, as described in the next section, "Uninstall Unused Applications." If you have any documents that you are sure you no longer need — particularly large media files — either move them to an external hard drive or USB flash drive, or send them to the Trash and then empty the Trash folder.

Uninstall Unused Applications

If you have an application that you no longer use, you can free up some drive space and reduce clutter in the Applications folder by uninstalling that application. When you install an application, the program stores its files on your Mac's hard drive, and although most programs are quite small, many require hundreds of megabytes of drive space. Uninstalling applications you do not need frees up the drive space they use and removes their icons or folders from the Applications folder.

In most cases you must be logged on to your Mac with an administrator account to uninstall applications.

Uninstall Unused Applications

1 Click **Finder** (📁).

2 Click **Applications**.

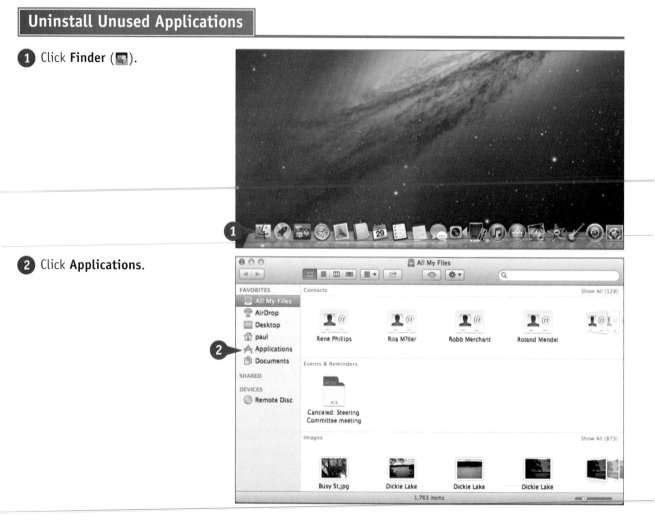

3 Click and drag the application or its folder and drop it on the **Trash** icon ().

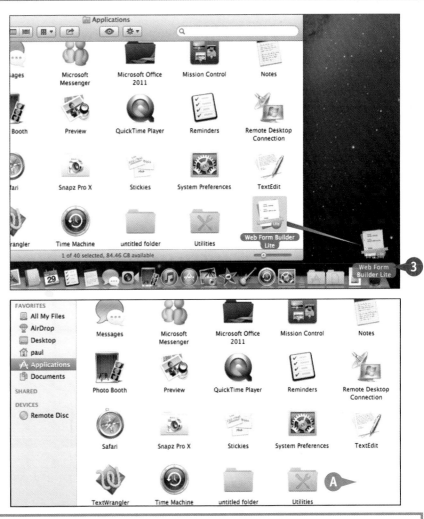

If your Mac prompts you for an administrator password, type the password and then click **OK**.

A Your Mac uninstalls the application.

TIPS

Is there another way to uninstall an application?
Yes, in some cases. A few Mac applications come with a separate program for uninstalling the application:

1 Follow steps **1** and **2**.

2 Open the application's folder, if it has one.

3 Double-click the "Uninstaller" icon and then follow the instructions on-screen.

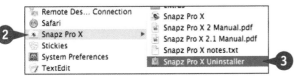

How can I restore an application that I uninstalled accidentally?
If you used the application's uninstall program, you must reinstall the application. If you sent the application to the Trash, and that was the most recent operation you performed, click **Finder** (), click **Edit**, and then click **Undo Move of "*Application*"** (where *Application* is the name of the application you want to restore). Otherwise, click **Trash** (), and then use the Trash folder to drag the application back to Applications.

Set a Software Update Schedule

You can ensure that your Mac and the applications that come with your Mac are up to date with the latest features and fixes by setting a schedule for updating the software. Apple makes OS X updates available from time to time. These updates fix problems, add new features, and resolve security issues. You can reduce computer problems and maximize online safety by setting up your Mac to download and install these updates automatically.

By default, your Mac checks for updates weekly. You can configure Software Update to check for updates daily or only once a month.

Set a Software Update Schedule

1 Click **Apple menu**.

2 Click **System Preferences**.

Note: You can also click **System Preferences** ( ) in the Dock.

The System Preferences window appears.

3 Click **Software Update**.

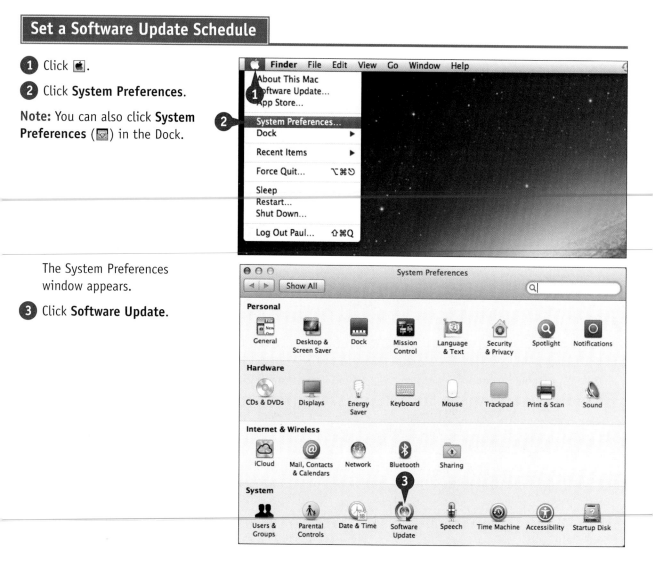

The Software Update preferences appear.

4 Click **Check for updates** (☐ changes to ☑).

5 In the Check for Updates pop-up menu, click ⬓ and then click the schedule you want: **Daily**, **Weekly**, or **Monthly**.

Software Update checks for new and updated versions of your software based on information about your computer and current software.

Check Now

Last check: No new software updates were available.
Thursday, May 24, 2012 1:41 AM

Daily
4 ☑ Check for updates: ✓ Weekly **5**
☐ Download updates Monthly
You will be notified when the updates are ready to be installed.
☐ Automatically update system support files

Click the lock to prevent further changes.

6 Click **Download updates automatically** (☐ changes to ☑).

7 Click **Automatically update system support files** (☐ changes to ☑).

Your Mac checks for updates on your selected schedule and downloads updates automatically.

Software Update checks for new and updated versions of your software based on information about your computer and current software.

Check Now

Last check: No new software updates were available.
Thursday, May 24, 2012 1:41 AM

☑ Check for updates: Weekly ⬓
6 ☑ Download updates automatically
You will be notified when the updates are ready to be installed.
7 ☑ Automatically update system support files

Click the lock to prevent further changes.

TIPS

Do I have to let Software Update do the checking automatically?

Technically, no, you do not have to rely on Software Update's automatic checking. Instead, you can check for software updates manually, as described in the next section, "Update Software Manually." However, this is not a good idea because you should always keep your Mac software up to date, and this might not happen if you have to remember to check for updates.

How does Software Update work?

When the time comes for an update check, Software Update first examines what Apple applications and system software you have installed on your Mac. Then, for each program, Software Update queries an Internet database on the Apple website to see if the program has an update available. If it does, Software Update adds the program to the update list. If the update is considered important, Software Update immediately downloads the update. The Software Update icon then bounces in the Dock to let you know that updates are available.

Update Software Manually

To make sure that your Mac and the applications that come with your Mac are currently up to date with the latest features and fixes, you can update the software manually. By default, your Mac checks for new software updates automatically on a regular schedule. If you turned off this feature or configured it to be less frequent, you can still keep your Mac up to date by checking for — and if necessary, installing — updates yourself.

See the previous section, "Set a Software Update Schedule," to learn how to configure the Software Update schedule.

Update Software Manually

1 Connect to the Internet, if you have not already done so.

2 Click **App Store** (▣).

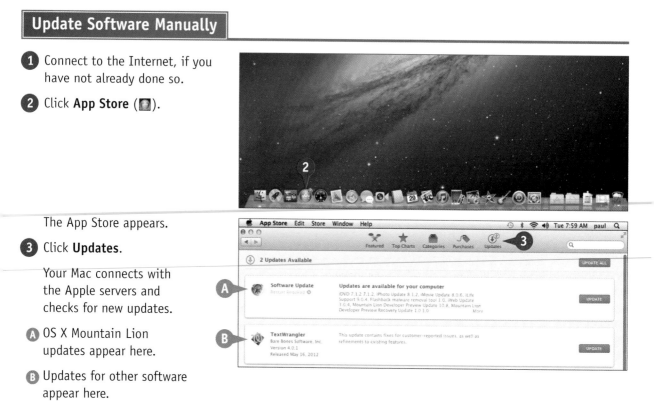

The App Store appears.

3 Click **Updates**.

Your Mac connects with the Apple servers and checks for new updates.

Ⓐ OS X Mountain Lion updates appear here.

Ⓑ Updates for other software appear here.

C If you want to install all the available updates, click **Update All**. Skip to step **6**.

D If you want to install all the available OS X updates, click this **Update** button. Skip to step **6**.

E If you install any updates that display the Restart icon (⊙), you must restart your Mac to complete the installation.

4 To install individual updates, click **More**.

Your Mac displays the list of available OS X updates.

5 Click **Update** beside each update you want to install.

F The App Store displays the update download and install progress.

For some updates, your Mac prompts you to restart the computer.

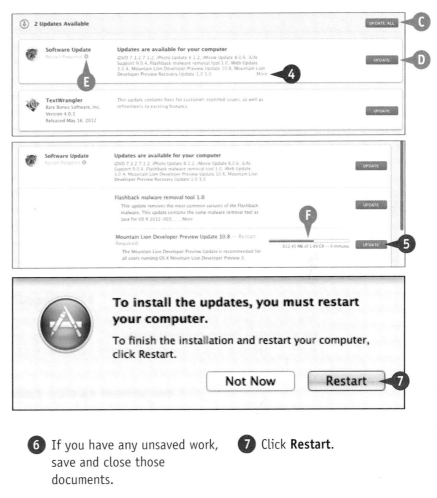

6 If you have any unsaved work, save and close those documents.

7 Click **Restart**.

TIPS

Should I always install every available update?

As a general rule, yes. However, some exceptions exist. For example, if an update is available for an application that you never use, you can safely skip that update. Also, if your Internet connection is slow, you may prefer to install the updates one at a time.

Is the Mountain Lion Update important?

Yes, any update named Mountain Lion Update is very important. These are major updates to your Mac's operating system, and they generally improve system stability and security. Because such an update affects your entire Mac and is usually quite large — often several hundred megabytes — you should install this update on its own.

Force a Stuck Application to Close

When you are working with an application, you may find that it becomes unresponsive and you cannot interact with the application or even quit the application normally. In that case, you can use an OS X feature called Force Quit to force a stuck or unresponsive application to close, which enables you to restart the application or restart your Mac.

Unfortunately, when you force an application to quit, you lose any unsaved changes in your open documents. Therefore, you should make sure the application really is stuck before forcing it to quit. See the second tip on the next page for more information.

Force a Stuck Application to Close

1 Click .

2 Click **Force Quit**.

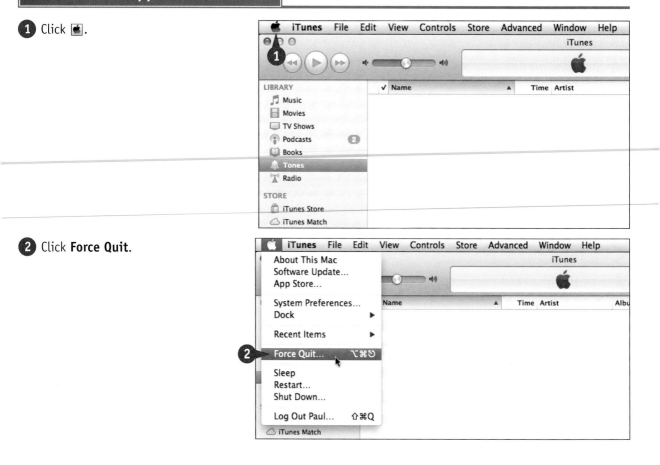

The Force Quit Applications window appears.

3 Click the application you want to shut down.

4 Click **Force Quit**.

Your Mac asks you to confirm that you want to force the application to quit.

5 Click **Force Quit**.

Your Mac shuts down the application.

6 Click **Close** (◉) to close the Force Quit Applications window.

TIPS

Are there easier ways to run the Force Quit command?

Yes. From the keyboard, you can run the Force Quit command by pressing `Option`+`⌘`+`Esc`. If the application has a Dock icon, press and hold `Control`+`Option` and then click the application's Dock icon. In the menu that appears, click **Force Quit**.

If an application is not responding, does that always mean the application is stuck?

Not necessarily. For example, some application operations — such as recalculating a large spreadsheet or rendering a 3-D image — may take a few minutes, and during that time the application can appear stuck. Similarly, your Mac may be low on hard drive space or memory, which can also cause an application to seem stuck. In this case, try shutting down some of your other applications to free up some memory.

Configure Time Machine Backups

One of the most crucial Mac maintenance chores is to configure your system to make regular backups of your files. Macs are reliable machines, but they can crash and all hard drives eventually die, so at some point your data will be at risk. To avoid losing that data forever, you need to configure the OS X Time Machine feature to perform regular backups.

To use Time Machine, your Mac requires a second hard drive. This can be a second internal drive on a Mac Pro or Mac mini, but on most Macs the easiest course is to connect an external hard drive, which you learn about in this section.

Configure Time Machine Backups

Configure Backups Automatically

1 Connect an external USB, Thunderbolt, or FireWire hard drive to your Mac.

A Your Mac adds an icon for the hard drive to the desktop.

Your Mac asks if you want to use the hard drive as your backup drive.

2 Click **Use as Backup Disk**.

Note: If your Mac does not ask to use the hard drive, continue with the following steps.

Configure Backups Manually

1 Click **System Preferences** (⬚).

2 Click **Time Machine**.

The Time Machine preferences appear.

③ Click **Select Backup Disk**.

Time Machine displays a list of available backup devices.

④ Click the external hard drive.

⑤ Click **Add Backup Disk**.

Time Machine enables backups and prepares to run the first backup automatically in 2 minutes.

⑥ Click **Close** (◉).

TIP

How do Time Machine backups work?

Time Machine makes backing up your Mac easy because backups are handled automatically on the following schedule:

- The initial backup commences 2 minutes after you configure Time Machine for the first time. This backup includes your entire Mac.

- Time Machine runs another backup every hour. These hourly backups include just those files and folders that you have changed or created since the most recent hourly backup.

- Time Machine runs a daily backup that includes only those files and folders that you have changed or created since the most recent daily backup.

- Time Machine runs a weekly backup that includes only those files and folders that you have changed or created since the most recent weekly backup.

Restore Files Using Time Machine

If you have configured your Mac to make regular Time Machine backups, you can use those backups to restore a lost file. If you accidentally delete a file, you can quickly restore it by opening the Trash folder. However, that does not help you if you have emptied the Trash folder, if you overwrite a file with another file with the same name, or if you improperly edit a file.

Because Time Machine makes hourly, daily, and weekly backups, it stores older copies and older versions of your data. You can use these backups to restore any file that you accidentally delete, overwrite, or improperly edit.

Restore Files Using Time Machine

1 Click **Finder** (![icon]).

2 Open the folder you want to restore, or the folder that contains the file you want to restore.

Ⓐ If you want to restore your entire hard drive, choose **Macintosh HD** in the sidebar.

Note: Restore your entire hard drive only if your original hard drive crashed and you have had it repaired or replaced.

3 Click **Time Machine** (![icon]).

The Time Machine interface appears.

Ⓑ Each window represents a backed-up version of the folder.

Ⓒ This area tells you when the displayed version of the folder was backed up.

Ⓓ You can use this timeline to navigate the backed-up versions.

4 Navigate to the date that contains the backed-up version of the folder or file.

Note: See the following tip to learn how to navigate the Time Machine backups.

5 If you are restoring a file, click the file.

6 Click **Restore**.

If another version of the folder or file already exists, Time Machine asks if you want to keep it or replace it.

7 Click **Replace**.

Time Machine restores the folder or file.

TIP

How do I navigate the backups in the Time Machine interface?

Here are the most useful techniques:

- Click the top arrow to jump to the earliest version; click the bottom arrow to return to the most recent version.
- Press and hold ⌘ and click the arrows to navigate through the backups one version at a time.
- Use the timeline to click a specific version.
- Click the version windows.

Recondition Your Mac Notebook Battery

To get the most performance out of your Mac notebook's battery, you need to recondition the battery by cycling it. *Cycling* a battery means letting it completely discharge and then fully recharging it again. Most Mac notebook batteries slowly lose their charging capacity over time. For example, if you can use your Mac notebook on batteries for 4 hours today, later on you will only be able to run the computer for 3 hours on a full charge. You cannot stop this process, but you can delay it significantly by periodically cycling the battery.

You should cycle your Mac notebook battery once a month or so.

Recondition Your Mac Notebook Battery

Display the Battery Status Percentage

1 Click the **Battery status** icon (⊡).

2 Click **Show Percentage**.

Your Mac shows the percentage of available battery power remaining.

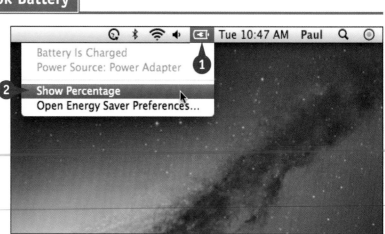

Cycle the Battery

1 Disconnect your Mac notebook's power cord.

A The Battery Status icon changes from ⊡ to ⊡.

322

2 Operate your Mac notebook normally by running applications, working with documents, and so on.

3 As you work, keep your eye on the Battery Status percentage.

When the Battery Status reaches 4%, your Mac warns you that it is now running on reserve power.

4 Click **OK**.

5 Reattach the power cord.

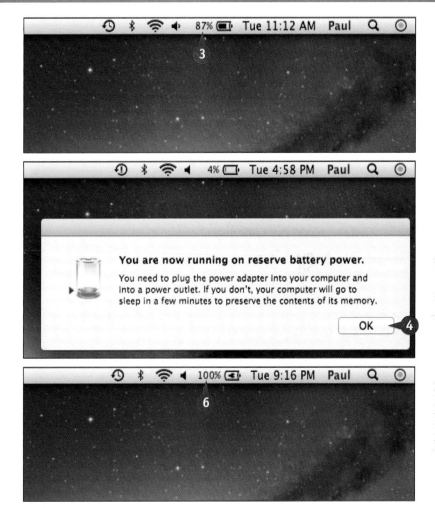

Your Mac restarts and the Battery Status icon changes from 🔋 to 🔌.

6 Leave your Mac plugged in at least until the Battery Status shows 100%.

TIPS

I do not see the battery status in my menu bar. How do I display it?

Click **System Preferences** (⚙) in the Dock to open System Preferences, and then click the **Energy Saver** icon. In the Energy Saver window, click **Battery** and then click the **Show battery status in the menu bar** check box (☐ changes to ☑).

Do Mac notebooks suffer from the memory effect?

Not anymore. Older portable computers used rechargeable nickel metal hydride (NiMH) or nickel cadmium (NiCad) batteries. The NiMH and NiCad types were phased out because they can suffer from a problem called the *memory effect*, where the battery loses capacity if you repeatedly recharge it without first fully discharging it. All the latest Mac notebooks have rechargeable lithium-ion (Li-ion) or lithium-polymer (Li-Po) batteries. These batteries are lighter and last longer than NiMH and NiCad batteries and, most importantly, do not suffer from the memory effect.

Restart Your Mac

If a hardware device is having a problem with some system files, it often helps to restart your Mac. By rebooting the computer, you reload the entire system, which is often enough to solve many computer problems.

For a problem device that does not have its own power switch, restarting your Mac might not resolve the problem because the device remains powered up the whole time. You can *power cycle* — shut down and then restart — such devices as a group by power cycling your Mac.

Restart Your Mac

Restart Your Mac

1 Click the **Apple** icon (🍎).

2 Click **Restart**.

| 🍎 | Finder | File | Edit | View | Go | Window | Help |

About This Mac
Software Update...
App Store...

System Preferences...
Dock ▶

Recent Items ▶

Force Quit... ⌥⌘⎋

Sleep
Restart...
Shut Down...

Log Out Paul... ⇧⌘Q

Your Mac asks you to confirm.

3 Click **Restart**.

Note: To bypass the confirmation dialog, press and hold (Option) when you click the **Restart** command.

Are you sure you want to restart your computer now?

If you do nothing, the computer will restart automatically in 49 seconds.

☑ Reopen windows when logging back in

Cancel 3 → Restart

Power Cycle Your Mac

1 Click 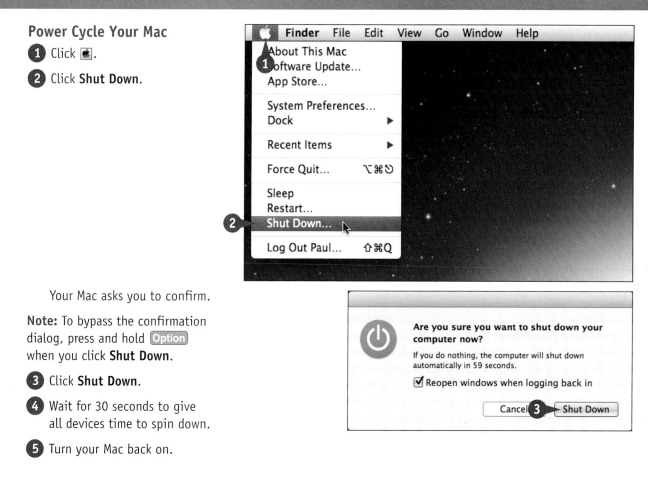.

2 Click **Shut Down**.

Your Mac asks you to confirm.

Note: To bypass the confirmation dialog, press and hold Option when you click **Shut Down**.

3 Click **Shut Down**.

4 Wait for 30 seconds to give all devices time to spin down.

5 Turn your Mac back on.

TIP

What other basic troubleshooting techniques can I use?

- Make sure that each device is turned on, that cable connections are secure, and that insertable devices (such as USB devices) are properly inserted.
- If a device is battery powered, replace the batteries.
- If a device has an on/off switch, power cycle the device by turning it off, waiting a few seconds for it to stop spinning, and then turning it back on again.
- Close all running programs.
- Log out of your Mac — click ; click **Log Out** *User*, where *User* is your Mac username; click **Log Out**; and then log back in again.

Index

Numerics

30-pin connector, disconnecting, 43

A

About This Mac window, 5
accounts
    e-mail, 184–185
    user, 280–281
Add Bookmark dialog, 176
Add Printer dialog, 37–41
Administrator account type, 281
AirPlay mirroring, 246–247
Album List view, iTunes, 85
albums of photos, 116–117
alert notifications, 244
all-day events, 31, 223
app folders, creating in Launchpad, 278–279
App Store
    Dock icon, 59
    gift cards, 229
    installing programs using, 228–229
    manual software updates from, 314–315
    web page editing software, 19
Apple e-mail accounts, adding, 184
Apple ID, creating, 100, 201, 250–253
Apple iWork Keynote, 19
Apple iWork Numbers, 19
Apple iWork Pages, 18
Apple.com Start page, 174
application windows, 63
applications. *See also specific applications by name*
    Dock, 59
    Force Quit, 316–317
    installing using App Store, 228–229
    opening file attachments in, 199
    restoring from Trash, 311
    shutting down, 61
    starting, 60–61
    switching between, 62
    uninstalling unused, 310–311
appointments, scheduling, 31
aspect ratio, 277
At a Location option, Reminders, 235

audio

audio
    graphic equalizer in iTunes for, 89
    listening to with Bluetooth headphones, 51
    volume settings in iTunes, 87
audio out port
    iMac, 7
    Mac mini, 9
    Mac Pro, 11
    MacBook Air, 15
    MacBook Pro, 13
audio port
    in iMac, 7
    in Mac mini, 9
    in Mac Pro, 11
automatic backups, 318

B

background images
    changing, 271
    fixed, 270–271
backups, configuring, 318–319
banner notifications, 244
batteries
    cycling, 322–323
    displaying battery status percentage, 322
    status, viewing in menu bar, 323
Bcc (blind courtesy copy), 259
bit rate, 93
Bluetooth devices
    connecting
        with Passkey, 50–51
        without Passkey, 48–50
    headphones, 51
    mouse, 49
    removing, 51
Bluetooth Setup Assistant, 49, 50
bookmarking web pages, 176–177
bulleted lists in notes, 231
Burn Settings dialog, 97
burning music to CDs, 21, 96–97
buying
    music from iTunes Store, 20, 100–101
    on Web, 27

Index

Q